# *Natural Wonders of*
# TENNESSEE

## — SECOND EDITION —

*Exploring Wild and Scenic Places*

ARDI LAWRENCE AND H. LEA LAWRENCE

## COUNTRY ROADS PRESS
*NTC/Contemporary Publishing Group*

**Library of Congress Cataloging-in-Publication Data**

Lawrence, Ardi.
    Natural wonders of Tennessee / Ardi Lawrence and H. Lea Lawrence.
    — 2nd ed.
        p.    cm. — (Natural wonders)
    Includes bibliographical references and index.
    ISBN 1-56626-196-1
        1. Tennessee—Guidebooks.    2. Natural history—Tennessee—
Guidebooks.    3. Natural areas—Tennessee—Guidebooks.    4. Parks—
Tennessee—Guidebooks.    5. Botanical gardens—Tennessee—
Guidebooks.    I. Lawrence H. Lea, 1930–  .    II. Title.    III. Series.
    F434.3.L39    1998
    917.6804'53—dc21                                                          98-39698
                                                                                              CIP

Cover and interior design by Nick Panos
Cover photograph: Cade's Cove, Great Smoky Mountains National Park.
Copyright © Ric Ergenbright
Interior illustrations and map copyright © Barbara Kelley

Published by Country Roads Press
A division of NTC/Contemporary Publishing Group, Inc.
4255 West Touhy Avenue, Lincolnwood (Chicago), Illinois 60646-1975 U.S.A.
Copyright © 1999 by H. Lea Lawrence and Ardi Lawrence
Manufactured in the United States of America
International Standard Book Number: 1-56626-196-1
99  00  01  02  03  04  ML  19  18  17  16  15  14  13  12  11  10  9  8  7  6  5  4  3  2  1

*For*
*Hig, Dorsey, and Ashley*

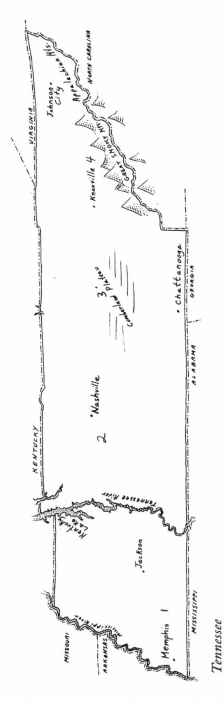

*Tennessee*
*(Figures correspond with chapter numbers.)*

# Contents

Acknowledgments VII
Introduction IX

## 1 Western Tennessee Delta Country 1

An Ocean Has Come to This 1
Reelfoot Lake 2
In and Around Memphis 10
Heart of Delta Country 29
Where the River Runs Through It 41
Land Between the Lakes 48

## 2 Middle Tennessee 57

Bluegrass and Other Surprises 57
In and Around Nashville 58
Natchez Trace Parkway and Corridor 89

## 3 Cumberland Plateau 97

A Wealth of Wild Places 97
Upper Cumberland and Big South Fork 98
Along the I-40 Corridor: Six Easy-Access Sites 126
South Cumberland and Sequatchie 137
Chattanooga and the Tennessee River Gorge 160

# 4 Great Valley and Blue Ridge 187

Call of the High Country 187
The Tennessee Overhill 188
In and Around Knoxville and Oak Ridge 200
A String of Pearls 218
Cumberland Gap National Historical Park 226
Great Smoky Mountains National Park 230
East of "Eden" 254

Reading Guide: Author's Short List 277
Index 281

# Acknowledgments

We thank these individuals for their input and assistance as we gathered information for this book:

Jenny Andrews, the late James Lovell Bailey, Gary Barnett, Terry W. Bonham, Pat Boren, Arminta Bowen, James C. Brown, Ronnie Burk, Mary Jane Burnette, Joan Burns, Linda Butler, Linda Caldwell, Lissa Clarke, Buell and Patsy Cox, Gene Cox, F. Lynn Craig, Roy Davis, Don DeFoe, David D. Dickey, Kenneth H. Dubke, Richard Evans, Jennifer Fain, Willie Freeman, Paige Funk, Joe W. Giles, Agnes Gorham, Herman and Judy Haecker, Linda Harris, Jim Harrison, Joyce Harsson, R. I. C. and Marcy Hawley, Randy Hedgepath, Dickie and Stephanie Hinton, Mary Hively, John Hooper, Landon Howard, Julia Johnson, Reg Johnson, Gina Jones, Jay R. Jorden, Joe Kelly, Jim Kennedy, Becky M. Koella, Pam Kubilus, Jerry Lamastus, Edward T. Luther, Johnny and Pat Lynch, Terry Maddux, the late Valary Marks, Dawne Massey, Steve McAloon, Don McGonigal, Claudia Moody, Joe Moore, Ted Murdoch, Jimmy Newman, Donald J. (Jamie) Nicholson Jr., Ronnie Nixon, James David Oliver, Barbara Parker, John Parrett, Mack S. Prichard, Pauline Prosser, Doug and Rita Pruett, Mary Robbins, Tammy Rowe, Ken Rush, Rick Schwartz, Marty Silver, Jennifer Smith, Jimmy Neil Smith, Saundra Owens Smith, Jack Snapp, Anne Stamps, Walt Stewart, Mary Beth Sutton, Joe H. Taft, Charlie Tate, Shannon Tignor, Bo Townsend, Robert Turan, Amy Williams, Jennifer Bauer Wilson, and Ray Zimmerman.

# Introduction

Welcome to this updated and expanded edition of *Natural Wonders of Tennessee*. As we all prepare to move into the 21st century, it's timely to consider what values we want to carry forth. High on the list would be an appreciation of the natural environment.

And now, imagine for a moment that you are living in another galaxy in space and are beaming a powerful listening device toward Planet Earth. Say you are aiming it on an area we call Tennessee, in fact zooming in on a part that is remote from the cities and towns. What do you suppose you might hear?

No doubt, the sounds of rivers tumbling over rocks. Perhaps the wind rushing past trees on high mountain peaks. Birdsongs. Logs crackling in campfires. Squawks and whistles of eagles, or wolf howls echoing over vast ravines. A beaver slapping water in the darkness . . . you get the picture.

But listen again: there's something else, like the intake of a thousand breaths, overriding all other sounds. We call it "the Tennessee Gasp," and it's instinctive. It's what we do whenever we round a bend or climb a peak and come upon unexpected beauty. It's also what we do when we look at fields of flowers.

You can practice it, too. Just come for a visit and see! Prepare to be impressed by the vastness of the wild country here, the great diversity of ecosystems, and the many outstanding natural features of record-book dimension. But this guide is also about Tennessee's cities and their zoos, natural-history museums, arboretums, botanical gardens, and nature centers.

Before we started writing, we visited each location, asking about seasonal and special events and other items of interest to people from "ages 2 to 92." We wanted to have the most current information possible, see everything for ourselves, then take you, the reader, with us on a path of discovery throughout the state.

Have you noticed how interested children are these days in the environment? School classes, Scouts, and other groups from preschool on up love to learn about animals and plants, weather systems, and how to preserve our natural resources. They want to understand why rain forests can become deserts and why some species need to be protected. So, if there are children in your family, what better way is there to teach them about nature than to take them where they can experience it with you?

Readers should be aware of two things about this book. First, we couldn't include every location that you'd want to know about. For example, Tennessee has more than 50 state parks. We have mentioned many of them, but an omission doesn't mean that a particular park is less desirable than others. The same holds true for rivers and lakes. Tennessee is one of the most visited states for fishing and water sports, with opportunity almost everywhere. We tried to select an interesting variety of locations, but we suggest that people planning a visit contact tourism offices about other places to include in their itinerary. For even quicker information, check out the locations on the Internet's Web addresses we've included.

Second, there are some outstanding parks and outdoor recreation areas that we share with other states. In describing them, we emphasized what our state has to offer, but we didn't always stop at the border. Great Smoky Mountains National Park is half in North Carolina; the peak of "the Roan" (Roan

Mountain) is in North Carolina; Cumberland Gap National Historical Park is mostly in Kentucky and Virginia; Big South Fork National River and Recreation Area is partly in Kentucky; Land Between the Lakes is in both Tennessee and Kentucky; Pickwick Lake goes into Alabama and Mississippi, and so does the Natchez Trace Parkway; and we share Lookout Mountain with Georgia. For more information on all of these, refer to the Natural Wonders series companion books for each state.

We've divided Tennessee into four regions identified by geologic features that give each a particular character. The western regions divide themselves neatly in a north-south direction. The Cumberland Plateau, however, is shaped more like a top-heavy wedge; and the eastern region has a southwest-to-northeast orientation, bordered by the Blue Ridge physiographic region of the southern Appalachians. Most of the roads in that area take a parallel route (and so do the locations in this book).

For consistency (and not to digress with explanations), "we" could refer to the author, the coauthor, or both of us. "We" hope that you enjoy this discovery tour and that it will inspire you to see some of the locations firsthand.

# 1

# Western Tennessee Delta Country

## An Ocean Has Come to This

Gaze over the relatively flat lands of western Tennessee Delta Country where soybeans, corn, winter wheat, and cotton grow in fields, and your imagination will probably not supply a sea monster on the horizon. Yet, for millions of years—and periodically until 40 million years ago, when the sea subsided for the last time—this part of Tennessee was a portion of the Gulf of Mexico.

So, we could answer the charge that Tennessee has no seashore with, "Well, maybe not now, but there's evidence that it *did*." More species of marine shells and vertebrate remains from the Upper Cretaceous period have been found in one place in west Tennessee than anywhere else in the world.

Tennessee, although not among the largest states, is certainly longer than most. Memphis and Bristol are so far apart that Memphis is closer to the Gulf of Mexico and Bristol is closer to Ontario, Canada, than they are to each other. Along its length, Tennessee borders eight other states and spans nine distinct geologic regions. A compelling story of how these regions were formed is told by geologist Edward T. Luther in *Our Restless Earth: The Geologic Regions of Tennessee.*

And now for the most recent dramatic event:

Forty million years of comparative stability ended when, in the winter of 1811–12, a devastating series of earthquakes occurred along the New Madrid Fault where Missouri, Kentucky, and Tennessee meet. They included the most violent quake ever recorded in North America, so powerful, in fact, that for a time the Mississippi River ran backward. When they were all over, Reelfoot Lake—5 miles wide and 14 miles long—had been formed. This jewel is now a premier environment for wildlife and one of the most visited spots in Tennessee.

The Delta Country region encompasses three major geologic areas: the Mississippi River Floodplain, the West Tennessee Plateau Slope, which rises gently from the river to a wide line of sand hills miles to the east and then meets the Western Valley of the Tennessee River, better known now as Kentucky Lake.

Rivers here flow gently. The Hatchie swamp river, entering Tennessee near Pocahontas and skirting Bolivar, Brownsville, and Fort Pillow, has been designated a Tennessee Class I Natural River Area; and the placid Wolf River, taking a fairly straight path from near Grand Junction through Memphis, is a favorite float stream for beginners.

# Reelfoot Lake

## *Reelfoot Lake State Park*

On a sunny morning in May, we were navigating a Reelfoot boat (a local invention called the "stump jumper" for its prowess over submerged obstacles) in a remote part of Reelfoot Lake near Tiptonville. The little inboard motor powered us slowly past bulbous trunks of bald cypress trees and brought us to an area where wild climbing roses were growing on the trees. It was the first rose garden we had ever seen in a lake! Not far away, a snake had found a depression in the trunk of a tree and was coiled there. It might have been a cottonmouth, but there *are* look-alikes. Dragonflies darted around us like little iridescent helicopters, and ospreys watched from their treetop nests.

The scent of cypress and roses, the breeziness of the day, and the colors and sounds of this mysterious place that seemed to be full of secrets—the folklore of this area hints at many—all added to the pleasure of being there. We snapped photographs recklessly, as we always do when we see cypress trees and wildlife in our viewfinders.

That was another year, though clear as yesterday. It illustrates why irresistible Reelfoot Lake draws us back again and again.

Reelfoot is the largest natural lake in Tennessee: some 27,000 acres, although only about 13,000 are actual lake. Sloughs and swamps account for most of the remaining territory. Because of its location on the Mississippi flyway, its wetland character, fertile soil, and effective management programs by federal and state agencies, Reelfoot is a haven for wildlife of nearly every description.

People come here year-round for fishing, wildlife viewing, lake cruises, camping, naturalist-guided tours and programs, waterfowl hunting, and special events; and Reelfoot Lake State Park is host to many of the activities that take place here. The park is scattered in 10 individual locations around the lake, sharing the shoreline with summer cottages, fishing camps, wildlife refuges, and the town of Tiptonville.

The park visitors center is at the southwest end of the lake on State 21/22. A museum here has exhibits that relate the natural and cultural history of the area. A photo display illustrates wetlands. An earthquake simulator shakes and groans on cue. Included also are an aquarium, live reptile exhibits, a small auditorium, and a gift shop. Naturalists are on duty throughout the year to conduct programs and tours and to answer questions. Adjacent to the center is a 400-seat, air-conditioned auditorium.

Behind the center is a large caged area that holds animals that were rehabilitated from injuries but cannot be returned to the wild. Some are used for environmental education activities. A bald eagle there lets out a series of loud squawks and then a series of whistling sounds. The attendant says that eagles "talk" when they're eating or when they like the weather. On this cool and breezy September day, we feel like whistling, too.

At the water's edge a cypress-boardwalk nature trail goes out over part of the lake and loops back. Signs along the way interpret natural features. Here the mirrored surface of emerald green water doubles the effect of the ghostly cypress trees.

Near the northern end of the lake is the state Airpark Inn resort complex. A 3,500-foot all-weather landing strip is next to the inn. A restaurant, meeting rooms, and chalet-type cottages sit on pillars over the water, connected by a wide concrete pier. Each sleeping unit has a private deck that provides lush bayou views. A year-round campground is nearby.

We talked there with Ranger Jerry Lamastus about the American bald eagles that winter on the lake. The eagles start moving in when cold fronts push down. Jerry says that in a hard winter 200 or more eagles may be in an area from Hickman, Kentucky, to the Dyer County line. In mild winters fewer birds will come down, so the population may number more like 100 to 150.

Eagle tours begin December 1, close during the Christmas holidays, then resume from January through mid-March. Daily "eagle watch" bus tours depart from the Airpark Inn and last about two hours. Reservations for the tours are required and should be made well in advance. You can also look for eagles as you take a self-guided auto tour that follows the lakeshore. When the lake isn't frozen, you may be able to take a boat tour. During January and February, the most active months for eagle watching, park interpretive specialists and other experts from the region present special weekend talks and live bird shows.

Right after the eagle tours end, the fishing season starts. Until the first of June, fishermen in boats dot the lake and later tell fish stories at local cafés, then fishing drops off during summer and fall.

In May, a three-day Spring Escape includes Swamp Tromps—short walks that require wading through swampy natural areas to see nesting areas of great blue herons, American egrets, and other birds. Archaeology and geology tours go to Indian mounds, earthquake domes, and other historical features. Live bird shows demonstrate "Raptors of Reelfoot"; pontoon boats give guided cruises; and roads and trails lead to observation of birds, reptiles, and wildflowers.

From Memorial Day weekend through Labor Day, visitation is heavy. Campgrounds and cottages are full, interpretive programs are offered on weekends, and many people are using the outdoor recreational facilities. Pontoon boat tours leave from the visitors center from May 1 until October 1, weather permitting. These include long morning cruises with a lunch stop at the historic Caney Island Indian Mound, short afternoon tours, a two-hour sunset cruise on Fridays, and a moonlight cruise when the moon is full and the weather is right.

Two excellent places to view wildlife are east of State 78 between Tiptonville and the airpark, in the Reelfoot Wildlife

Management Area (WMA) managed by the State of Tennessee. They are identified on the State Park Auto Tour brochure. In winter, watch for ducks and eagles especially; in spring, look for herons, egrets, and other wading birds.

*Where:* Northwest corner of Tennessee at Tiptonville near the junction of State 78 and State 21/22. Take State 22 west from Union City or State 78 north from Dyersburg. The visitors center is east of the junction on State 21/22, and the airpark is 10 miles north on State 78.

*When:* Park open year-round; daily, 8 A.M. to 10 P.M. in summer (closes at sundown in winter); visitors center open year-round, 8 A.M. to 4:30 P.M.; inn, restaurant, spillway motel, and eagle tours are closed during Christmas holidays (inquire about dates); airpark campground is year-round; southern campground, April 1 to November 30.

*Admission:* Park is free. Modest fees for camping, tours, cruises, boat rental. Senior-citizen discounts for 62 and older.

*Amenities:* Inn, cabins, two campgrounds, restaurant, gift shop, museum, meeting rooms, snack bars.

*Activities:* Swimming, tennis, picnicking, boat rentals, boat-launch ramp, fishing, interpretive center, boat cruises, nature trails, playground, miniature golf, kiddie rides, recreation building.

*Special events:* Eagle-watch tours (December to March), Spring Escape (May), Round House Reunion (September), Arts and Crafts Festival (October).

*Other:* Barrier-free access.

*For more information:* Superintendent's Office, Reelfoot Lake State Park, Route 1, Tiptonville, TN 38079. Inquiries and eagle tour reservations, 901-253-7756. Accommodations, 800-250-8617. Website, http://www.state.tn.us/environment/parks/ then select.

## Reelfoot and Lake Isom National Wildlife Refuges

Beyond the park, there is more to learn about why Reelfoot is one of the most outstanding hunting and fishing preserves in the nation as well as a mecca for wildflower lovers, photographers, birders, and other nature enthusiasts. A good place to visit first is the Reelfoot National Wildlife Refuge (NWR) visitors center, 10 miles east of the park boundary and a mile north of State 22 on State 157. The center is open Monday through Friday from 8 A.M. until 4 P.M. (but daily during winter). It has wildlife exhibits, displays about historic events at Reelfoot, and informative leaflets about the birds, mammals, reptiles, and amphibians that are found here and at the smaller Lake Isom NWR, three miles south of Reelfoot Lake.

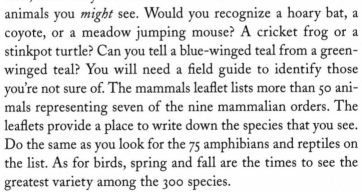

Reading the leaflets can add meaning to your visit, since they list the animals you *might* see. Would you recognize a hoary bat, a coyote, or a meadow jumping mouse? A cricket frog or a stinkpot turtle? Can you tell a blue-winged teal from a green-winged teal? You will need a field guide to identify those you're not sure of. The mammals leaflet lists more than 50 animals representing seven of the nine mammalian orders. The leaflets provide a place to write down the species that you see. Do the same as you look for the 75 amphibians and reptiles on the list. As for birds, spring and fall are the times to see the greatest variety among the 300 species.

For quantity, it is not unusual to see a sky shadowy with ducks, geese, eagles, and other birds during fall and winter. Hundreds of thousands are attracted to this place. Even though some areas of the refuge are closed during parts of the year to prevent undue stress on the migratory waterfowl and eagles, plenty of other locations provide viewing opportunities.

The Reelfoot NWR is split into two sections separated by the Upper Blue Basin of Reelfoot Lake. The Long Point Unit is north of the basin and extends into Kentucky. Gravel roads lead through open fields and woods, where you can view migratory birds in fall and spring. Canada geese and many kinds of ducks live here in winter. Access is from the Kentucky side. Sportfishing is permitted here also, from March 15 through November 15.

The Grassy Island Unit is south of the basin not far from the NWR visitors center and includes the Buzzard Slough area of Reelfoot Lake. It is open to the public except during the waterfowl-hunting season. The Grassy Island Wildlife Drive leads to a boardwalk and observation platform and a nearby boat-launching ramp. A late-day visit that lasts until sunset can give you some excellent practice on that legendary "Tennessee Gasp."

Little Lake Isom allows fishing and wildlife viewing from March 15 to October 15 and hunting in specific seasons. You'll find croplands, a lake, and forested wetlands here. A public boat-launching ramp is available for lake access.

Animals need to be protected because their biggest threat is loss of habitat. The ecosystem must meet their needs for food, water, cover, and other important elements. The Reelfoot area refuges are examples of what people can do to provide habitat that supports waterfowl, marsh and water birds, fish, and certain mammals. Water levels are controlled here to preserve the wetland character. The forests are managed through selective cutting that preserves mast-producing trees—those that bear acorns and nuts—and animal dens. Fields of grain provide food for migrating and wintering waterfowl. If any of these elements were missing, this area would not attract and feed large numbers of waterfowl.

# Saving the Eagles

Reelfoot Lake was for many years a favorite winter home and nesting location for hundreds of American bald eagles which prey on fish, waterfowl, and other wildlife. Beginning in the 1950s, DDT contamination precipitated a nationwide decline in the eagle population, and nesting at Reelfoot stopped in 1963.

In 1980 Tennessee started reintroducing the bald eagle through a process called *hacking*, which involves releasing young wild birds into a new area. These birds are initially moved from their birth nests before they can fly and placed in cages on hacking towers, or platforms, where they have no contact with humans.

When the young birds are 12 weeks old and ready to fly, they are let out of the cage. When birds of prey become sexually mature and are ready to establish nests and raise their young, they normally return to the area where they learned to fly, so this method gradually built a nesting population at Reelfoot Lake.

In 1983 Reelfoot had its first hacking success—a nest that produced young *and* from which the young birds learned to fly. The survival rate for hacked eagles is 55 percent the first year and 90 percent each succeeding year. By 1988, the nesting population of eagles was reestablished. Now, up to 250 birds winter here.

***Where:*** Visitors center is on State 157 a mile north of State 22 between Union City and Samburg.

*When:* Refuge open year-round; daily, during daylight hours; visitors center, 8 A.M. to 4 P.M. Monday through Friday (daily in winter); Grassy Island Auto Tour, March 15 to November 15; Grassy Island Walking Trail, year-round; Lake Isom, March 15 to October 15.

*Admission:* Free.

*Amenities:* Visitors center, observation platforms, boat-launching ramps, hiking trail.

*Activities:* Wildlife viewing, photography, self-guided two-and-a-half-mile wildlife auto drive, fishing, Grassy Island Walking Trail.

*Other:* Hunting by permit for squirrel, raccoon, deer, and wild turkey.

*For more information:* Refuge Manager, Reelfoot NWR, Federal Building, Room 129, 309 North Church Street, Dyersburg, TN 38024. Phone, 901-287-0650. Fax, 901-287-0468.

Refuge Manager, Lake Isom NWR (same as preceding).

Free booklet, "National Wildlife Refuges: A Visitors Guide," U.S. Fish and Wildlife Service, Publications Unit, MS-130 Webb Building, 4401 North Fairfax Drive, Arlington, VA 22203 (also available at refuges).

Websites, National Wildlife Refuge System home page, http://bluegoose.arw.r9.fws.gov/; National Wildlife Refuge Association, http://www.refugenet.org/.


# In and Around Memphis

The city of Memphis grew from its strategic location on the Mississippi River, where barges were (and still are) the lifeblood of commerce for a wide area of America's heartland. Today this city is a large center of business and culture surrounded by miles of fertile farmland. If you have only driven *past* Memphis, as we have done so many times, we invite you to spend a few days here and see what the city has to offer to the nature enthusiast.

## Memphis Zoo and Aquarium

The Memphis Zoo, which recently underwent a $30 million expansion and renovation, should be on every visitor's itinerary. Perhaps it is, since it is a top tourist attraction here. If your impression of city zoos is that they are places where animals are kept in dreary cages with concrete floors—well, that was the old style. This is a place to see what a zoo can and should be.

This zoo, which had its first permanent building dedicated in 1909, sits on 72 wooded acres in the heart of the city (in Overton Park), where nearly 3,000 animals representing 400 species from around the world call it home. It's been recognized internationally for its animal breeding programs that have helped preserve the lowland gorilla, snow leopard, and Pere David deer and has breeding pairs of Sumatran tigers, cheetahs, clouded leopards, and rare yellow back duikers.

The zoo has created several state-of-the-art areas that they describe in one word, "Exzooberance." Since 1993, when the talk of the town was the newly developed four-acre Cat Country, the zoo has been adding similar habitat areas for other species. All the animals roam freely within their domain, restrained usually by high-tension wire and moats.

Colorful Egyptian motifs of hieroglyphs and columns at the entrance set the theme that is repeated throughout the zoo—in the orientation plaza, administration building, Elephant's Trunk Gift Shop, Discovery Center, and Education Building.

In Cat Country, the habitats are very exotic and contain caves, pools, rock outcroppings (kopjes), grassy savannas, subtropical plants such as bamboo, and waterfalls. To give a sense that these are real places that people have inhabited, an Egyptian temple, the ruins of an ancient city, and an Asian pagoda bridge are part of the setting.

As you enter Cat Country, you see the African lions from East Africa and the Kalahari Desert. A sign says that the females of a pride often stay together all their lives, while the males are usually ousted within three years. The males defend their territory, and the lionesses do the hunting.

Directly across is the fishing cat from Asia, given this name because it dives headfirst into the water to catch fish, frogs, and mollusks. This cat likes tidal marshes, so there is a lot of water, including a waterfall, fallen trees for walking bridges, and plenty of vegetation.

We walk over a footbridge passing through tall bamboo plants, while signs along the way tell us about prehistoric cats and today's cats. What is the one characteristic all nocturnal animals have? The signs explain.

One by one, the habitats delight your eye and tell you a story. The Sumatran tiger, the largest of all living cats, is an endangered species. The clouded leopard is a natural gymnast that can hang from a limb by its hind feet. The spotted leopard is becoming very rare and is found only in remote areas from Africa through the Middle East and India to China and Asia. One of the yellow-spotted leopards here is a female that carries the black gene and so could have black cubs.

Indian muntjac deer make a barking sound and have "tusks" (actually, protruding teeth) that they use in territorial fights. The red panda, a very rare species, is related to the raccoon and is active mainly at night, feeding on bamboo, acorns, and other vegetation. The snow leopard, which comes from high in the Himalayas, would probably welcome a blizzard, we think. Its furry paws act as natural snowshoes.

We enjoy viewing the spotted jaguars from the several vantage points that are provided. It is the only surviving big cat in the Western Hemisphere. Across from the jaguar habitat (but out of sight) is one of its favorite prey, the capybara, a huge rodent from South America that weighs about 100 pounds. Just try to imagine a giant guinea pig! It shares its home here with the crested screamer, a bird similar to ducks and geese, which nests in marshes and grasslands. It can be tamed and, in fact, makes a pretty good "watch animal," we are told.

The jaguarundi is a sleek brown cat that loves to swim and is usually active at dusk. It ranges from Arizona to Texas and on down to South America. The caracal lynx has pointed black ears that give it an inquisitive air. It is very quick and loves to climb and jump.

The cheetahs, from sub-Saharan Africa, are endangered in the wild, but here they move about freely and even have room to do what they enjoy most—sprinting. Three cheetah cubs were born in 1996 and quickly became favorites with visitors. Across from the cheetahs are the meerkats, said to be the "animal of the '90s" because they are so entertaining. Together in colonies, they chatter constantly.

Nearby is the Cat House Café. The historic facade incorporates gold-leaf lion statues from the old Carnivora Building (the former home of the cats) that were saved to decorate this new 3,000-square-foot building. It has a colorful Moroccan decor inside and huge window walls that overlook a lush animal habitat on one side and a kiddie playground and patio on another. The restaurant seats 165 people indoors and 85 on the patio.

Animals of the Night, which opened in 1995, features nearly 40 species of mammals, birds, fish, reptiles, amphibians, and invertebrates in freestanding exhibits. It is exciting to view because the lighting schedule turns day into night, so the animals are active during normal visiting hours. Entering, you are in partial darkness and sense that this is the sunset hour. This turns to "night" as you enter the forest area and move along. In the cave and deep forest settings, you can see vampire bats, Jamaican fruit bats, blind cave fish, Arabian wildcats, fennec foxes, bandicoots, kinkajous, and other fascinating nocturnal creatures such as naked mole rats (bucktoothed, but cute). The animals in this exhibit represent all kinds of living things—species that fly, swim, climb trees, or live underground. Watching the aardvarks eat gets the crowd excited every time, while the "glow-in-the-dark" bodies of Emperor scorpions present an eerie picture. As you leave, the exit area portrays a sunrise. It's time for your biological clock to readjust.

Primate Canyon is a showplace for some sociable creatures—gorillas, orangutans, colobus monkeys, lemurs, siamangs, and lion-tailed macaques—that always intrigue us with their antics. It is a spacious, outdoor habitat even larger than Cat Country. These animals play in natural settings that we can view from three levels as they climb and swing on towering structures. Or we can look at them nose-to-nose through a glass window. Do they like their new home? No doubt, since two colobus monkeys produced their first offspring just a few months after moving in—the first-ever colobus monkey birth at the zoo. That they are an endangered species of black-and-white colobus (*Guereza kikuyuensis*) made the event especially noteworthy.

On the heels of the two areas just mentioned was the opening of *Once Upon a Farm*. In this interactive exhibit of a working farm, we find out why farm animals are important to civilization as we know it. We see demonstrations of farming activities and learn about seven animal species. Contrast the wild boar of 9,000 years ago with the friendly and intelligent potbellied pig of today. Or, compare a primitive sheep with today's Babydoll Southdown sheep, raised for their prized fleece. Find out all the interesting facts about the Nubian goat, miniature zebu cattle from India, Dexter cattle from Ireland, various unusual types of chickens, and even prairie dogs, to heighten your understanding of how farming and wildlife fit in the picture together. You will even learn what these seemingly mismatched pairs have in common: cotton and cabbage, papyrus and peanuts, garlic and grapes, roses and radishes, and pine trees and peppermints.

You can get farm food at "The Roost," a concession area near the farm exhibits. Corn bread and beans, ham and biscuits, and farm-style pies are among the offerings here.

At our visit, we were entertained by the zookeepers feeding the seals, and we recommend arriving early in the morning when many of the animals are feeding and being generally more active.

Achievements such as this don't happen overnight, or without both public and private funding and the support of the whole community. Memphis can be proud of this one!

*Where:* Overton Park. Enter the park from Poplar Avenue, or follow signs from I-40.
*When:* Daily. March 1 through last Saturday in October, 9 A.M. to 6 P.M.; last Sunday in October through February, 9 A.M. to 5 P.M. Closed Thanksgiving, Christmas Eve, Christmas Day.
*Admission:* Adults through 59, $7.00; 60 and over, $5.50; 2 through 11, $4.50.
*Amenities:* Restaurant, snack bars, gift shop.
*Special events:* Zoo Boo, Winter Lights, Zoo Grass, Senior Day (free to over 60). Inquire.

*Other:* Barrier-free access, stroller and wheelchair rental.
*For more information:* Memphis Zoo, 2000 Galloway Avenue,
Memphis, TN 38112. 901-276-9453. Website, http://www.mem
phiszoo.org/ then select.

## Memphis Pink Palace Museum

The Memphis Pink Palace Museum was housed for years in
a mansion built by Piggly Wiggly founder and philanthropist
Clarence Saunders and called the Pink Palace because of its
marble exterior. Completed in 1923, the 35,223-square-foot
structure sat on a 155-acre estate on the outskirts of Memphis.
In the late 1920s it was converted into the museum; the city
grew around it. Later all but 10 acres of the original property
were sold.

Today's modern two-story museum, situated in front of the
mansion, has a planetarium and 30,000 square feet of permanent and touring exhibits about the natural and cultural history of the Mid-South. A 26,000-foot underground education
wing has been added, with classrooms, geology and biology
labs, an auditorium, and a four-story-tall IMAX theater.

The mansion, which houses the museum's headquarters,
was completely renovated and reopened its doors to the public in 1996. A permanent exhibit focuses on life in Memphis
in the early 20th century. Included is an Entrepreneur Hall of
Honor highlighting careers of Memphians "whose vision
changed the way the world does business."

The museum has a spacious lobby leading to the planetarium, museum shop, and snack area and the natural-history
exhibits. Right away, we know this will be a hands-on experience. We enter an area called Small Worlds that displays
examples of what people have seen through microscopes,
starting with instruments from around 1600. All of the
microscopes are displaying the image of a flea. It starts out

being very blurred, and as the microscopes get more advanced, the image becomes increasingly sharp, until finally we're scanning with an electron microscope where the color is gone and the image is three-dimensional and white. We also learn about scientists who were important in the development of the microscope.

Did Tennessee have dinosaurs? Yes, and the Coon Creek Fossil Exhibit tells the story. In 1950 a young scientist was following an exposed section of a meandering creek bed near Milledgeville in McNairy County when he discovered a deposit of marine shells and vertebrate remains. The skeletal remains date from the Upper Cretaceous period, about 70 million years ago.

Three things made this find extraordinary. First, these are no ordinary fossils that have turned to stone. Because of the sandy sediment that covered them, they have been preserved exactly as they were when they lay on the ocean floor. And because they have not been altered by time, all the details remain, showing how closely they resemble today's living saltwater animals. Second, among the fossils were scattered parts of a mosasaur, a seagoing, short-necked predator that sometimes reached 40 feet in length. Third, nowhere else in the world have so many shells and skeletons from this period been found in a single location. A two-foot-square block of soil can contain hundreds of them. More than 600 species have been found, including clams, oysters, crabs, snails, sharks, and huge seagoing reptiles. The best examples from this world-famous find are on display in the museum.

The museum owns the Coon Creek Science Center, where access for study purposes is by reservation only through the education department (901-320-6320).

The other exhibits we saw were:

**Birds.** Walk up a ramp with your hands on a "flight rail" and feel how birds flap their wings. Listen to bird sounds and see how they look on an oscilloscope. Did you know that there are more than 8,000 species of birds and 20 billion individuals in North America alone? Learn about habitat, communication, nests and eggs, the Mississippi flyway, and bird survival. The special section about birds of prey displays mounted specimens of many of them.

*Oxbow Lakes.* These little crescent-shaped lakes are formed when rivers change their path. Many displays here show different environments around the oxbow lakes, including their inhabitants. We see things that are underwater and what is above, and we learn about plant succession and its stages.

*Mammals of the Mid-South.* Here are mounted animals in realistic woodland scenes. Learn what you can tell from a mammal skeleton (how they move, what they eat); study the pouched animals (can they fly?); view flesh eaters, predators, and prey (where did wild hogs come from, and what happened to the bison?); and see small-window views of rodents (is an armadillo a rodent?).

*Geology: 4.6 Billion Years of Earth History.* The Restless Earth shows how continents formed on Earth as plates separated, where these plates will be 150 million years in the future, and what is happening on the west coast of North America today. A Walk Through Time is about geologic history. It starts at 4 billion 600 million years ago and goes through all the geologic periods through the Ice Age—four episodes of glaciation that ended in the Mid-South about 12,000 years ago. We see casts of skeletons of gigantic prehistoric creatures, including a mastodon which towers above us and a huge dilophosaurus of the early Jurassic period.

The geology display also identifies another Tennessee site that has fossil remains: Somerville, in Fayette County. Forty-five million years ago it was a subtropical river delta similar to the bayous in present-day north Florida. Fine-grained mud preserved more than 25 species of trees and shrubs. Thousands of leaf impressions are found in the bluffs north of the Loosahatchie Bottoms. The plant families they represent can still be seen today.

Upstairs in the museum are cultural history exhibits and an old-time Piggly Wiggly store. Children will love the miniature animated circus in a nearby area. It operates for half an hour each morning and twice on Saturdays. Also, a touring science exhibit offers hands-on experiments and games to play.

The Sharpe Planetarium schedules many types of shows. We saw Cosmic Whispers, about radio astronomy, what the world's most famous radio observatories are doing, and some of the latest discoveries in this exciting field.

*Where:* 3050 Central Avenue, Memphis (between East Parkway and Highland Street).

*When:* Daily. Monday through Wednesday, 9 A.M. to 5 P.M.; Thursday through Saturday, 9 A.M. to 9 P.M.; Sunday, noon to 5 P.M.; closes one hour earlier Monday through Thursday from Labor Day through Memorial Day (school-year schedule). Sharpe Planetarium, one or more shows daily (request schedule). Closed New Year's Day, Thanksgiving, Christmas Eve, Christmas Day.

*Admission:* Adults, $5.50; seniors, $5.00; 3 to 12, $4.00 (special events and planetarium admission extra).

*Amenities:* Museum shop, Sharpe Planetarium, snack area, Union Planters IMAX Theater, Pink Palace Mansion.

*Activities:* Exhibits, IMAX-format movies, planetarium shows, puppet shows, music laser-light concerts.

*Special events:* Adult explorer day trips; children's "Science Saturdays" and weekend "Camp-In" sleep-overs. Inquire.

*Other:* Nonsmoking; barrier-free access.

*For more information:* Memphis Pink Palace Museum, 3050 Central Avenue, Memphis, TN 38111-3399. 901-320-6320. General IMAX information, 901-763-4629. Website, http://www.memphismuseums.org/ then select.

## Lichterman Nature Center

It's a 65-acre wildlife sanctuary and environmental education facility, but if you could see out through the trees, you'd be looking at high-rise office buildings. Not to worry: this peaceful environment could just as well be a hundred miles from Memphis, because what you *do* see is a southern hardwood forest, a sprawling lake, fields, and marshes. More than 350 varieties of plants, 200 kinds of birds, 45 kinds of reptiles and amphibians, and 35 species of small mammals are here, too.

You can wander on trails through all these areas. The main trails lead to loop trails that are self-guided, with descriptive signs along the path and illustrated brochures. Most of these self-guided loops take less than an hour to complete. The Forest Ecology Loop teaches about the plant life and creatures of the forest and how to "read the woods." The Tree and Shrub Loop teaches how to identify 14 different species. The Native Plant Loop contains forest wildflowers that are common to this region. The Marsh and Ecology Loop follows a causeway and boardwalk between two ponds, then circles back along either a spillway or a cove (your choice). Either way, this trail teaches about wetlands and their inhabitants, and you may see mallards, wood ducks, turtles, kingfishers, and signs of beavers. There is also a Sensory Trail that is paved and accessible for wheelchairs and strollers.

The interpretive center is a historic log structure with stone fireplaces, built in 1929. The large reception area has an information desk and a gift shop.

Down the hall is a Discovery Room for small children.

They can learn about the anatomy of a honeybee, see cross sections of tree trunks and animal skeletons, look into discovery boxes and find things, identify animal tracks, and look at bird pictures on the windowsills to see if the same birds are outside.

Across from the Discovery Room is an excellent ecology exhibit that shows the relationship between living things and their environment. It explains how an ecologist combines the work of other scientists to learn how the pieces in nature fit together. The forest ecosystem, different layers of habitat, predators and prey, the marsh, recycling, decomposition, succession—all these concepts are presented in interesting ways.

At the other end of the center is a night room. Take a flashlight inside and get the feeling of nighttime in the outdoors. Feel things in the dark, or shine your light to read about what happens in the night. There's even a tent.

Behind the building is a butterfly garden, with a greenhouse next to it. Bees and butterflies are working here on the flower blossoms. Birds are everywhere, too.

This facility also rehabilitates injured wildlife. Laws prohibit showing animals as they are being treated, but we are allowed to see some that cannot be returned to the wild. Here were a red-tailed hawk that had flown into a utility wire, two owls with partially severed wings, and a great horned owl that had become too tame and preferred to be with people instead of living in the wild.

Special events, including guided nature walks, occur throughout the year. Friday-night fireside programs are open to the public. Here's what might be offered: Zzub Zzub! (an entertaining puppet show about bees), Tall Tales with the Storytellers, Night Hike! (look for beavers, raccoons, owls, and other nocturnal creatures), and Stargazing at the Night Skies (look through telescopes at stars and planets). These are after-hours programs. An admission fee applies.

There is also a regular Sunday-afternoon wildlife program. The week we visited, the interpretive specialists were planning to include a boa constrictor as part of the show.

Another kind of special event is the twice-yearly sale of native plants. This is an excellent way to acquire plants that furnish food or shelter for songbirds, butterflies, and hummingbirds, or simply beautify the landscape.

The Lichterman Nature Center is first of all an education facility. It was the first nature center in the United States to be fully accredited by the American Association of Museums.

Tip: if you spend the day here, bring your lunch. There are no concession stands or vending machines.

*Where:* 5992 Quince, Memphis (between Ridgeway and I-240).
*When:* Year-round. Tuesday to Saturday, 9:30 A.M. to 5 P.M.; Sunday, 1 P.M. to 5 P.M. Closed New Year's Day, Thanksgiving, Christmas Eve, Christmas Day.
*Admission:* Adults, $2.00; 3 through 18 and seniors, $1.00. Group rates.
*Amenities:* Interpretive center, gift shop, wildflower greenhouse, amphitheater, 10-acre lake, self-guided nature trails.
*Activities:* Nature walks, guided tours, picnicking, viewing exhibits, nature-oriented activities.
*Special events:* Spring and fall wildflower sales; adult-education classes. Pre-K First Saturdays, Puddlejumpers, and summer ecology camps. Kindergarten S.N.O.O.P.S. classes. Family Fireside Series.
*Other:* Nonsmoking; barrier-free access and paved trail; vending machines not provided.
*For more information:* Lichterman Nature Center, 5992 Quince Road, Memphis, TN 38119. 901-767-7322. Website, http://www.memphismuseums.org/ then select.

## Memphis Botanic Garden

In the minds of many, Memphis and gardens just seem to go together—especially in spring, when azaleas are blooming everywhere. Given such a city, it's not surprising to find a 96-acre botanic showplace in its midst.

From the spacious parking lot at the Memphis Botanic Garden, enter the visitors center lobby on the east side of the Goldsmith Civic Garden Center to pick up information and start your tour. The center has an art exhibition hall, a horticultural library, an auditorium, meeting rooms, and a gift shop where you can purchase garden-related gifts and accessories.

Outside, you'll enjoy viewing lush lawns, wooded plots, serene lakes, and display gardens. The individual gardens are showpieces designed and tended by local garden clubs and plant societies. One of the largest public iris gardens in the United States is here, along with an impressive rose garden with 1,500 bushes and the largest collection of Asian magnolias in the Southeast.

*Seijaku-En* (Garden of Tranquility) is the name of the Japanese garden, redesigned in 1989. As in all Japanese gardens, everything is symbolic, so the emphasis is not only on the objects but also on what they represent.

# *Seijaku-En,* a Japanese Garden

Look for the symbolism in the zigzag bridge. According to Japanese folklore, demons can only walk a straight line, so when you cross the bridge, any troubles that are following you will fall into the water.

The arch of the Red Drum (half-moon) Bridge reflects in the water below, creating the image of a full circle of unity.

Tortoise Island, near the Red Drum Bridge, represents strength and a long life, while Crane Island bestows good luck on all admirers.

The multicolored koi (carp) in Lake Biwa also symbolize strength. Their movement adds life to the water, and they lift their mouths above the surface for visitors to feed them. (These fish were first used in Japanese gardens as an offering to the god of ponds.)

The Moongazing Pavilion gets its name from the way it is positioned on a small hill, allowing a view of the rising moon.

Trees are stunted and contorted to appear windblown. They are prized for their attractive evergreen foliage, their flowers, or their autumn color.

Stones are carefully grouped to suggest scenes from nature, and traits may be attributed to them. The vertical "Guardian Stone" near the lake is said to be very wise.

---

The Sensory Garden is close to the entrance and has wide paved paths that accommodate wheelchairs, canes, and walkers. It has received the Founder's Fund Award from the Garden Club of America for meeting the unique needs of people with disabilities while emphasizing how all five senses help us discover the natural world.

Aromatic plants—roses and other flowers, herbs, junipers—encourage the sense of smell. Sour fruits, sweet berries, and edible plants are for tasting. Birdsongs, breezes, and rippling water create sounds. The variations of color and shape and the sparkle of the water are visually pleasing. And plant textures and garden sculptures invite the visitor's touch.

The planting design emphasizes visual contrast, which aids people with impaired vision, and the large letters on plant labels are also easier to see. Blind people can "see" the garden model as they touch it. Raised beds bring plants closer to those in wheelchairs. And all can appreciate the convenient benches in shady places.

Another area that might be unexpected among formal plantings is the five-acre wildflower woodland with its native flowers, ferns, trees, and shrubs, and its natural woodland paths. More than 350 species and varieties of American native plants grow here, many of them rare or endangered. This area also attracts birds and other wildlife.

Here's a short list of what you can find in different seasons: conservatory plants, indoor cactus collection, and Japanese garden year-round; pansies and ornamental cabbage in winter; magnolias in late February and March; 75 cherry trees blooming in March; dogwood and 40 varieties of azaleas in April; iris mid-April to mid-May; herbs and perennials from April through October; roses from May until frost; daylilies in June; organic varieties (plants grown without using pesticides or commercial fertilizer) summer and fall; and mums in October.

There are two picnic areas that can be reserved. One, a covered pavilion surrounded by shade trees, is on the shore of Lake Audubon. The other has picnic tables in a grassy area among tall pine trees; both are pleasant places to do lunch.

Something special is going on nearly every week. Adult workshops are very popular. Most are about two hours long, and they cover a wide range of subjects such as horticulture, landscape design, flower arranging, photography, cooking, attracting birds, and calligraphy. Modest registration fees apply.

A two-day Good Earth Festival (May or June) is a major event that has themes of environment, ecology, and health and includes a trade show. There is also an environmental playhouse for children, providing activities such as solar cooking, natural bird feeder construction, and worm composting.

Other recurring events emphasize music and art, and there

are semiannual plant sales and special children's activities such as Story Time in the Gardens.

*Where:* 750 Cherry Road, Memphis (in Audubon Park: turn north from Park Avenue).

*When:* Daily. Monday through Saturday, 9 A.M. to 6 P.M.; Sunday, 11 A.M. to 6 P.M. (November through February, closes 4:30 P.M.). Closed major winter holidays.

*Admission:* Adults, $2.00; 65 and over, $1.50; 6 to 17 and full-time students, $1.00; under 6, free.

*Amenities:* Gardens, library, auditorium, gift shop, meeting rooms. Tram operates seasonally.

*Activities:* Botanical walks, wildlife viewing, photography, classes for adults and children, picnicking, fishing (16 and under, 65 and over).

*Special events:* Concerts, tours, festivals, plant sales. Inquire.

*Other:* Barrier-free access except across Red Drum Bridge.

*For more information:* Memphis Botanic Garden, 750 Cherry Road, Memphis, TN 38117. 901-685-1566. Website, http://aabga.mobot.org/AABGA/Member.pages/memphis.bot.gdn.html.

## Meeman–Shelby Forest State Park

North of Memphis, the Chickasaw Bluffs rise above river bottoms and bayous that flank the Mississippi River. Meeman-Shelby Forest State Park has towering trees and bluff roads that have some roller-coaster dips and curves. The western park boundary follows the river shoreline for about eight miles.

For recreation, you can choose from many picnic areas, a riding stable, a golf course, an Olympic-size swimming pool, volleyball, badminton, softball, and other outdoor activities.

Enjoy the more than 20 miles of walking and horseback trails and a 5-mile paved bicycle trail, which is also suitable for wheelchairs.

The campground has 50 sites, each with a table, a grill, and electric and water hookups. A bathhouse has hot showers, and a dump station services self-contained trailers. Reservations may be made through the visitors center.

Six two-bedroom furnished cabins, along the wooded shore of 125-acre Poplar Tree Lake, have kitchenettes and fireplaces, central air and heat, and color TVs. Cabin guests can fish right outside their door (fishing license required for ages 13 to 65) and swim in the park's Olympic-size pool.

Fishing is allowed year-round in the lake. Some outstanding largemouth bass have been taken, as well as bream and catfish. Rent jonboats at the park boat dock, or fish from the bank or pier.

The rustic Meeman Interpretive Center is open from Memorial Day through Labor Day and has natural-history exhibits that feature woodlands and wetlands. Naturalists conduct programs about park history, ecology, and the environment.

Other activities are varied: guided tours, pioneer-living demonstrations, organized games, movies, hayrides, square dances, and many other events. Schedules are available at the park office.

Wildlife is abundant, and there are many opportunities for viewing animals from the system of trails. A trail map is available at the visitors center.

The Chickasaw Trail is the longest—eight miles, following the bluffs from the Mississippi River Group Camp at the northern end, south to Poplar Tree Lake. You are likely to see raccoons, squirrels, and signs of beavers. Look to the skies for red-tailed hawks, barred owls, and eagles.

The Woodland Trail has three one-mile connected loops, starting at the interpretive center. The first loop passes through ferns and towering oak trees and descends the bluff to the Piersol Group Camp. You can return or continue on, following a stream that has formed small oxbow lakes. The trail then climbs the bluff, where you can choose to continue on the third loop to the Woodland Trail Shelter.

The Pioneer Springs Trail is five miles long and follows the base of the Chickasaw Bluffs through mature cypress, cottonwood, and poplar trees.

Even though visitation is heaviest in summer, we think the cooler days of early spring and late fall are excellent times to hike the trails.

*Where:* Thirteen miles north of Memphis. Exit north from I-240 on State 388 (North Watkins Road). Go west until Watkins Road dead-ends into Benjestown Road. Go left to Bluff Road (first stop sign). Go right one-half mile to the park entrance on the left.

*When:* Year-round, 8 A.M. to 10 P.M. in summer (closes at sundown in winter).

*Admission:* Free. Fees for cabins, camping, boat rental.

*Amenities:* Visitors center, cabins, campgrounds, interpretive center, snack bars, two fishing lakes, boat-launching ramps, boat rentals, stables.

*Activities:* Year-round picnicking, fishing, playground, field games (free equipment checkout), nature trails, bike trails, bicycle rental, horse trails, backpacking. Seasonal (Memorial Day through Labor Day) swimming.

*Other:* Barrier-free access. Motorized vehicles prohibited on trails. Electric motors only allowed on lake. Managed hunts for small game, waterfowl, deer, and turkey (call Tennessee Wildlife Resources Agency: 901-423-5725).

*For more information:* Visitors Center, Meeman-Shelby Forest State Park, Box 10, Grassey Lake Road, Millington, TN 38053-5099. 901-876-5215. Website, http://www.state.tn.us/envi ronment/parks/ then select.

# Heart of Delta Country

## Cypress Grove Nature Park

Throughout the state are places designated as Wildlife Viewing Areas. The sign that identifies all of them is a brown square with white binoculars in silhouette. It was by noticing the binoculars that we found Cypress Grove Nature Park. The Cypress Grove sign on U.S. 70 west of Jackson is large enough, but the gray signboards flanked by stone pillars are easy to overlook.

This park, managed by the Jackson Recreation and Parks Department as part of its greenbelt development, is full of the unexpected. It is a 165-acre tract at the edge of the city in a river bottomland that has open meadows, a mature cypress forest, and two fishing lakes. At the entrance is a visitors center, and nearby is a picnic pavilion. Meandering through the property is a one-and-three-tenths-mile elevated boardwalk that provides excellent vantage points for viewing wildlife, trees, and plants. Right on the boardwalk is a raptor center— six large enclosures built on platforms that house permanently injured birds of prey. There is also a large teaching pavilion in this area where naturalists conduct programs and workshops.

The raptor center is on Jewelweed Trail, a spur of the main boardwalk, where we are in for a surprise. The tall jewelweed plants are covering the ground and blooming at our feet.

Looking at the orange flowers, we suddenly notice a lot of movement and then realize that all over the jewelweed are hummingbirds, more than we have ever seen in one spot. Because of the boardwalk's elevation, we are looking down at the birds all around us. It is an unusual perspective.

This trail passes close to a large open meadow and provides good views of it. We are again surprised, this time by the masses of colorful flowers that are obviously there to tantalize photographers and impressionist painters. It's September, but we sometimes prefer to connect wildflowers with spring and forget that *other* season! Joyce Harsson, who is in charge of the park, explains that fall—September through mid-October—is the peak time to see flowers in bloom. Among the many varieties are tickseed sunflower, partridge pea, and Virginia meadow beauty.

Joyce's recommendation of the best time to come might surprise many people.

"Visitation is heavy in summer," she said, "and even heavier in spring and fall—yet, the most interesting time to come is in the dead of winter. Especially for viewing wildlife. In winter all the foliage is gone, and the deer have herded up. Also, many kinds of waterfowl pass overhead as they go from their roosting place to a feeding area on down the river. We're right on their path.

"In the winter," she continued, "we have night programs. One of the most popular is the Owl Prowl. On a February night I take a group of people down the boardwalk to an area where the birds are nesting. I call the barred owls, who often come out and scold me."

This park is a haven also for songbirds, hawks, two species of herons, turkey vultures, cottontail rabbits, gray squirrels, mink, raccoons, frogs, and turtles.

The forest is thick with very tall trees. Besides cypress, we identified white ash, red maple, sweet gum, and water tupelo.

When leaves are on the trees, it is quite dark underneath. In this setting look for cardinal flowers—vivid scarlet blooms on upright stems that create small bright spots in the landscape.

The main trail splits, and the left fork ends at Killdeer Pond. Jewelweed is here, too (and of course, more humming-birds). The pond has that air of languor that comes when mist rises and floats off in little wisps and the air is filled with the sound of bees on flowers. A hammock would be nice!

Retracing our steps, we head for Wood Duck Lake and the Rockwell Observation Tower. On the way, the boardwalk makes a small circle around Cypress Knee Loop. It encloses a little forest of cypress knees—the curious-looking woody projections that rise abruptly from roots of trees standing in water.

The boardwalk goes out across the lake to the tower. From the third level we have a good view of the lake and its islands. No ducks here today, but we're certain that in the lake are bluegills, bream, crappies, and bass.

The park offers short workshops once or twice a month on Saturdays. Some are free, others ask for "empty aluminum cans" as an entrance fee, and sometimes there is a modest materials charge.

Joyce noted, "The best-attended workshop is in early March. People come and learn how to build bluebird nesting boxes, how high to place them, which direction they should face, what to watch for, and how to take care of the boxes in the winter."

Among other workshops for adults and children are The Flower Press (pressing and framing wildflowers), Under-standing Animal Talk, Tree I.D., and Project Suet (instruc-tions, samples, and a recipe for beef suet cakes).

**Where:** Jackson, U.S. Route 70 West, about one and a quarter miles west of the intersection with U.S. Route 45 Bypass.

*When:* Year-round, daily. April through September, 8 A.M. to
7:30 P.M.; October through March, park closes at 5 P.M.
*Admission:* Free.
*Amenities:* Visitors center, raptor center, pavilion, observation
tower.
*Activities:* Wildlife viewing, walking, photography, picnick-
ing, fishing.
*Special events:* Workshops each month.
*Other:* Barrier-free access. Group tours by appointment (free).
*For more information:* Cypress Grove Park Naturalist, Jackson
Recreation and Parks Department, 400 South Highland, Jack-
son, TN 38301. 901-425-8364.

## Big Hill Pond State Rustic Park and Natural Area

The park, about 45 miles south of Jackson and 70 miles east
of Memphis, is bordered on the north by State 57 and on the
south by the Tuscumbia River and Cypress Creek, less than 2
miles from the Mississippi border.

The entrance on State 57 is well marked. We turn in and see
a sign, "Watch for Deer Crossing." That turns out to be very
good advice.

It's a misty, cool morning, with the temperature hovering
around 60 degrees and tinges of fall color on the trees. As we
go down a steep hill and up another one, we realize that we've
left the highway for a totally different world.

The park's 4,500 acres embrace hills and valleys, meadows,
lakes, rivers, floodplains, and swamps. All the trees are second
growth—chestnut oak and blackjack oak on the ridges, and
black gum, oak, willow, elm, tulip poplar, cedar, birch, and
pine in the valleys. The wetlands have bald cypress, cottonwood, alders, several kinds of oak, sweet gum, bitternut,
weeping willow, and tupelo.

This is a hiker's paradise, with 35 miles of marked loop and interconnecting trails that are classified as both Tennessee and National Recreation Trails. The six individual hiking trails range from ½ mile to 7 miles in length and follow the ridges and valleys, sometimes climbing 200 feet up steep hills and descending again. Hilltops and rocky overhangs offer splendid views, and an 80-foot tower on Tuscumbia Trail overlooks the entire park. No bicycles, horses, ATVs, or trail bikes (or vehicles of any kind) are allowed on the trails. Four primitive overnight shelters are reached only from the trails, and the carry-in, carry-out litter policy is observed.

Park Manager Jim Harrison said, "We cater to a whole different clientele than most other state parks. People come here to enjoy the outdoors by hiking the trails, camping, fishing, or just to view nature."

Some historical notes: this place was occupied by the Chickasaw Indians before 1819, but white traders occasionally passed through. You can see evidence of an old Indian village at one location within the park. In 1857 the Southern Railroad constructed an embankment for its tracks that restricted drainage from the low-lying areas that include what is now the park. This created swampland and a shallow 35-acre lake—Big Hill Pond—for which the park is named.

In the 1970s Dismal Branch was dammed to create the 165-acre Travis McNatt Lake, where you can now enjoy fishing for catfish, bass, and bluegills from the bank or from boats (there is a boat-launching ramp). The bass limit is 10 per day, and bass must be 15 inches long. Private boats are allowed, but they are restricted to electric motors only. Below the dam is the large Dismal Swamp. A boardwalk on the trail allows foot traffic through this area and excellent views of wetlands and waterfowl.

Not everything is primitive here, though. The campground, with 32 sites, is right on the main park road. It has rest rooms with showers, but water and electric hookups are not available at every site. And there are recreation areas nearby: a large picnic ground, a blacktop basketball court, a jungle gym for children, and an archery range.

Wildlife is abundant. Quail, wild turkeys, squirrels, otters, and raccoons have been seen—though we didn't see any—and mink and coyotes are present. Down by the lake we saw a young doe, and as we were leaving the park, we saw two mature does and a half-grown fawn. These deer are pretty shy, since they are hunted on 900 acres of the park during statewide hunting seasons. Hunting is off-limits around the lake, but hikers are advised that Turkey Call Trail (south of the railroad) is not closed to hunting.

This is also a place to find wildflowers. Come at the right time of year and look closely: you may see wild azaleas, the rare dwarf iris, or wood orchids.

Spring and fall bring the ospreys to the big lake, and you can have fun watching them dive for fish.

During the summer—Memorial Day through Labor Day —many daily activities are conducted by the park ranger and seasonal naturalists.

Winter is an excellent time to view migrating waterfowl. It's a musical time, too. An annual event on a December Friday and Saturday is Christmas Down by the Lake. Luminarias along the road light the way, and choirs and other groups perform Christmas music.

**Where:** State 57 between Pocahontas and Ramer (70 miles east of Memphis).
**When:** Year-round. Visitors center, Monday through Friday, 8 A.M. to 4:30 P.M. (closed all major holidays). Campground and public rest rooms, March 1 through November 30.
**Admission:** Free.
**Amenities:** Visitors center, campground, nature trails and overnight shelters, boat-launching ramp, boat rentals.

*Activities:* Hiking, backpacking, picnicking, fishing, camping, and interpretive and recreational activities.
*Special events:* Annual Christmas Down by the Lake.
*Other:* Barrier-free access to some locations. Deer, quail, squirrel, and turkey hunting allowed in statewide seasons.
*For more information:* Park Manager, Big Hill Pond State Rustic Park, Route 1, State Highway 57, Pocahontas, TN 38061. 901-645-7967. Website, http://www.state.tn.us/environ ment/parks/ then select.

## Natchez Trace State Park

This is a great park in more than one sense of the word. It's a 48,000-acre tract of land between the city of Jackson and Kentucky Lake that is a resort park, wildlife management area, and state forest. And, since I-40 runs right through it, getting there couldn't be easier.

Emphasis here is on forestry, wildlife, and history.

The modern visitors center, south of I-40, is in a grove of very tall, aromatic pine trees. Inside you'll find impressive displays about forests: The Forest Primeval, The Old Forest, The Community of Living Things, Indians Who Lived in This Area, The Old Natchez Trace, What Happens When Forests Are Ravaged (and what happened here), The Forest Reborn, and The Forest Sustaining.

This park is quite a few miles west of the Natchez Trace Parkway, so why does it bear the same name? From a little-known fact: the famous Nashville-to-Natchez trading route of the late 18th and early 19th centuries began as not just one wagon road but a series of trails and paths used by Native Americans (and maybe by buffalo, too). They gradually merged into a main route, but as robbers—"highwaymen"— on the trace became an ever-growing threat to travelers, peo-

*Wild Turkey, Natchez Trace State Park*

ple started using some of the earlier routes as alternates. One of these, called the Western Natchez Trace, came through this area.

History has taught some important lessons about land management and forestry. Early settlers used farming practices that changed the forested sandy clay hills into deep, eroded gullies—some of the most heavily abused land in the state. In less than 100 years, this land became incapable of producing decent crops. Although much of it has been reclaimed, the Fairview Gullies, one and a half miles south of I-40, are left to illustrate what occurred here.

Many people visit this park to view the Big Pecan Tree, which is the largest in the state and in 1973 bore the distinction of "world's largest" according to the American Forestry Association's Social Register of Big Trees. Soon, though, Louisiana and Virginia reported larger specimens. It is said that one of Andrew Jackson's men returning from the Battle of New Orleans gave a pecan to Sukey Morris, who planted it here in the spring of 1815. This cannot be proven. At any rate, the tree still lives and even produces some pecans. It is four miles north of I-40 on a paved loop drive that also goes by historic Mount Comfort Church and Cemetery and Maple Creek Lake.

Twenty-five old cemeteries are on the park property, reminders of early settlers. Most of these are found along hiking trails.

All Tennessee resort parks have a wide range of facilities, and this park lives up to that standard. On the wooded shores of Pin Oak Lake are the luxury Pin Oak Lodge and a restaurant noted for Southern cuisine. Swimming pools, tennis courts, a recreation room, a playground, and private meeting rooms are here also. Several miles away on Cub Lake are 18 air-conditioned rental cabins and a day-use area with a public beach.

Fishing is popular here on the four park lakes: Cub (58 acres), Pin Oak (690 acres), Maple Creek (90 acres), and Brown's Creek (167 acres). The last two are managed by the Tennessee Wildlife Resources Agency (TWRA). Cub Lake offers rowboat and pedal-boat rentals, and the other lakes have launching ramps for privately owned boats. The lakes hold bluegills; catfish; crappies; and largemouth, rock, and hybrid bass.

Three campgrounds provide a total of 145 sites plus water and electrical hookups, bathhouses with hot showers, and all the amenities expected in modern campgrounds. Availability is on a first-come, first-served basis. Equestrian camping is provided, too, at Wrangler Camp.

During the summer the park offers daily interpretive programs and recreation activities. Among annual events are a crafts fair and a Senior Citizens Shenanigan in April, a fishing rodeo the Saturday before July 4, and a two-day horseback ride in September.

The forest provides much of the park's appeal and many learning experiences. At one clearing, for instance, a sign explains that long, narrow openings provide food and cover for a variety of animals, especially small game such as rabbit and quail. Early successional native plants are growing here, and brush piles provide escape and nesting cover. Wild turkeys feed on the insects and seeds. Deer graze and bed in the openings and eat the woody browse around the edges of the fields.

Dirt fire trails crisscross the area through wooded places and fields and along lakeshores and streams, offering many miles of changing views. There is even a long overnight hiking trail for backpackers. Many backcountry trails are also open to motorcycles and other off-road vehicles, and a stable provides rental horses.

Wildlife management is practiced even on the trails. We notice a sign: "Do not take horses or vehicles on this trail because it has been planted in food for wildlife."

Kudzu management is another story, though. Like many other southern states, Tennessee has its "kudzu moments" (places where this aggressive vine has covered all the ground, shrubs, and trees with an otherworldly, destructive mantle). The park has areas covered with kudzu but also places where the kudzu is being destroyed—an expensive and time-consuming process.

In passing fields of kudzu in bloom, we had noticed a delicious fragrance in the air that was hard to identify. Now we took a close look at the flower clusters, which are similar in size and shape to pinecones and have individual pealike flowers about an inch long. As they bloom, the flowers change from violet to a magenta rose and back to violet, and they have a golden yellow patch at the base when fully open. We were able to identify the fragrance: grape lollipops! At least, there is *something* appealing about kudzu.

# Kudzu, the Mistake That Won't Go Away

Imagine digging 12 feet into the ground to kill the taproot of a vine that grows a foot a day and can be 60 feet long. You can't burn or cut the root, and it's resistant to herbicides. So kudzu just keeps on forming blankets over all vegetation in its path, blocking out the sunlight and strangling the native species it covers.

Blame the U.S. Soil Conservation Service, although it meant well. In the 1930s the agency got 73 million kudzu seedlings from Asia and planted them in the Southeast to control soil erosion along roadways. The irony is that because of kudzu's long taproot it does a poor job of erosion control!

It can be eradicated, at least in small areas, but that takes years and is very expensive—and while one plot of land is being rid of the pest, kudzu is invading other places at a dizzying rate with potato-like tubers that sprout prolifically.

When invasive exotics such as kudzu are introduced into an area, the biological controls—weather and insects—that keep them in check in their native ranges are often not present in the new location. This can create a disaster by disrupting the balance of nature.

The Tennessee Parks and Recreation Association and 13 other agencies strongly recommend that government agencies cease planting invasive exotics. Natchez Trace State Park is a good place to learn more about this problem.

---

*Where:* I-40 between Nashville and Jackson (exit 116).

*When:* Year-round. Summer, 8 A.M. to 10 P.M.; winter, 8 A.M. until sundown. Restaurant, March 1 to December 23.

*Admission:* Free.

*Amenities:* Visitors center, environmental learning center, inn, restaurant, gift shop, recreation hall, cabins, campgrounds, tennis courts, swimming pool, picnic sites, playgrounds, park store, service station, boat rentals, boat-launching ramps, stable, equestrian trails, hiking and biking trails, firing range.

*Activities:* Fishing, hiking, mountain biking, backpacking, OHVs, camping, swimming, tennis, horseback riding, outdoor games. Organized recreation and nature interpretation programs in summer.

*Special events:* Crafts fair, Senior Citizens Shenanigan, fishing rodeo, two-day trail ride.

*Other:* Barrier-free access. Caution: hunting allowed during statewide seasons; safety zones provided.

*For more information:* Park Manager's Office, Natchez Trace State Park, 24845 Natchez Trace Road, Wildersville, TN 38388. 901-968-3742.

Park Inn, 901-968-8176; toll-free reservations, 800-250-8616; information package, 800-421-6683.

Website, http://www.state.tn.us/environment/parks/ then select.

# Where the River Runs Through It

Lines that define the regions of a state are usually invisible, but in Tennessee there's a prominent exception. The middle and western parts are separated by the Tennessee River, a broad band of water that splits the state while flowing north from the Mississippi-Alabama border all the way to Kentucky and beyond. Along the way, it is mostly a lake. Near Tennessee's southern border it is Pickwick Lake, which extends southward into the two neighboring states. After a few miles on a northward course, it becomes Kentucky Lake, created by the Kentucky Dam some 30 miles north of the Tennessee-Kentucky border.

Kentucky Lake is a lot more than just a dividing line, though: it's the second-largest man-made lake in the world. With more than 160,000 surface acres of water and 2,300 miles of shoreline, it's a recreational playground that offers an immensely varied menu of opportunities. There are dozens of boat docks and marinas; two state parks; several federal and state waterfowl refuges and wildlife management areas; numerous recreational areas, some of which provide camping and RV sites; and public boat-launching ramps scattered up and down the lake. You can fish, hunt, swim, sail, water-ski, hike, view wildlife, and explore. You can either camp here or stay in cabins or rooms at the parks or various upscale resorts.

The Tennessee River follows a curious course that begins in the Blue Ridge province of the southern Appalachians in east Tennessee, heads in serpentine fashion southwest to Chattanooga, creates a great canyon there, then continues southwest past Huntsville, Alabama, takes a northwesterly course to the Tennessee line, and finally turns decisively north all the way to the Ohio River—but that's another story and another state!

## Pickwick Landing State Park

We both enjoy this park, but it's a special place for Lea because it offers him the chance to fish in Pickwick Lake and also in the tailrace below the dam, which is very close by. Both are very productive places, and when the wind makes the lake's surface too choppy for comfort, the tailwaters are always an alternate choice.

While fishing is a major attraction, the fully equipped marina can handle crafts of all sizes. Motorboating, sailing, and waterskiing are popular activities. Also, because Pickwick is on the mainstream Tennessee River navigational channel, it's a favorite port for yachters and houseboaters who are traveling up or down the river. For swimmers and waders, there are three public beaches at the park and a pool at the inn that is for park guests only.

Pickwick's ultramodern inn overlooks Pickwick Lake and has 75 single and double sleeping rooms and a dining room that seats 195. There's additional seating for 300 in the private dining room area. The inn also has a gift shop, lighted tennis courts, kiddie swimming pools, and a playground.

Those who prefer different kinds of accommodations have several alternatives. Ten two-bedroom deluxe cabins are fully equipped for housekeeping, each with central heating and cooling, TV, and a fireplace. A family camping area has 48 sites, each with a table, a grill, electrical and water hookups, and a dump station. Finally, a 347-acre primitive camping area has campsites, a modern bathhouse, a swimming beach, and a boat-launching ramp. A fee is charged for the use of this area.

There's much more. The park has a par 72, championship 18-hole golf course with a pro shop that rents clubs and carts. Other recreational activities include volleyball, badminton, horseshoes, archery, and field games.

***Where:*** Thirteen miles south of Savannah, Tennessee, on State 57 at the intersection with State 128 (20 miles north of Corinth, Mississippi).

***When:*** Year-round. Daily, 6 A.M. to 10 P.M. The inn and marina provide 24-hour service.

***Admission:*** Free. Modest fees for camping.

***Amenities:*** Resort Inn, restaurant, gift shop, cabins, campsites, marina, boat rentals, boat-launching ramp, snack bars, nature trails, playground, three swimming beaches (unsupervised).

***Activities:*** Boating, fishing, swimming, tennis, golf, hiking, picnicking, wildlife viewing, photography.

***Special events:*** Kid's Fishing Rodeo (August; see the following entry); inquire about others.

***Other:*** Barrier-free access.

***For more information:*** Pickwick Landing State Park, PO Box 15, Pickwick Dam, TN 38365-0015. Office, 901-689-3129; inn and shelter reservations, 901-689-3135; golf pro shop, 901-689-3149; toll-free reservations, 800-250-8615. Website, http://www.state.tn.us/environment/parks/ then select.

## Pickwick Tailwaters

The waters below Pickwick Dam literally teem with game fish. This tailrace gets more attention from resident and visiting anglers than any other in the state. Present are largemouth and smallmouth bass, crappies, white bass, yellow bass, striped bass, saugers, catfish, bluegills, and several other species.

There's virtually year-round fishing, plus two special annual events. During July and the first half of August, the National Catfish Derby Fishing Rodeo is held here. Weekly prizes are awarded for the biggest catfish caught that week, and other prizes are offered, too. At the conclusion of this event, a one-day National Catfish Derby Kid's Fishing Rodeo is held at Pickwick Landing State Park for kids 4 through 16. In midwinter a sauger tournament supplies action for cold-weather fishermen. Fall fishing is excellent, while spring is very productive except for times when rains create unusually high water conditions.

As with all of the dams which generate hydroelectric power, water levels can fluctuate radically and without warning. Anglers who are wading or in boats must exercise extreme care. When you're on the water, approved life vests are required by law.

*Where:* Thirteen miles south of Savannah, Tennessee, on State 57 at the intersection with State 128 (20 miles north of Corinth, Mississippi).

*When:* Year-round (there is no closed season on fishing).

*Admission:* Free.

*Amenities:* A TVA (Tennessee Valley Authority) public camping area below the dam with picnic tables, rest rooms, water and electrical hookups, and a boat-launching ramp.

*Activities:* Fishing, picnicking, camping.

*Special events:* National Catfish Derby Fishing Rodeo (summer); sauger tournament (winter).

*For more information:* Team Hardin County, Inc. (tourism information), Savannah, TN 38372. 800-552-3866.

Tennessee Wildlife Resources Agency, PO Box 40747, Nashville, TN 37204. 615-781-6500.

Catfish Derby E-mail, whiskers@usit.net.

## Tennessee and Cross Creeks National Wildlife Refuges

The state's national wildlife refuges (NWRs) can also be *people* refuges, because in addition to their primary purpose of serving as sanctuaries for waterfowl, they offer special havens where nature lovers can get a bird's-eye view of an amazing variety of wildlife. Designated refuge trails and auto routes lead you to the best spots for wildlife viewing and photography. During the winter months all entry is barred at some locations in order to minimize disturbance to waterfowl and other wildlife and for public safety.

The array of wildlife found on the refuges is mind-boggling: waterfowl, wading birds, shorebirds, ospreys, owls, and game birds are just a few of the 228 species of birds. Throughout the seasons, look for some of the 27 species of waterfowl, 25 species of warblers, and 14 species of raptors, some common and others considered to be quite rare. You may see endangered American peregrine falcons as they migrate through, or bald eagles that winter on the refuge. Among the 46 species of mammals present are white-tailed deer, squirrels, rabbits, skunks, raccoons, opossums, beavers, muskrats, and mink.

While the major portions of the refuges provide full protection of all wildlife, they are managed in such a way that hunters and fishermen have plenty of opportunity. However, neither camping nor fires are permitted.

Public-use areas at the refuges are open during daylight hours except as modified by hunting regulations. Check with the specific location for information, since the rules aren't the same at all places.

Two refuges lie on the Kentucky Lake corridor: the Tennessee NWR with three units on Kentucky Lake, and the Cross Creeks NWR on Barkley Lake to the east.

Tennessee NWR's northernmost unit is the 21,356-acre Big Sandy Unit, which has an auto-tour route, a wildlife foot trail, a marina, and numerous boat-launching ramps. The visitors contact point is on a secondary road located off State 69 near the town of Big Sandy.

The largest of the units, Duck River, encompasses 26,730 acres and features a marina and several boat-launching ramps.

Access to the visitors center is from U.S. 70 near New Johnsonville.

Busseltown, with 3,272 acres, is the southernmost unit, and the only facility is a boat-launching ramp. It is four miles east of State 69 between I-40 and Parsons (south of I-40). Turn on Broadys Landing Road to the launching ramp.

Cross Creeks National Wildlife Refuge totals 8,862 acres, about one-third of which is in hardwood forests, with the rest in water areas, brush, and farmland. Like its sister refuge, the Tennessee NWR, Cross Creeks was established mainly as an area for migrating waterfowl. In addition, it provides suitable habitat for more than 245 other bird species that include wading birds, shorebirds, hawks, ospreys, owls, bobwhite quail, mourning doves, and an abundant variety of songbirds. Mammals often seen are white-tailed deer, gray and fox squirrels, gray and red foxes, coyotes, beavers, mink, muskrats, opossums, and woodchucks. Also present are many species of reptiles, amphibians, and insects. Animal species number 480. Rare or endangered species likely to be sighted are the bald eagle, least tern, and American peregrine falcon.

Since Cross Creeks NWR straddles Barkley Lake, fishermen have plenty of opportunity. Sixteen launching ramps provide access. Limited hunting for deer and squirrels is permitted on certain parts of the refuge during the fall months.

Although no camping or fires are allowed, the refuge has many environmental and educational activities for all ages. Wildlife exhibits and audiovisual programs are offered at the visitors center three miles east of Dover off State 49. Much of the area is open for wildlife viewing; photography; nature study; boating; and mushroom, berry, and grape picking. Bicycling and horseback riding are permitted on established roads, and there are an auto tour and two interpretive foot trails. No swimming is permitted, but wading is allowed in specified places.

*Where:* Cross Creeks NWR: two miles east of Dover on State 49 (follow signs to the visitors center). Tennessee NWR—Big Sandy Unit: from the town of Big Sandy on State 69A north of Camden, take Lick Creek Road north to Lick Creek, then Bennetts Creek Road to the visitors center (about eight miles total); Duck River Unit (south of New Johnsonville): from U.S. 70, go south on Long Street to the dead end, turn left, then take the first right to the refuge entrance on the left (three and a half miles total).

*When:* Daylight hours only, and closed seasonally according to schedule (inquire). Cross Creeks visitors center open Monday through Friday year-round, 7 A.M. to 3:30 P.M.

*Admission:* Free.

*Amenities:* Cross Creeks NWR: visitors center; Tennessee NWR: visitors center, marina, boat-launching ramps, kiosks.

*Activities:* Wildlife viewing, bird-watching, photography, self-guided auto and walking tours, some guided tours, environmental education, boating, hunting, fishing, water-oriented recreation, limited bicycling and horseback riding.

*Nearby accommodations:* Cross Creeks NWR area: Leatherwood Resort & Marina, Route 2, Box 499, Dover, TN 37058 (931-232-5137).

Tennessee NWR area: Paris Landing State Park, Route 1, Buchanan, TN 38222 (901-642-4311); Buchanan Resort, Route 1, Box 440, Springville, TN 38256 (800-225-6302); Mansard Island Resort, Route 1, Box 261, Springville, TN 38256 (800-533-5590).

*Other:* Inquire about current conditions (bottoms may be flooded). Limited hunting permitted.

*For more information:* Cross Creeks NWR: Refuge Manager, Cross Creeks National Wildlife Refuge, 643 Wildlife Road, Route 1, Box 556, Dover, TN 37058. Phone, 931-232-7477. Fax, 931-232-5958.

Tennessee NWR: Refuge Manager, Tennessee National

Wildlife Refuge, 810 East Wood Street, Suite B, PO Box 849, Paris, TN 38242. 901-642-2091. Website, http://www.fws.gov/. E-mail, r4fw_tn.tns@mail.fws.gov.

## Land Between the Lakes

Visitors driving or hiking through the Tennessee Valley Authority's massive Land Between the Lakes Recreation Area never know what might lie around the next bend or over the next hill. One moment a brilliant bluebird might capture their attention, only to have it diverted seconds later by the sight of a herd of shaggy buffalo. That's simply an example, since there's an enormous diversity of birds and animals on this 270-square-mile national recreational and environmental education area. It's also a place where eagles, hawks, owls, Canada geese, wild turkeys, white-tailed deer, fallow deer (the oldest established herd in America), beavers, otters, and bobcats are likely to be seen—not to mention countless songbirds. It's known as a haven for 54 mammal and 230 bird species, and the current "hot" wildlife hangouts are noted on the Land Between the Lakes Web page.

Lbl, as it is commonly called, lies on a 40-mile-long inland peninsula between Kentucky and Barkley Lakes in Tennessee and Kentucky. Before the lakes were impounded, this was a remote and sparsely populated area referred to locally as "the land between the rivers." Kentucky Dam on the Tennessee River was built first, then Barkley Dam on the Cumberland. Since the dams were close together, the two navigable rivers were joined by a canal instead of having separate lock systems.

In the meantime, tva acquired 170,000 acres of the rolling fields and woodlands between them and began work on what was to be one of the nation's largest public playgrounds, designed to provide individuals and families with the opportunity to see and experience nature and enjoy a broad array of outdoor activities. No one who has visited the area can deny that TVA has succeeded magnificently. It was the third-most visited attraction in Tennessee in 1995 and 1996 (and the second-most visited in Kentucky). It has also gained world attention: in 1991 it was declared a biosphere reserve under the UNESCO Man and the Biosphere Program. As such, it is recognized as an international laboratory for environmental problem solving and a place dedicated to conserving natural resources.

There are features and activities for all outdoor interests and age groups. Fishermen and boaters have access to both lakes at launching ramps that are located all around the 300 miles of undeveloped shoreline. For hunters, LBL offers open seasons on waterfowl and 10 species of upland game. The white-tailed deer and wild turkey are particular favorites.

Roughly a third of the LBL territory is in Tennessee, and that is the part we will focus on most here (although, we'll have to discuss the exciting new area called the Elk & Bison Prairie in Kentucky). You can find out more about the Kentucky part in Ardi's companion book, *Natural Wonders of Kentucky*.

Visitors wishing to stay awhile have several camping choices, from tent camping to developed campgrounds that offer RV sites and full amenities. Piney Campground is easy to get to from U.S. 79, 19 miles east of Paris, Tennessee. Turn north on Fort Henry Road just east of the Scott Fitzhugh Bridge. This is an 11-mile paved road that curves east above Piney, provides access to the Fort Henry hiking trails, then goes east to the South Welcome Station on The Trace (the main road that runs the entire length of LBL).

Piney Campground has 322 sites with electrical hookups. These are well defined and can handle large motor homes. It also offers basic sites for tent campers and even some camping shelters for people who want to camp but don't have tents. They are one-room buildings equipped with beds, tables and chairs, electric outlets, and ceiling fans. Practically everything is provided in the campground to make your stay enjoyable: fishing pier, boat-launching ramps, fish-cleaning station, swimming beach, archery range, ball fields, shelters, playgrounds, bike skills court, campfire theater, equipment checkout station, hike and bike trails, swimming area, dumping station, rest rooms and showers, and public telephones. The fishing pier has barrier-free access. You can rent regular bicycles, mountain bikes, tents, and camping supplies at the campground's Outpost Supply Center.

Rushing Creek Campground is a less-developed site at the northwest corner of the Tennessee portion that is open year-round. It has 40 gravel campsites suitable for tents or RVs, drinking water, a multipurpose play court, picnic tables, grills, shelters, showers, modern rest rooms, a boat ramp, and courtesy docks. It does not have electricity or a dumping station.

For even more primitive camping, there are fee-access lake sites at Ginger Bay and Boswell Landing on Kentucky Lake, and at Gatlin Point and Neville Bay on Lake Barkley. Boswell Landing and Gatlin Point have chemical toilets, drinking water, picnic tables, grills, and launching ramps. Ginger Bay and Neville Bay have fewer amenities. If you're seeking even more primitive conditions, you can take advantage of LBL's open-camping policy that permits backcountry camping almost anywhere in the 170,000 acres of solitude. You will need a Backcountry Camper Use Permit (valid for 12 months from March 1 through February 28).

If you prefer more luxurious accommodations, you'll find them just west of LBL in nearby Paris Landing State Park, which has a modern inn, a restaurant, a swimming pool, a marina with boat rentals, a golf course, tennis courts, a gift shop, a recreation building, and nature trails. To the east are the towns of Dover and Clarksville. There are full-facility marinas outside LBL on Kentucky and Barkley Lakes.

Trails are provided for hikers, backpackers, and bicyclists throughout LBL, and off-highway vehicles (OHVS) are allowed on 2,500 acres of trails at Turkey Bay's OHV area in Kentucky (you can camp there, too). Also in the Kentucky portion are two trails especially for mountain bikes. All in all, LBL offers more than 200 miles of trails that can take you through meadows, forests, and wetlands and over flat or hilly terrain. You'll find road and trail maps at any of the welcome stations.

For hikers, the 65-mile North-South Trail sometimes follows old logging roads and meanders through valleys, beside streams, and along the lakeshore. You can hike shorter portions from several access points along The Trace. The Fort Henry Trail, a series of interconnecting loops, is 26 miles long and follows the Civil War retreat of Southern forces from Fort Henry to Fort Donelson. There are 35 miles of special trails for horseback riding in Kentucky at Wranglers Campground. Bicyclists can take advantage of lightly paved and little-traveled roads. Biking is prohibited on horseback and foot trails except where marked. During hunting season, blaze orange should be worn. You might want to avoid the early-morning and late-afternoon hours when hunters are most active.

Motorists can see much of LBL by car on The Trace. In Tennessee, access it from U.S. 79 about five miles west of Dover. The South Welcome Station is near the southern park entrance. In Kentucky, the Golden Pond visitors center (the main welcome facility) is at the intersection with U.S. 68/80.

The Trace also leads to The Homeplace-1850, an interpretive center just south of the Kentucky border that shows how rural families lived in the 19th century as they worked the land, planted crops, raised livestock, made cloth, and produced nearly everything they needed for food, clothing, and shelter. You will go back in time and learn about the environmental ethic of people who lived here. Did they live well? This old recipe for bread fritters might give a clue:

*Boil a quart of milk with cinnamon and sugar to taste. When done, stir in a tablespoon of rose water. Cut some slices of bread into a circular shape, soak them in milk until the milk is absorbed, then drain. Beat some yolks of eggs until frothy. Dip the bread slices into the yolks and fry them in butter. Serve them up dusted with powdered sugar.*

This property dates back to a Revolutionary War land grant, from which 40 acres were assigned to William Pryor, whose family settled here in 1808. It is still a working farm that grows corn and tobacco and raises sheep and hogs. Sixteen log structures are here, including 14 original structures moved to this site from nearby locations. They are typical of the mid-19th century—single- and double-pen houses, an ox barn, a springhouse, and other buildings. Daily programs, depending on the season, demonstrate butter making, fall plowing, tobacco firing, bread making, spinning, dyeing, weaving, and oxen working.

In June, the Four Rivers Folk Festival offers music, storytelling, and crafts demonstrations. In October, the Apple Festival salutes the American apple. Baking contests, demonstrations, cider making, wagon rides, storytelling, and music are all included.

Near The Homeplace is the Great Western Furnace, one of two iron furnaces remaining from the 1800s, when the LBL area was the center of a major iron-producing region by 1850. Iron furnaces took a great toll of timber, which was converted to charcoal to fuel the huge smelters. With new production methods, new ore deposits discovered elsewhere, and the local timber effectively depleted, iron production came to a standstill here by 1880.

In Kentucky, The Nature Station north of the Golden Pond visitors center is a mecca for people who want to see and photograph a wide variety of animals, birds, and reptiles. Available to both adults and children are the staff-led programs, audiovisual presentations, and hands-on exhibits that encourage involvement with the natural world. During most of the year, The Nature Station hosts regular events—hikes, canoe floats, boat cruises, photography weekends, waterfowl watching, and nature festivals. Among the most popular events—sellouts each year—are the guided tours from mid-January to mid-February in search of migratory bald eagles that winter in this area. Lake excursions depart from Kenlake Marina, and van tours take to the back roads near the lake. You'll need reservations well in advance.

Also, just two-tenths of a mile north of the Golden Pond visitors center is an exciting new area, the Elk & Bison Prairie, where 750 acres are being restored to the natural prairie that existed 200 years ago. Then, grassland was extensive in this area and estimated to encompass around 2.4 million acres in Kentucky alone. It was a lush environment for bison and elk, providing edibles of tall grasses and shrubby plants. Herds numbered in the thousands.

A huge effort is under way to restore the prairie ecosystem here, using controlled burning techniques that open up the landscape and allow dormant seeds of tall prairie grasses to voluntarily spring up. Individuals, agencies, corporations, and associations are all involved in this project. Today, you can drive through, read interpretive message boards, view the animals, and get an idea of how it will look in the future.

Until June 1996, when the bison at LBL were moved to the new prairie location, they were kept on a Buffalo Range across from The Homeplace-1850. Now they coexist with elk brought from Elk Island National Park in Alberta, Canada. You can learn a lot about these interesting animals and their prairie habitat on a visit here.

One last caution about LBL: in the woods are ticks, ticks, ticks! If you didn't bring tick spray, you can buy it here. You are strongly encouraged to do so.

***Where:*** In Tennessee, reach The Trace, the main north-south road through LBL, from U.S. 79, 5 miles west of Dover and 19 miles east of Paris. Watch carefully for a large brown sign directing you north on a road that becomes The Trace in about 4 miles, at the South Welcome Station. Reach the Golden Pond visitors center in Kentucky from U.S. 68/80 west of Cadiz and east of Aurora (from I-24, take exit 65 and go west), or drive up The Trace from Tennessee.

***When:*** Year-round (including Wranglers and Rushing Creek Campgrounds and all trails). Energy Lake, Hillman Ferry, and Piney Campgrounds, The Homeplace-1850 (9 A.M. to 5 P.M.), and The Nature Station are open March 1 through November 30 (Homeplace closed Monday and Tuesday in March and November). Golden Pond Planetarium, March 1 through December 15 (show times vary).

***Admission:*** Free. Fees for campgrounds and back-country camping, canoe trips, guided group tours, OHV permits, hunting. Modest admission fee to The Nature Station, The Homeplace-1850, Golden Pond Planetarium, and Elk & Bison Prairie.

***Amenities:*** Welcome stations; visitors center; planetarium; wildlife habitat areas; nature center; farmstead; campgrounds; hiking, equestrian, bicycle, mountain biking, and OHV trails; boat-launching ramps; fishing piers; playgrounds; environmental education centers.

*Activities:* Fishing, boating, canoeing, guided trail rides, hunting, camping, hiking, wildlife viewing, scenic auto tours, photography.

*Special events:* Full schedule. Day with the Eagles boat tours and van tours (January, February). In Tennessee: River Sounds Traditional Music Festival (June), Independence Day Celebration (July), Children's Heritage Festival, Family Living History Experience (August), Harvest Celebration (September), Homeplace Wedding, Snap Apple Night (October), Christmas Workshop, Harvest Home (November).

*Other:* Anyone who intends to hunt or fish should request a *Hunting and Angling Guide* (published annually and available at welcome stations). Elk & Bison Prairie is off-limits to hunting, game calls, bicycles, and horses. Special regulations apply to pets.

*For more information:* Recreation Services Section, Land Between the Lakes, 100 Van Morgan Drive, Golden Pond, KY 42211. 502-924-2000. Reservations and activity schedules (planetarium, guided bike treks, guided hikes and nature tours, Homeplace-1850 workshops, canoe floats), 502-924-2020. Wranglers Campground guided trail rides, 502-924-2211.

LBL Website, http://www2.lbl.org/lbl/.

Bike World, Inc., 848 Joe Clifton Drive, Paducah, KY 42001-3746 (LBL mountain bike races). 502-442-0751.

# 2

# Middle Tennessee

## Bluegrass and Other Surprises

Middle Tennessee's wooded hills, croplands, and pastures create a pleasant landscape, but what is hidden underneath has been important to the development of this region.

In the late 1700s, for instance, the western part of the region was found to have many iron deposits, and a smelting industry grew and prospered for several decades of the 1800s. Then a higher-grade ore was discovered around Lake Superior, and the smelting in Tennessee stopped. The remains of iron furnaces are still visible, particularly along the Natchez Trace Parkway and places such as the Narrows of the Harpeth and Montgomery Bell State Park.

Two large geologic zones, the 7,500-square-mile Western Highland Rim and the 5,000-square-mile Central Basin, account for many of the features that are found from Kentucky to Alabama and around Nashville in all directions.

The Western Highland Rim is a tilted plateau that is 300 feet above the Western Valley and 400 feet above the Central Basin to the east. Forty million years ago, there was an uplifted area called the Nashville Dome where the basin is now, but erosion from streams gradually whittled it down.

What is left is bluegrass country—an area larger than all the bluegrass found in the entire state of Kentucky. Because of the underlying limestone and other minerals, the pastures of middle Tennessee are ideal for raising cattle and horses.

The rivers? There are scenic float streams and impoundments that provide opportunity for fishing, boating, and other water sports. The Cumberland River is navigable, with a system of locks that supports barge traffic, upstream to a port on Cordell Hull Lake near Gainesboro on the Cumberland Plateau. Riverboats and privately owned craft, too, travel down the Cumberland through Nashville, west through Barkley Lake to the Ohio River, then on to the Mississippi and all the way down to New Orleans.

# In and Around Nashville

As Memphis grew up on the Mississippi River, so Nashville started as a fort—Fort Nashborough—on the banks of the Cumberland. It is the state capital and a center for green industries: insurance, printing, and universities are all well established here, and in recent years it has become a "third coast" for music, video, and TV production.

## Cumberland Science Museum and Sudekum Planetarium

For children and parents who like science and nature and want to make exciting hands-on discoveries, this is the place. When you enter, the first thing you notice is that it is not quiet! That's because North America's largest science sculpture, a two-story Kinetic Coaster, is continually demonstrating the science of motion: kinetic energy, trajectory, and loud collisions every few seconds. It takes very little energy to *find* the museum, though. It's just off I-40 on the south side of downtown.

Gina Jones was our host the day we visited, and she explained what visitors can see and do:

"About three times a year we get a traveling blockbuster exhibit like *Dinosaur Park* in '93. In early '94 we had *Mission to Mars*, then *Whales*. We relate our regular live animal shows to these programs. When the dinosaur exhibit was here we tailored our Animals Alive show and called it 'Dinosaur Descendants.' It was about the birds of today and how they descended from the dinosaurs.

"The Animals Alive program goes year-round. We bring out animals that we keep in the museum. We have an alligator, birds, a rabbit, and other kinds of animals. The show explains about the animals and lets the audience touch them and ask questions. One of the interesting things I learned in the show is that an alligator won't grow any bigger than its surroundings allow, so they keep our alligator where it will stay just three feet long.

"We emphasize both science and nature. For example, one of our permanent exhibits is *The Science Game*. It has 12 interactive games that everyone can play and test their science skills. We also have a permanent recycling exhibit. We think it's important to encourage recycling to help preserve our earth and reduce the waste. The exhibit includes a shopping game, showing kids which products they can buy and then recycle to help our environment. It's approached in a fun way—touch and feel and see.

"For younger children there is a Curiosity Corner. It has several areas. In an old country store they can put on an apron and be the shopkeeper, use an old cash register, and measure and wrap the groceries. In the Nature Area they can visit the cocoon room or fox den and match animals to their homes.

Wonder boxes hold interesting things to handle and explore, and in the Japanese Room they put on kimonos, take off their shoes, and sit at a low table to read or play games."

We thought the Curiosity Corner was one of the best discovery centers we had seen.

There are many more exhibits, including a Health Hall Talking Cow that offers tips on nutrition, and a paleontology lab.

One of the newest permanent exhibits is *Mission Earth*, including the Deep Sea Adventure with 12 simulated underwater experiment stations of imaginary Pelican Bay. Visitors explore oceanography and perform computer-aided studies such as identifying whales, conducting plankton surveys, dealing with an oil spill, and exploring scuba diving safety. A companion exhibit, *Rainforest Adventure*, teaches about South American plants, animals, and ecology.

Another one of the newest permanent exhibits is *Discovery House*, a scale model that shows how homes are actually constructed, with cutaway views that let you see elements such as wiring and plumbing that are normally hidden from view.

Besides the exhibits, the museum has many scheduled events. Two recurring ones that are always well received are Trains! and Discovering the Splendid Light (lasers and holograms).

The Sudekum Planetarium has regular shows that are both educational and entertaining. Each Saturday, Skies Over Nashville is shown in the 40-foot star theater where a projector reproduces the motions of stars, sun, moon, and planets as seen from anywhere on Earth at any time—past, present, or future. Other shows run for three or four months. The museum staff creates its own planetarium programs. Planet Patrol gives new information about our sun's planets; WSKY Radio Station of the Stars explores the universe uniquely; Rusty Rocket's Last Blast explores rocket physics on a tour of the solar system; and Star Stealers invites viewers to join the planetarium's celestial detectives and crack a cosmic case ("but don't get too close to a black hole!").

*Where:* 800 Fort Negley Boulevard, Nashville. From I-40, take exit 210C and follow museum signs. From I-65, take exit 81 (Wedgewood) to Eighth Avenue South, right on Eighth, right on Chestnut, left on Fort Negley.

*When:* Year-round. Memorial Day to Labor Day, Monday through Saturday, 9:30 A.M. to 5:00 P.M.; Sunday, 10:30 A.M. to 5:30 P.M. (September 1 through May 31, closed Monday; Sunday hours, 12:30 P.M. to 5:30 P.M.). Closed Easter, Thanksgiving, Christmas Day, New Year's Day.

*Admission:* Adults, $6.00; 3 to 12 and 65 and over, $4.50 (planetarium $1.00 with admission). Planetarium only, $3.00. Discounts for seniors over 65.

*Amenities:* Museum, gift shop, computer lab, free parking.

*Activities:* Hands-on exhibits, daily workshops and shows, scheduled planetarium shows.

*Special events:* Scheduled weekend festivals, weeklong summer camps.

*Other:* Barrier-free access. Reservations recommended for 10 or more, 615-862-5177.

*For more information:* Cumberland Science Museum, 800 Fort Negley Boulevard, Nashville, TN 37203. Phone, 615-862-5160. Fax, 615-862-5178. Planetarium, 615-401-5092.

## Nashville Wildlife Park at Grassmere

It's a zoo, a nature center, a discovery place for children and their parents, and the site of nature-oriented activities for preschoolers through seniors. It's on a 200-acre tract of land south of downtown Nashville that owners Margaret and Elise

Croft had willed to the Cumberland Museum, stipulating that it be kept as a wildlife park. The entrance is on Nolensville Pike, easily reached from I-24, I-65, or I-440.

Actually this park, established in 1990 as Grassmere Wildlife Park, is in a state of transition that will be complete by 2002 when the Nashville Zoo finishes relocating here (though retaining its present location for projects related to species survival). This place will then be known as "Nashville Zoo and Wildlife Park at Grassmere" and the present zoo north of Nashville will be a premier breeding compound for endangered species.

Meanwhile, Grassmere is a home for many of the animals that are native to North America and especially to Tennessee.

Along a seven-tenths-mile trail the animals are kept in large habitat areas: elk, bison, gray wolf, black bear, North American otter, cougar, bald eagle, golden eagle, beaver, white-tailed deer, wild turkey, and American white pelican. You can also see the Przewalski's horse, the only true wild horse remaining on the planet.

All this will change in the near future as a fast-track renovation prepares for the zoo's full relocation. It is an exciting time, and repeat visits are certain to reward you with new surprises.

For one, Grassmere has what may be the largest jungle gym ever constructed in the largest playground in the universe! Well, you judge. It's a 66,000-square-foot playground that can accommodate more than a thousand playful children at any given time. And there's plenty of "play" material for exploring: a 35-foot-tall Tree of Life (treehouse structure); a concrete garden containing a bat cave, a giant snake tunnel, concrete hippo sculptures, a jungle village, a koi fishpond, and other intriguing elements—all designed by world-renowned playground architect Robert Leathers (his largest project to date). The jungle gym took three months and 6,000 volunteers working 40,000 total hours to complete, and it's a masterpiece.

The main building, Croft Center, has an indoor aviary, aquariums, a discovery room, galleries, a theater, nature exhibits, a gift shop, and a restaurant (but who knows what will await your visit in the months ahead?). Recently, the entire lower level was redesigned and converted into The Unseen New World, an exhibit hall showcasing rare aquatic species, reptiles, and insects from throughout the Western Hemisphere. It is an expansion of the original "indigenous species" concept for the park, now reflecting life on additional sections of our planet.

Outside are the animal habitats, a large festival field, the Lawson Forest Loop Trail, a picnic grove, an amphitheater, and the old Croft farmhouse, newly renovated and becoming a true showplace and working farm. The house, regularly open to the public, has been restored to its 1885 splendor in Italianate style with tall doors and windows and other appropriate architectural elements. As a working farm, it gives a true picture of life as it was in the farm's most productive time. The gardens are planted with heirloom plants for authenticity. An herb garden and orchard are being added.

The pathway to the animals is a wide blacktop. Most of this area is wooded, and the trees have botanical markers. All pens are large and provide room to roam, rocks and fallen trees to climb, and places to hide. Signs tell about the species, their lifestyles, and where they are found today in the wild.

The first habitat on this path is the pelican pond. The four pelicans that are being kept here were injured in the wild. Nonbreeding pelicans do occasionally visit Tennessee wetlands, although only seven have been sighted in the area since 1915. A fairly recent sighting was in January 1994, when one appeared on a pond in Fountain Square, a commercial development in Nashville.

The elk and bison are in two fields of several acres each. From a viewing platform, we observe the activity in both places. All along the path are "experiment stations" where learning is fun. Ever wonder how it feels to carry a heavy set of antlers on your head? Here is a handle: push it and feel the weight.

Walk along a boardwalk across a ravine and have a good view of the American black bears. These animals can weigh up to 230 pounds and be five and a half feet long. There are boxes with hinged lids that answer questions. What does a bear eat? Raise the lid, and there's the answer. Alongside the path just beyond the bears is a "bear's den" that has tracks leading up to it, and you can peek inside.

Otters are many people's favorites, with their antics and exuberance. You can view this area from two levels: underwater or above. We saw four otters taking advantage of their swimming hole, maneuvering deftly around submerged trees.

Outside the bald eagles' pen is a simulated eagle's nest, and you can climb up into it. Nests can be 9½ feet across and 20 feet deep (larger than this one!). Another experiment lets you compare your eyesight with that of an eagle by looking through magnified eyeholes.

The cougar's habitat holds two of these cats. Although cougars are still in the wild in the West, in eastern North America the only recognized population is in southern Florida, where they are called Florida panthers. A display compares jumping distances, from a 40-inch bullfrog jump to a 40-foot cougar leap.

The Przewalski's horse was quite a find. In the 1800s it was believed that the ancestor of the domestic horse had disappeared, but a Russian explorer (Nikolay Przhevalsky) found a small herd of these horses in Mongolia. It has a dark, erect mane and no forelock, a yellow winter coat that turns light reddish brown in summer, and light zebra stripes on the front legs. Prehistoric wild horses roamed throughout Tennessee; and the park is participating in a species survival plan for this wild horse.

Read about the Nashville Zoo (later in this chapter) to get a sense of other animals that will be relocated here.

Inside the Croft Center is a spectacular two-story aviary where many kinds of birds sing from treetops and walk around on the ground. Included are cardinals, mourning doves, cedar waxwings, fulvous whistling ducks, cinnamon teal, bluejays, eastern bluebirds, house finches, red-headed woodpeckers, barn swallows, sharp-tailed sparrows, meadowlarks, goldfinches, ovenbirds, red-winged blackbirds, and brown-headed cowbirds.

Many free activities go on here: otter feeding, fish feeding, animal encounters, and talks by animal keepers.

Special events include wildflower weekends, senior walks, Scottish Festival and Highland Games, Native American festivals, nature photography workshops, Bird Day, and an annual Halloween Howl and Monster Bash. There are also preschool Family Funshops covering nature subjects in ways three- to five-year-olds can appreciate.

Grassmere, closed for a time but definitely rejuvenated and moving forward at a fast clip, also has a new reptile house and an aviary of birds from Central and South America. Ultimately, Grassmere will house some of the rarest animals in the world and will have a superlative African Continent habitat area.

*Where:* 3777 Nolensville Road, Nashville. Exit I-24 or I-65 at Harding Place and turn north on Nolensville Road; or exit I-440 onto Nolensville Pike and drive south.

*When:* Year-round, daily. April through September, 9 A.M. to

6 P.M.; October through March, 10 A.M. to 5 P.M. Admission until one hour before closing. Closed Christmas Day and New Year's Day.

*Admission:* Adults, $6.00; seniors and ages 3 to 12, $4.00. Parking $2. Group rates available.

*Amenities:* Zoo, entry village, nature center, aquarium, aviary, exhibits, technology center, gift shop, restaurant, concession stands, amphitheater, picnic area, wetlands, seven-acre children's zoo, jungle gym playground.

*Activities:* Wildlife viewing, photography, nature trails, picnicking, historic tours (Monday through Friday), animal shows.

*Special events:* Twilight Safari and Reptile Mania (both in March), Wildflower weekends, senior walks, photography workshops, Bird Day, Ghouls at Grassmere (October). Reserved areas available for corporate and birthday parties (615-371-6462).

*Other:* Barrier-free access. Stroller rental, free wheelchairs (limited availability).

*For more information:* Nashville Wildlife Park at Grassmere, 3777 Nolensville Road, Nashville, TN 37211. 615-370-3333. To book family reunions or private parties, 615-746-3449; for corporate events, 615-833-1534. Website, http://www.nashville zoo.org/.

## Radnor Lake State Natural Area

Tennessee's Natural Areas Planning Act of 1971 came just in time to save this 1,100-plus-acre watershed ecosystem from development. It is in the southern part of Nashville—a deep lake surrounded by wooded hills teeming with wildlife and wildflowers. The high, wooded limestone knobs around Radnor Lake—reaching more than 1,100 feet in altitude—are dissected remnants of the Western Highland Rim (Nashville sits on the northwest edge of the Central Basin).

What is perhaps astounding is that such property even existed within the city limits at that late date. It had been owned by the L&N Railroad, which created the 85-acre Radnor Lake in 1914 by building a 20-foot-high earthen dam in a deep natural gorge. The lake supplied water to the Radnor Yards a few miles away, providing up to a million gallons a day until the 1950s, when diesels replaced steam engines. Later it was operated as a private fishing club.

In 1973, with federal and state funds, private donations that came from a community-wide fund drive, and the help of the Nature Conservancy, the Radnor Lake purchase made it Tennessee's first official State Natural Area.

It is also the most-visited natural area, with easy access from Otter Creek Road, which follows the south shore of the lake, providing a paved lakeside walkway. Large paved parking areas are at each end of the lake, one and one-tenth miles apart. The road is closed daily between the two parking lots from 7 A.M. to dark to increase safety and enjoyment for park visitors. A modern visitors center is at the west parking lot. Displays, exhibits, a meeting room, and a gift shop are here.

The seven-mile trail system is extensive. A self-guided spillway interpretive trail leads from the west parking lot to the dam, where a nature center overlooks the lake. From there, a lake trail follows the north shoreline and connects with other trails along the way, and a gravel road over the dam leads to Otter Creek Road. The Spillway and North Lake Trails are both easy, and unlike trails in most natural areas, they are covered with wood-chip mulch and have boardwalks and graveled segments that allow use during rainy weather.

The other trails climb hills and are the narrow, natural kind you'd expect to find. From the North Lake Trail, you can take the Ganier Ridge Trail loop to the top of a ridge. You can also branch off this trail and descend to the east parking lot, where there are modern rest rooms. Another trail, South Lake Trail, gains altitude for panoramic views of the lake and gives access at each end to the South Cove Trail, a loop that takes you into coves and on top of a high ridge top.

It is possible to hike for half a day, following all the trails and loops and retracing your route in only a few short segments. If your aim is to observe nature, you can easily spend the entire day here. Picnicking is not allowed, but a modern market is on Granny White Pike, just a block away from the west parking lot.

You are certain to see wildlife. The lake and shore are home to turtles, water snakes, bullfrogs, muskrats, tree frogs, toads, raccoons, bass, bluegills, shellcrackers, crappies, and catfish. Its winter visitors include up to 23 species of migratory waterfowl, and in summer wood ducks, Canada geese, little green and great blue herons, and belted kingfishers take up residence. Woods and meadows support white-tailed deer, red and gray foxes, coyotes, bobcats, beavers, rabbits, shrews and voles, mice, opossums, and gray squirrels. Birding is excellent in summer and during spring and fall migrations.

Wildflowers cover the ground in spring and are showy in fall, and the forest is colorful in different seasons with dogwood, redbud, honeysuckle, and other flowering shrubs, and autumn leaf color. The occasional snow-covered winter landscape provides a different beauty and the opportunity to see animal tracks.

This park sponsors a variety of guided activities throughout the year. Typically, you can sign up for canoe floats, wildflower and fruit hikes, nature and birding walks, rappelling workshops, Native American storytelling, and off-site tours. Some activities are for specific age groups.

***Where:*** 1160 Otter Creek Road, Nashville. Exit I-65 at Harding Place, go west to Granny White Pike, then south to Otter

Creek Road and left on Otter Creek one block to the visitors center. Alternately, go south from Harding Place on Franklin Road, then right on Otter Creek Road to the east parking lot.
***When:*** Year-round, 7 A.M. to sundown in summer, 8 A.M. to sundown in winter. Visitors center, 8 A.M. to 4 P.M. daily (depends on volunteer staffing on weekends).
***Admission:*** Free.
***Amenities:*** Visitors center, nature center, trails, three rest room locations.
***Activities:*** Hiking, birding, nature observation and study, photography.
***Special events:*** Canoe floats, guided walks, bird and wildflower hikes, nature programs, archaeology awareness programs.
***Other:*** Barrier-free access at visitors center and along Otter Creek Road. Otter Creek Road closed in the park during daylight hours.
***For more information:*** Area Manager, Radnor Lake State Natural Area, 1050 Otter Creek Road, Nashville, TN 37220. 615-373-3467. Event registration, 615-377-1281. Website, http://www.state.tn.us/environment/parks/ then select.

## *The Warner Parks*

For Nashville nature enthusiasts, 1973 was a memorable year. Not only was Radnor Lake purchased in May, but also the Warner Park Nature Center opened that October. The two adjoining parks, Edwin Warner Park and Percy Warner Park (called simply "the Warner Parks"), have a total of 2,665 acres and together form one of the largest municipal parks in the United States. They are on State 100 at Old Hickory Boulevard southwest of downtown Nashville. They offer miles of scenic drives, horseback and hiking trails, picnic areas, playgrounds, a polo field, a steeplechase, a model airplane field, a fishing lake, and two golf courses in a mix of hillsides, fields, and forests. Much of the stonework for entrances, rock walls, and shelters was done in the 1930s.

The nature center, just past Old Hickory Boulevard on the left as you travel west, is one of Tennessee's finest and a recommended stop when visiting. At the center are a research library, a natural-history interpretive center, and gardens. Both facilities are open Monday through Friday, although the grounds are open every day from sunup to sundown.

The center was created to resemble an old farmstead and is landscaped with native plants. A bird-feeding area has both feeding stations and growing plants that furnish wild food. Throughout the grounds are bluebird nesting boxes. (The park has had a nesting box program continuously since 1936, and brochures about this are available.) There is also an organic garden with a composting area alongside, an official weather station donated by the U.S. Weather Service, a small pond, a wildflower garden that contains more than 360 species, and movable-frame beehives (which should be observed from a distance).

In the parking lot and on nearby Hungry Hawk Trail are bat boxes. The nature center conducts entertaining programs about bats and gives away handouts about this interesting flying mammal.

The trail information station at the visitors center has maps, booklets, schedules, and park brochures in a weatherproof container. There are six trails in Edwin Warner and two in Percy Warner.

The trailhead for the Percy Warner trails is in the Deep Well Picnic Area off State 100. The Warner Woods Trail is a two-and-a-half-mile loop through deep, secluded woods; at one point you can walk a paved road to a high summit and then return to the trail. The Mossy Ridge Trail goes four and a half miles through wooded hills, hollows, and open meadows, crossing several springs. Two short spurs provide scenic views.

Edwin Warner has two trailheads, with most trails starting at the visitors center. The old roadbed here is actually the historic Natchez Trace (the Natchez Trace Parkway now begins a few miles away, farther out on State 100).

The Little Acorn Trail is less than three-tenths of a mile and has a self-guiding booklet for children six and under. An interesting three-trunked red oak tree is on this trail.

The Hungry Hawk Trail is another easy trail three-tenths of a mile long. It goes by a wet-weather stream and through woods and an open field. It has a bird blind, a wildlife tracking station, and a well house from an old homestead.

The Amphitheater Trail, 200 yards one way, passes the same old homesite and ends at a secluded platform that is used for programs and meetings.

The Nature Loop is a moderate trail seven-tenths of a mile long. It has a guide written for adults that discusses many plants, the geology and biology of Vaughn's Creek, and some facts about the Natchez Trace.

The longest trail in Edwin Warner is the Harpeth Woods Trail, a two-and-a-half-mile loop accessed from either trailhead. It offers a rich variety of forest types, crosses a rock quarry, and follows the old Trace for seven-tenths of a mile.

The second trailhead is by the Little Harpeth River at Owl Hollow. The easy, self-guided Owl Hollow Trail starts here (though it also connects with the Harpeth Woods Trail as a three-tenths-mile loop). It tours a hollow where barred owls, eastern screech owls, and great horned owls may be present.

The nature center offers many activities, including a Junior Naturalist program. Throughout the summer, many kinds of hikes take place—family walks, fun runs, nature hikes, bike hikes, trail horseback rides. There are programs for adults, for families, and some just for children. For ages 6 to 12, these include fishing in Willow Pond, a kid's gardening workshop, animal identification, night hikes, recycling activities, predicting the weather, stargazing, and nature-oriented slide shows.

*Where:* 7311 Highway 100, at Nashville's western city limits.
*When:* Year-round. Park, sunup to 11 P.M.; nature center, Monday through Friday, 8 A.M. to 4:30 P.M. (grounds close at sundown daily).
*Admission:* Free.
*Amenities:* Nature center, interpretive center, hiking and horseback trails, stables, picnic shelters, two golf courses, steeplechase, sports fields, fishing lake.
*Activities:* Hiking, wildlife viewing, scenic drives, fishing, outdoor sports, golf, picnicking, daily activities at nature center.
*Special events:* Annual hot-air balloon weekend.
*For more information:* Warner Parks Nature Center, 7311 Highway 100, Nashville, TN 37221-3003. 615-352-6299. Website, http://nashville.citysearch.com/E/V/NASTN/0002/22/14/ (current-event schedule is posted).

## Cheekwood, Nashville's Home of Art and Gardens

Cheekwood is more than a premier showplace, although this 55-acre estate with its three-story mansion and elegant formal gardens dating back to the early 1930s is certainly that, too. Materials from Europe were incorporated into the house (doors from the Duke of Westminster's Grosvenor House and a staircase from Queen Charlotte's palace at Kew, to name two), and the grounds were landscaped with fountains, pools, streams, wisteria, and large boxwoods.

In 1957, Cheekwood was converted into a botanical garden and art museum. Today it is a prestigious fine-arts center that holds a permanent collection of 19th- and 20th-century American art, Worcester porcelains, antique silver, oriental snuff bottles, and period furniture. It also hosts major traveling exhibitions and specially mounted shows of national prominence.

Nature lovers, however, probably come here more to see the flowering trees, wildflowers, roses, perennial borders, and display gardens that change with the seasons. The acreage sits on a rise of land that overlooks the Percy Warner Park hills, lending a panoramic backdrop to each garden view.

We suggest going first into Botanic Hall, where you can pick up self-guiding leaflets about the different gardens and greenhouses, enjoy the atrium with its interesting specimen plants, and browse through the special exhibits that may be on display. Also, an excellent botanical reference library is open to the public.

Behind Botanic Hall is the Rose Garden, where you will see blooming plants from May through October. From there, go left to the four greenhouses. The Cloud Forest has plants from the mountains of Panama: orchids, bromeliads, peperomias, anthuriums, and others. The camellia greenhouse is especially interesting from October to April when these flowers are in bloom, although summer-blooming plants are here, too. There are two orchid houses: a warm house and a cool house (the latter for orchids that grow at higher elevations).

One thing we particularly like about Cheekwood's garden leaflets is that they not only describe the plants but also give tips on how to grow them and what varieties will be most successful locally.

The self-guided garden tour brochure gives a complete orientation to the 13 principal garden areas. Among the featured varieties are daffodils (marigolds in summer); herb study (herbs that grow in the area); perennials such as anemones, mums, roses, and tulips; irises (a Dykes Medal collection); daylilies; peonies; ornamental grasses; and crape myrtle. In the formal Swan Garden are large boxwoods as well as a swan fountain, pools, and streams. The plantings are extensive, and this short list doesn't begin to name them all.

Our tour guide was Cheekwood's wildflower horticulturalist, Jenny Andrews. We started at the award-winning Howe Wildflower Garden, which is on about an acre of ground. Much of what is here came from a well-known garden in east Nashville. Even the stone walls, rocks, an iron bench, and a little stone toolhouse were moved here.

Jenny is always experimenting with new plants to see what will grow well, and her goal is "to have a garden that looks like someone's taking care of it but that is also very loose, somewhat wild and romantic." In one area is a little pond with a tiny waterfall to relieve the summer heat. A rustic wooden bridge is nearby, and a low rock wall borders the area.

Some wildflowers are blooming through most of the year, but the peak time is February through May. Then visitors get a visual feast of bloodroot, bluestar, celandine poppy, Dutchman's-breeches, dwarf crested iris, dwarf larkspur, false rue anemone, fire pink, foamflower, golden ragwort, jack-in-the-pulpit, Jacob's ladder, mayapple, shooting star, Solomon's plume, Solomon's seal, spring beauty, toothwort, trillium, trout lily, twinleaf, Virginia bluebells, wake-robin, wild columbine, wild geranium, wild ginger, wild hyacinth, and wild sweet William.

To people who would like to grow native plants, Jenny says, "First, look at your site. Is it dry? Shady? Sunny? Does it have coarse clay? Rich loam? Whatever its characteristics, *something* will grow there, so try to match the plant's requirements. We suggest ordering from a mail-order house or getting them at a local nursery. When people dig in the wild, usually they don't get the whole root system, so the plant dies."

We add: if you are getting them from a commercial supplier, ask if they are "nursery *propagated*." These will have a better chance of survival than plants that are simply nursery or field grown.

Another way to acquire them is to come in April to Cheekwood's Wildflower Fair and purchase plants grown in the Howe Garden nursery. To learn more about growing native plants, Jenny recommends *Growing and Propagating Wildflowers* by Harry Phillips. It has more information in one volume than most other references, she says.

Other themed areas we enjoyed are the Herb Study Garden, the Carell Dogwood Trail, and the Wills Perennial Garden. The newest ones are the Color Garden (providing colorful displays year-round), the Seasons Garden, and the Water Garden (terraces and aquatic plants). Newest of all is the Woodland Sculpture Trail, an innovative concept that combines art and nature through placing sculptures in a forested setting.

Our last stop was *Shomu-en*, the Japanese Pine Mist Garden. A fragrant Tanyosho pine at the entrance has multiple trunks and is a handsome specimen. From here a walkway leads among plantings of bamboo and ginkgo trees to a viewing pavilion that is the observation point for the garden. Look at the garden as if it were a painting. Gravel has been carefully raked to represent a lake with water rippling on the surface. Other objects in the landscape could represent a boat dock, a lighthouse, and a waterfall. A large stone could be a mountain, and a stone tower might represent a secluded temple. The trees are carefully pruned to look windswept.

The "painting" changes with the seasons. Spring brings flowering cherry trees and azaleas. Summer offers green foliage in varied hues and smoke tree blossoms. The oranges and golds of maples and ginkgoes signal fall, and in winter, snow may lightly cover the lanterns and dark pine trees.

Many botanical classes and workshops are offered at Cheekwood, among them some hour-long sessions that might fit into a traveler's schedule. Decorating with gathered natural materials, ikebana, flower painting, lecture/demonstrations, landscape design, how to force bulbs, photography, and herb gardening are just a few of the subjects.

One special annual event since 1964, Trees of Christmas at Cheekwood, is on display nearly the whole month of December in Botanic Hall. There are usually 17 or 18 trees, all decorated to follow a theme such as Memories of Trees Past or A Storybook Christmas.

The Owl's Hill Nature Center, in Williamson County south of Nashville, is another site owned by Cheekwood. This 150-acre sanctuary and environmental studies center conducts scheduled programs on a reservation basis and is open to the public for some special events. It also offers a virtual hike on the Cheekwood Web page. You can see and hear the owls and learn about their binocular vision and other owl facts.

Before we left, we took a short stroll to the museum shop and the Pineapple Room Restaurant, past flower beds full of lemon yellow mums, gigantic scarlet burning bushes, tall grasses with silvery ornamental heads, and other blooms of red, purple, and white. The Pineapple Room is one of our favorite lunchtime dining spots for the superlative cuisine and the view. They will also prepare box lunches and picnic fare. We recommend it.

*Where:* 1200 Forrest Park Drive, Nashville. From I-65, exit Harding Place and go west. Turn left at Belle Meade Boulevard, go to the end, then right on Page Road. Where Page curves to the right, turn left onto Forrest Park Drive.

*When:* Year-round. Monday through Saturday, 9 A.M. to 5 P.M.; Sunday, 11 A.M. to 5 P.M. Hours extended April 15 to October 15 to 8 P.M. Monday through Thursday. Pineapple Room, daily 11 A.M. to 2 P.M.; reservations suggested. Closed Thanksgiving, Christmas Eve and Christmas Day, New Year's Eve and New Year's Day, and third Saturday in April.

*Admission:* Adults, $6.00; seniors and college students, $5.00; 6 to 17, $3.00. Group rates, 615-353-2155.

*Amenities:* Art museum, exhibit hall, library, restaurant, gift shop, educational building.

*Activities:* Viewing gardens and galleries, scheduled workshops, concerts.

*Special events:* Wildflower Fair, Scottish Highland Games, Trees of Christmas (reservations, 615-353-2150). At Owl's Hill: Bluebird Day (January), Walk the Earth (April), Open House (November).

*Other:* Barrier-free access. Complimentary on-site shuttle.

*For more information:* Cheekwood, 1200 Forrest Park Drive, Nashville, TN 37205-4242. 615-356-8000. Pineapple Room reservations, 615-352-4859. Trees of Christmas, 615-353-2150. Website, http://www.cheekwood.org/.


## Narrows of the Harpeth Scenic River

The Harpeth River meanders south and west of Nashville on its way from Rutherford County to Cheatham Lake on the Cumberland at Ashland City. A pleasant day trip can take you to some very interesting locations such as the Harpeth Narrows (for hiking or even a canoe trip), the Mound Bottom village site, on to Ashland City and the Cumberland River Bicentennial Trail, and your choice of recreation spots on the vast Cheatham Wildlife Management Area.

On the Harpeth River's course, just a few miles from U.S.

70 near Pegram, are the historic narrows of the Harpeth, where Montgomery Bell operated Patterson Forge in the early 1800s. It is called Narrows of the Harpeth State Park on road signs and Narrows State Historic Area on the Harpeth Scenic River in tourism publications.

The term *narrows* used in this context refers to a place where the Harpeth River, after making a loop for several miles around a limestone ridge and descending 17 feet in the process, nearly meets itself on its return. Only a high and narrow bluff stands in between. The bluff is several hundred yards long, varying in height from 60 to 250 feet and in width from 180 to 450 feet. One of the several short trails at this location takes you on top of the ridge where you have a 360-degree view of the valley and the river below.

The Harpeth is a very scenic Class I and II float stream, especially in the spring and summer when rains provide a good water flow. Outfitters at the U.S. 70 bridge supply trips lasting from 2 to 11 hours and from 7 to 35 miles, with the last takeout point at the back side of the narrows.

People also come to see the tunnel—16 feet wide and 8 feet tall—that Bell cut through the bluff to operate a water-powered grit mill. It was a masterful engineering feat because it had to be dug and blasted through horizontally stratified rock while taking advantage of the natural arch to prevent collapse. The tricky project was done well, and the tunnel remains to this day.

The tunnel provided a 16-foot fall that turned huge waterwheels. These drove heavy hammers, pounding pig-iron billets into malleable bars and plates for blacksmiths to use in their forges. Historians say this operation was spectacular: four giant hammers powered by eight waterwheels, sending sparks flying. The operation continued day and night, and the charcoal fires never died down.

Products of the forge were taken by ox-drawn wagons or pack mules to Nashville and Franklin, and some were floated down the Harpeth and Cumberland Rivers to Clarksville, loaded on steamboats and shipped to Natchez and New Orleans.

The water flowing from the tunnel created a pond, where today bits of iron can still be found. In the 1980s several years of drought lowered the water level and exposed one of the old millstones. It was removed and taken to Montgomery Bell State Park 10 miles west, just beyond the town of White Bluff.

Sometimes what you see isn't all you'd like to know. You can obtain some information about the forge from float operators where the Harpeth River crosses U.S. 70.

And sometimes what you don't see poses a fascinating mystery. Hidden somewhere at the narrows is a second tunnel that Bell began but didn't complete. An old map shows that it should be 226 feet from the first tunnel, but no one can find it now. You can see a reproduction of this map at the Montgomery Bell State Park visitors center, and there you can find out more about the whole iron industry of earlier times.

An interesting aside to the tunnel story is that tunnel building in America may have originated here. In fact, Bell's tunnel at the narrows—begun in 1818 and finished within a year—may be the oldest extant tunnel in the United States. Historians Archibald Black and Gösta Sandstrom credit the Auburn Tunnel on the Schuylkill Navigation Canal in Pennsylvania (also begun in 1818 but completed in 1821) as being the oldest. It was later replaced by an open cut.

On the way to the Narrows (a mile after leaving U.S. 70), look for a historical marker on the left next to a country cemetery. It tells about Mound Bottom, a Native American heritage site dating back to the Woodland Indians

(A.D. 900 to 1350). Paintings from the period can still be seen today on rocks and in caves. It is a divided site, with the two locations a mile apart. A state park, an interpretive center, and trails are in the planning stages.

*Where:* Off U.S. 70 west of Nashville. Exit I-40 at McCrory Lane, go north to U.S. 70, west about five miles, right on Cedar Hill Road for two and seven-tenths miles, then left at Narrows of the Harpeth Road.
*When:* Year-round.
*Admission:* Free.
*Amenities:* Historic tunnel, trails, canoe put-in and takeout, scenic drive.
*Activities:* Hiking, nature appreciation, photography, canoeing (outfitters nearby).
*Other:* Some areas not barrier free.
*For more information:* Cheatham County Chamber of Commerce, PO Box 354, Ashland City, Tennessee 37015. 615-792-6722.

See Montgomery Bell State Park, which follows (inquire about Harpeth Narrows). 615-797-9052.

Friends of Mound Bottom, Attention: David Zauner, PO Box 454, Kingston Springs, TN 37082. 615-662-1366.

Websites, http://www.cheatham.org/ and http://www.syca more-is.cheatham.k12.tn.us/indian.htm.

## Montgomery Bell State Park

Before Montgomery Bell blasted his famous tunnel through the Narrows of the Harpeth, he operated Cumberland Furnace in Dickson County near the site of this park that bears his name. The two properties maintain their historic connection, since Montgomery Bell Park manages Harpeth Narrows as a satellite location.

Montgomery Bell is a popular middle Tennessee destination. It offers an inn and restaurant/conference center overlooking 35-acre Lake Acorn; a swimming pool; year-round vacation cottages; 120 campsites in a wooded valley with nearby meadows and a stream; a challenging 18-hole golf course; lake swimming with a bathhouse and recreation pavilion; boat dock and rental; many picnic areas; 19 miles of foot trails, including an 11⁷⁄₁₀-mile overnight hiking "natural area" trail; and tennis, archery, and many other outdoor activities.

Naturalists and recreation personnel conduct programs throughout the summer. A typical week might include creative crafts such as making leaf-print pictures, clay animals, and pinecone feeders; morning and night nature hikes; "Frisbee golf" and volleyball games; and nighttime entertainment by a local band.

Near the visitors center is the Jim Bailey Nature Trail, named for one of Tennessee's foremost conservation educators for 40 years. As director of Educational Services for the Department of Conservation, he inspired thousands of Tennesseans to love and respect nature and care about environmental preservation. Ardi had the privilege of working under him when she was editor of the *Tennessee Conservationist* magazine. This self-guided trail explains natural features, history and archaeology, cycles of forest life, and the need for natural diversity.

Roam around the 3,782 acres in this park to find more traces of the long-silent iron industry that lured hundreds to middle Tennessee beginning in 1795 when General James Robertson established the Cumberland Iron Works. Within park boundaries are the remains of the old Laurel Furnace and ore pits, where men once scratched the earth for an ore that was more precious than gold to America's early builders.

***Where:*** U.S. 70, 35 miles west of Nashville between White Bluff and Dickson.

*When:* Year-round, 8 A.M. to 10 P.M. (closes at sundown in winter). Montgomery Bell Inn and Restaurant closed during Christmas holidays (check dates). Swimming and boat rental, summer only.

*Admission:* Free.

*Amenities:* Visitors center, resort inn, restaurant, gift shop, cabins, golf course, tennis and other outdoor courts, campgrounds, camp store, group camp (May through September), primitive overnight camping shelters, picnic sites and catering, pavilions, playground, nature trails.

*Activities:* Fishing (three lakes), wildlife viewing, boating, paddleboats, swimming, picnicking, shuffleboard, croquet, outdoor games, archery, hiking, backpacking, guided tours, arts and crafts, demonstrations, movies, organized games.

*Special events:* Theatrical productions, hayrides, campfire programs, slide presentations.

*Other:* Some areas not barrier free.

*For more information:* Montgomery Bell State Park, PO Box 39, Burns, TN 37029. 615-797-9052. Reservations, 615-797-3101. Website, http://www.state.tn.us/environment/parks/ then select.

## Cumberland River Bicentennial Trail and Cheatham Wildlife Management Area

All trails are not equal. Individually, their appeal can be widely varied, and some are even extraordinary. A short trip from Nashville to the Cumberland River Bicentennial Trail in Ashland City will verify this observation.

This three-and-seven-tenths-mile trail is an example of the "rails to trails" concept of converting old railroad beds into hiking trails. If you remember the era of train travel, you recall that the railways were the original "back roads" that typically, in hilly terrain at least, unveiled some wild and scenic landscapes, opening fresh vistas along each exciting mile. If the sights were spectacular, the sounds were memorable, too—wheels clacking rhythmically on rails and piercing, mournful whistles of steam engines echoing for miles.

Some of this romance of the rails is being revisited in a totally different way in the trails program, and the Cumberland River Trail, developed to celebrate the state's 200th birthday in 1996, typifies the best elements of the concept. Because it's on a railroad bed, the trail is easy and level for walking and hiking (appropriate, too, for bicycling and equestrian use), but it's certainly not humdrum. The sights are just as remarkable, and the sounds are of nature—tumbling waterfalls, exuberant quacks and honks of waterfowl, songbirds' trills—whatever the season tends to produce.

The wide, graveled trail overlooks Borum Pond, a waterfowl resting area that parallels the Cheatham Lake (the impounded Cumberland River) several miles above Cheatham Lock and Dam. Since the railroad bed was cut into hillsides, the rocky bluffs add other interesting characteristics to the trail and extend the types of plant and animal habitat.

Many people like to start at the western trailhead, where the trailhead sign is easy to spot and an ample parking area across the road is provided. A picnic table is provided at the trailhead, and after you've gone just a few hundred yards, the trail becomes a boardwalk over a long trestle remaining from the railroading days. Since this isn't a loop trail, you'll be able to gauge how far you want to hike before retracing your steps. Remember, the view will be completely different from the reverse direction!

Seasonal changes assure that return visits will present new discoveries, ever-changing wildflower displays, and always-tantalizing calls of the wild.

The prime waterfowl and wildlife habitat enjoyed along the

Bicentennial Trail represents just a small portion of what can be found in this rugged, rural county. Cheatham Lake (and Lock and Dam) is a recreation paradise popular for camping, fishing, boating, waterskiing, swimming, tennis, picnicking, and exploring an old nature trail near the dam.

The 20,000-acre Cheatham Wildlife Management Area sprawls southwestward from Ashland City over mostly upland terrain, providing countless recreational opportunities. The WMA offers hiking and riding trails, vantage points for birding and wildlife viewing, rifle and archery ranges, picnicking, primitive camping, and hunting. It is managed mostly for deer, and a picnic area on Petway Road, about eight miles from Ashland City, has a herd of penned deer for observation and study.

*Where:* Bicentennial Trail: from the Ashland City courthouse, go north on State 12 to Marks Creek Road (one mile, just past Marks Creek), west past the Sycamore Creek Recreation Area on the left, cross a concrete bridge, then turn right immediately on Chapmansboro Road. Parking (Cheatham Lake WMA) is one mile on the left; trailhead is across the road on the right (sign: Cumberland River Bicentennial Trail, Sycamore Harbor). WMA Headquarters and Picnic Area: from Ashland City, go west on State 49 about three miles, then turn left on Petway Road and continue for five miles; entrance is on the left at Dukes Market.

*When:* Year-round, sunrise to sunset.

*Admission:* Free.

*Amenities:* Bicentennial Trail: trail, parking area, picnic table, historic trestle. Cheatham Lake and WMA: fishing ramps, boat-launching ramps, picnic shelters, playgrounds, tennis court, campgrounds, swimming beaches, hunting, public shooting and archery range, nature trails.

*Activities:* Hiking, walking, horseback riding, bicycling, wildlife viewing, birding, wildflower study, photography, picnicking, swimming, tennis, camping, boating, waterskiing.

*For more information:* Cheatham County Chamber of Commerce, 108 South Main Street, PO Box 354, Ashland City, TN 37015. 615-792-6722 or 615-792-4211. Website, http://www.cheat ham.org/ then select.

Cheatham Lake, 1798 Cheatham Dam Road, Ashland City, TN 37015. 615-792-5697.

## Nashville Zoo

We didn't expect to be wowed by the Nashville Zoo on a previous visit, since at the time, it had been open only long enough to complete its first phase of development, but we found it to be a truly exciting place. That was a few years ago, and this zoo continues to live up to its promises, providing showcase naturalistic habitats for more than 500 animals from all over the planet.

Expansion is in the air, though. By 2002, the Nashville Zoo will have moved to the 200-acre Nashville Wildlife Center at Grassmere and will be called the "Nashville Zoo and Wildlife Park at Grassmere." Its present location will be a premier breeding compound for endangered species. Presently, it participates in a worldwide Species Survival Plan under guidelines set up by the American Zoo and Aquarium Association. Species currently supported at the Nashville Zoo are cheetah, red ruffed lemur, clouded leopard, snow leopard, red panda, and cotton-topped tamarin.

The zoo is 15 miles north of Nashville just off I-24. It sits on 135 acres of typical middle Tennessee landscape: hilly woodlands, pastures, and many small streams that give character and a variety of views. Fifty-one acres of the property are exhibit areas open to the public, another 25 acres are used exclusively for propagation of endangered species, and there are quarantine facilities and a veterinary hospital. Everything is clean and like new, with surprises that greet you right away.

From the entrance, a wide boardwalk goes over a pond (where we saw Canada geese and some ducks), passes a waterfall flowing over a rock, and leads you to the red pandas. Their habitat has a waterfall, too, flowing over an artificial rock cliff and into a large pool that has bamboo growing around it. The red pandas spend most of their day in trees and so are easy to view. The zoo has several of these animals and also operates a state-of-the-art panda breeding facility and research center.

The boardwalk continues past a large Indian grasslands area that includes many plains animals. Display boards offer interesting facts; for example: "Fallow deer, easily distinguished from other deer by the large flattened antlers of the stags, or males. . . ." There are also nilgai, axis deer, and black-buck antelope here.

Now, decision time: one choice is uphill to the children's petting zoo that holds sheep, goats, and other tame animals. Feed baby animals here. Nearby, ride elephants in summer. Watch capuchin and black-and-white colobus monkeys climb and play; pause at a viewing deck above a wide ravine; and go on past a kangaroo community to the magnificent clouded leopard. These animals are usually very high-strung and can be self-destructive in captivity, but the ones here are calm, healthy, and happy cats that have been hand raised and fed a diet that provides all the nutrients they need.

A descent to the Valley of the Cats rewards you with views of many kinds of wild felines. Animals are in large, fenced wooded areas, with elevated walkways between them, making it very easy to see and photograph them. We watch a Bengal tiger "stalk" its larger Siberian tiger neighbor. We also observe cougars just below us. They have been enjoying walking on logs across a stream that runs through their habitat.

Another fork in the walkway leads along a tree-lined creek past elk, mule deer, red deer, several camel species, and ostriches, and on to the educational building. Programs take place here from mid-March through mid-November in the 500-seat amphitheater just behind it.

Zoo director Rick Schwartz explained the education program: "Throughout the day we give presentations that allow kids to ask questions of the keepers. They can touch some animals, like pythons and birds of prey. Other scheduled events are classes, concerts, lectures, and crafts demonstrations. Also, buses bring children from Nashville for weeklong day camps or a succession of weekly programs about animals, conservation, and ecology."

Across from the educational building are a gift shop and an impressive reptile house with dozens of exhibits of rare live reptiles such as pythons, vipers, rattlesnakes, iguanas, green mambas, boas, and monitor lizards. Ardi's favorite was a giant blue-tongued skink (nonvenomous, ranging from Sumatra to New Guinea). A very fat eastern diamondback rattlesnake, the largest and arguably the most dangerous snake in North America, seems docile behind glass. (Ardi saw one nearly this size on Otter Creek Road at Radnor Lake back in the 1960s, but in many years of walking there she's never seen one since.)

Past the reptile house the walkway turns right, and a two-level pond is on the left where waterfowl are free to visit. Beyond is a concession area that serves hot and cold foods and provides tables and benches in a large patio. Upstairs is a thatched-roof open pavilion overlooking a 12-acre African savanna. Here are zebras, gemsboks, oryx, common eland, sable antelope, and giraffes.

Nearby are a pair of African lions and some lemurs from

Madagascar that entertain us. Red ruffed lemurs run on horizontal poles and walk on the ceiling wire of their cage. The ring-tailed lemurs have faces resembling raccoon and beautiful horizontally striped tails of pearl gray and charcoal. They make quick jumps and seem very curious about everything. The black-and-white lemur has striking color contrast and a distinctive ruff of fur around the neck.

A peacock has the run of the place, walking beside a cage containing Abyssinian ground hornbills. It retreats shyly around the corner, but its iridescent blue-and-green plumage makes its "disappearing act" a failed attempt.

This zoo has gained widespread recognition for its breeding programs. It was the first institution in the world to be successful with artificial insemination of the clouded leopard, a very endangered species.

Among the newer animals that have joined the Nashville Zoo "family" are several Bactrian (two-humped) camels, natives of the Gobi Desert in Mongolia; "Gilda," a significant red panda brought here from Spain, whose parents both originated in the wild; and a Cuvier's dwarf caiman, a crocodilian predator native to the Amazon and Orinoco basins.

One of director Rick Schwartz's most cherished dreams will be realized soon at the Grassmere location. He's been planning for a children's zoo that will include a learning center.

"Not the petting kind," he explained, "but an educational hands-on five-acre tract that has theme exhibits. One might be a camouflage exhibit showing the different species that do camouflage. Others could be a walk-in aviary and an Australian walkabout. It will have a lot of "using" things such as a large prairie-dog town with tunnels underground where kids can crawl, then pop up their heads in bubbles. Even though these have been tried in other places, ours will be on a much grander scale."

For the next few years, the Nashville Zoo will continue to showcase the African and European animals here. Visit soon, while you can enjoy two superlative zoo locations in Nashville.

*Where:* Northwest of Nashville. From I-24, exit west on New Hope Road (exit 31 at State 249). Turn north (right) on U.S. 41A, go two miles, and follow signs.

*When:* Year-round. April through September, 9 A.M.to 6 P.M.; October through March, 10 A.M. to 5 P.M. Closed Christmas Day and New Year's Day.

*Admission:* Adults, $6.00; seniors and ages 3 to 12, $4.00; 2 and under, free. Parking, $2.00 per vehicle (free for members and disabled). Group rates, call 615-746-3449.

*Amenities:* Gift shop, concession stands, picnic areas, stroller rental.

*Activities:* Animal viewing and photography, classes, programs, elephant and camel rides (seasonal).

*Special events:* Walk on the Wild Side (March), Zoo Fest (April), Campout at the Zoo (October), and others. Inquire.

*Other:* Barrier-free access (some steep hills). Some animals are not available for viewing in winter (dates depend on weather).

*For more information:* Friends of the Nashville Zoo, 761 Old Hickory Boulevard, Brentwood, TN 37027. 615-370-3333. To book family reunions or private parties, 615-746-3449; for corporate events, 615-833-1534. Website, http://www.nashvillezoo .org/.

# Natchez Trace Parkway and Corridor

Sixty years in the making, the present-day Natchez Trace Parkway travels 440 miles from Natchez to Nashville. It retraces a historic pathway that was an important wilderness road in the 18th and early 19th centuries. Today's travelers can relive some of the adventure and romance of that era.

This book is not exactly about history, yet history and nature have some interesting parallels. History gives us a look back at what attitudes were and how they have changed. Attitudes toward nature have come full circle from the reverence held by Native Americans, reliance on the natural environment by early settlers, then careless use of resources that came with the industrial revolution and a burgeoning population, and now a growing emphasis on the value of protecting the environment.

The development of the Trace by the National Park Service has re-created a vibrant chapter in our country's development. This modern parkway that closely follows the historic route has finally been completed to its northern terminus on State 100 about three miles southwest of Nashville.

The known story of the Trace goes back at least 250 years. Earlier, Natchez, Chickasaw, and Choctaw Indians created hunters' paths that gradually became a trail. In 1733 the French made a map that showed an Indian trail running northeast from Natchez. Fifty years later, farmers were floating their crops down the rivers to New Orleans and Natchez, where they sold their flatboats and returned on foot or horseback. The trail from Natchez was the most direct return route. As the trail gained more use, it was improved, and by 1810 it was the most heavily traveled road in the region. In the early 1800s many *stands*—the word for inns—were built, and by 1820 there were 20 of these.

Not surprising, as traffic increased, so did the gangs of robbers that operated along the Trace, adding to the hazards of swamps, floods, disease-carrying insects, and occasionally unfriendly Indians. This chapter in history ended just a few years after the arrival of steamboats in Natchez in 1812. Steamer travel to Nashville was a much faster and safer choice.

Today a peaceful, leisurely drive along the Trace is a way to see some beautiful countryside without the clutter of electrical wires and billboards. There are many stops along the way where remnants of the past still exist.

## A Day on the Trace

A cool day in August is a rarity in middle Tennessee, and when one came along, we looked at each other and said, in unison, "Natchez Trace!" We lived only 10 miles from the Mile 429 access point on State 96 west of Franklin, so in just a few minutes we had a cooler loaded with ham-and-turkey-on-rye sandwiches, chips, fruit tidbits, and diet colas, and were on our way. We intended to drive the 90 miles to the Alabama state line and make as many stops as we had time for.

If you try this now that the northern terminus is complete, be sure to exit on State 96 to get a look at the magnificent bridge nearly a third of a mile long and its two arches that span 582 and 460 feet. Workers were hoisting a 55-ton segment of precast concrete into place as we drove by. No wonder the sign warned "Do not stop under bridge."

The first sign we saw on the Trace said, "Speed Limit 40," and the next one said, "Tupelo, Mississippi 179 Miles." There's a correlation here: a friend had told us that all speeding tickets on the parkway must be paid in Tupelo, in person. The speed limit is OK, because it defeats the purpose to use this road as a quick route to one's destination (farther south, where there are fewer curves in the road, the limit increases to the standard 50 mph).

At first the road winds through hills and valleys, flanked by mixed hardwoods, pines, and cedars, and an occasional split-rail fence. The right-of-way is a manicured corridor of green, and today the sky has layers of clouds and patches of blue.

Just as Lea comments that we're passing through prime deer habitat, a doe and fawn appear. They stop, we stop, the doe crosses the road, then the fawn follows quickly. Actually, it would be unusual not to see deer on the parkway.

A few minutes later we pass a red fox sitting on a bank at the right side of the road, not 30 feet away. It is scratching its ear with a hind foot and pays no attention to us. Lea comments that in January and February red-tailed hawks perch in the trees along this road looking for rodents, and we might see four to six in a 10-mile stretch.

The poplars are turning yellow, we notice. It is one of the first trees to turn, especially if the summer has been dry.

Five miles past where we saw the fox, we meet three foxhounds trotting north as if they suspected that an interesting chase might be ahead!

Occasionally we see signs of habitation: bales of hay stacked in a field, a barn of weathered wood with a rusting tin roof, a field of tobacco. Then a jarring sight: a power line in the distance, the first we've seen for 20 miles.

We stop to see the Gordon House, a two-story brick home that was built in 1818. It is one of the few remaining buildings associated with the old Natchez Trace and is being restored. Scaffolding covers the entire front. Here, Captain John Gordon operated a trading post and a ferry across the Duck River in the early 1800s, having made an agreement with the Chickasaw chief George Colbert that allowed this.

Now thunderheads are forming, and there is more blue in the sky. We pass river bottomlands and cornfields. From this point on, there are interesting stops every few miles. We pull off at Jackson Falls. There are two trails here, one to the left that follows the top of this high valley to an overlook with sweeping views of the Duck River gorge, and a paved trail to the right that descends to the falls of Jackson Branch (named for Andrew Jackson), a beautifully sculptured cascade. Sometimes this creek is dry, but today the water is flowing.

Forty miles from our starting point, we come to an old phosphate mine. There was a brief flurry of mining at this spot in the late 1800s. On both sides of the parkway are abandoned mine shafts in limestone ledges. We take a five-minute walk to an abandoned railroad bed and a collapsed mine shaft in a limestone outcrop.

Meriwether Lewis Park, named for the explorer of Lewis and Clark fame and onetime governor of the Louisiana Territory, is our next stop. Lewis, known for periods of despondency, died in 1809 here at Grinder's Inn of a supposedly self-inflicted gunshot wound. A monument designed as a broken shaft marks his grave. This is a nice park, with campground, exhibit room, pioneer cemetery, picnic areas, hiking trails, and ball fields.

Two sites a few miles south have relics of an old iron industry. Metal Ford, on the Buffalo River, has a scenic spot for a picnic (but we'll eat at our favorite spot—Jack's Branch). We take a loop trail that goes beside the river to the McLish Stand exhibit and then returns along the old millrace, ending where the Steele Iron Works used to be. It's a very short but interesting stroll. The Napier Mine, what's left of an open-pit iron mine, is a mile down the road. Here are exhibits and informative display boards as well as short trails that lead to relics of old mining operations.

Jack's Branch has picnic tables in a shady grove beside a gurgling stream. You descend some stone steps to get there, and there is also a footbridge across the stream. Just beyond this stop is one of the access points to the old Natchez Trace. There's a warning not to pull a travel trailer on the old road. That's because you ford a stream at one point. We had no problem with our two-wheel-drive car, though. This two-

and-a-half-mile loop took us around
and under the Trace, providing
some nice views and a feeling
of being in an earlier era.

Several other areas have
short trails or other interesting fea-
tures. The Sweetwater Branch nature trail would be very nice
in spring, when a 20-minute walk takes you through brilliant
wildflowers. Some other locations point to low areas where
mud holes make the trail impassable during periods of heavy
rain.

The last 20 miles (below U.S. 64) were disappointing to us
because many roads crossed the parkway and the secluded
feeling was missing. We even saw a billboard as we
approached the 64 junction!

Two places where groceries and gas are easily available—
that is, within two miles—are at the exit for Meriwether
Lewis and the one for U.S. 64.

*Where:* The northern terminus is on State 100 three miles
southwest of Nashville. Access from State 46, 7, 50, 20, 221, 13,
and 227 and from U.S. 412 and 64.
*When:* Year-round; never closed.
*Admission:* Free.
*Amenities:* Scenic parkway with many natural and historic
sites. Tennessee section has 5 hiking trails, 2 nature trails, 3
history exhibits, an Indian history exhibit, two nature exhibits, 11 Old Trace exhibits, 11 picnic sites, a campground (32
sites, no hookups, first-come basis), and 8 rest room areas.
*Activities:* Hiking, walking, camping, auto tours, swimming,
horseback riding, bicycling, wildlife viewing, birding, nature
appreciation, historic research, photography.
*Other:* No gas, food, or accommodations on parkway. Information center at Meriwether Lewis Park (State 20 at the parkway: milepost 385⁹⁄₁₀).

*For more information:* Superintendent, Natchez Trace Parkway, RR 1, NT-143, Tupelo, MS 38801. 601-680-4205. Traveler information, 800-305-7417.

## Monsanto Ponds

Along the "Natchez Trace Corridor" (the seven counties through which the Trace passes) some interesting places await just a few miles from the exits. One of these is the Monsanto Ponds on State 50 west of Columbia, an award-winning wetlands next to the Duck River. We visited it on our return trip along the parkway.

This destination is not easy to find, because there are no road signs pointing to it. In such situations we are grateful to have the *Tennessee Atlas and Gazetteer* (published by DeLorme Mapping) which shows all small roads and trails and many other land features. From the parkway, exit onto State 50 and go 11⁴/10 miles east, passing two unincorporated communities: Williamsport, on the Duck River, and Sawdust. Turn left on Monsanto Road—just before the junction with State 43.

Monsanto Road takes you right to the ponds. For 50 years, from 1937 to 1986, the Monsanto plant was the world's largest producer of elemental phosphorus. As early as 1942 the company was initiating environmental restoration, planting trees on the mined land and making settling ponds for the ore tailings. This increased the natural food supply for wildlife and provided cover and nesting sites.

The Monsanto Wildlife Enhancement Area is a joint project of the Monsanto Corporation, the Tennessee Wildlife Resources Agency, and the Tennessee Ornithological Society. Some 200 acres are open to the public, and an additional 5,000 acres are reserved for wildlife habitat enhancement. The public-access area has five ponds and several acres of freshwater marshlands, forming a wetland habitat that is unusual in middle Tennessee and that provides an outstanding attraction for many birds rarely seen here—at least 160 species sighted so far. The extensive series of ponds attracts waterfowl during spring and fall migrations. More than a dozen species of ducks and geese stay here in winter. The surrounding woodlands are visited by a wide variety of songbirds in all seasons.

The Rail Pond was named for an immature Virginia rail that was spotted there. The four-acre cattail marsh next to it supports unusual nesting species such as the least bittern. A tundra swan was seen here from Thanksgiving to January one year, and one March two greater white-fronted geese were present.

Some of the rare songbirds seen nesting here include the green-and-white tree swallow and the willow flycatcher. Warbling vireos also breed here each year.

*Where:* West of Columbia off State 50W on Monsanto Road.
*When:* Daily, sunup to sundown.
*Admission:* Free.
*Amenities:* Observation tower blinds, information kiosk.
*Activities:* Wildlife and waterfowl viewing.
*Other:* Barrier-free access to one viewing blind.
*For more information:* Monsanto Wildlife Enhancement Area, Monsanto Ponds, Monsanto Road, Columbia, TN 38401. 931-380-9300.

# 3

# Cumberland Plateau

## A Wealth of Wild Places

East of middle Tennessee's central basin are two giant "stair steps." The first jumps up 300 feet to the Eastern Highland Rim, which is roughly 25 miles wide. The second is more a leap than a step to the Cumberland Plateau 1,000 feet higher, 50 miles across, and 2,000 feet above sea level. It is part of the Appalachian Plateau that extends from New York to central Alabama. The two geologic zones represented by the stair steps did not wear down like the Nashville Dome because the caprock is much harder here. High escarpments are on both sides of the plateau and within it, where the Sequatchie Valley cuts a straight, slightly diagonal north-south line through the middle of the plateau's southern half.

In the 18th and early 19th centuries few pioneers settled here or even went through the area, preferring to take wide detours through the Tennessee, Ohio, and Cumberland river systems to reach the fertile bluegrass country of middle Tennessee.

As you will see, this part of Tennessee offers much to people looking for wild and scenic country. Throughout the area are waterfalls, caves, cliffs for rappelling and hang gliding, wild rivers, rugged mountains as high as 3,500 feet, vast wilderness tracts, and many scenic drives and hikes.

Today I-40 and I-24 ascend the plateau with fairly steep grades (twice between Nashville and Knoxville, and at Monteagle Mountain, respectively), and I-75 skirts the tops of Pine Mountain and Hell's Point Ridge on its way from Knoxville to Kentucky. I-40 goes through 50 miles or so of plateau but gives only a hint of the rugged country through which it's passing. Travelers are in for a very pleasant surprise when they leave this superhighway and take the scenic routes.

When you're on the Cumberland Plateau, nearly *every* road offers enough breathtaking views to fill a photo album. Mile after mile, roads wind and dip. You round a curve, and a rock overhang looms overhead. A river tumbles below, and you hear the rapids before you see them. Top a hill, and distant mountains appear like magic. Each time, we seem to hear Beethoven's Fifth Symphony making the announcement: "dah-da-da-dummm!"

# Upper Cumberland and Big South Fork

The Upper Cumberland Plateau is north of U.S. 70, roughly between Smithville and Harriman, and points northeast. Here are deep, clear lakes, scenic state parks, untamed rivers, and remote natural areas. The centerpiece, literally, is the Big South Fork National River and Recreation Area (NRRA).

## *Big South Fork National River and Recreation Area*

It's big, it's wild, and a river has carved great gorges here. It's also a very new kid on the block as national recreation areas go, created by the federal Water Resources Development Act of 1974 and turned over to the National Park Service (NPS) in 1989: 106,000 acres mostly in Tennessee but with a sizable portion also in Kentucky.

Multiple use and protection are the two goals of the Big South Fork NRRA. This rugged area is a mecca for many kinds of outdoor recreation, including high-adventure sports such as kayaking and rock climbing. Visitors also come to enjoy back-country camping, horseback riding, hiking, swimming, fishing, hunting, and sight-seeing. There are 150 miles of hiking trails and more than 130 miles of horseback-riding trails. Mountain bikes are allowed on all horse trails and primitive and gravel roads, but dedicated hiking trails are off-limits to these bikes and to off-road vehicles. The Big South Fork provides roads for four-wheel-drive and all-terrain vehicles. People who are less active can enjoy the scenery by automobile and take short walks to easy-to-reach overlooks.

Canoeing, kayaking, and rafting are popular seasonal activities that depend on natural water flow. The Big South Fork of the Cumberland River and its main tributaries, Clear Fork, North White Oak, and New River, are free-flowing streams that drain over 1,300 square miles of Tennessee and Kentucky. More than 80 miles of navigable river flow through this NRRA. At times, the waters move with great force, over the centuries helping to create many cliffs, natural arches, and waterfalls.

You might wonder how this area has remained relatively remote through most of the 20th century. Actually, quite a bit has been going on here. Exploration was under way in the late 1700s, and a few settlers were moving in by 1800. For 100 years they homesteaded small farms, operated gristmills and moonshine stills, and mined potassium nitrate ("nitre") for gunpowder. In the 1900s a frenzy of coal mining and lumbering began and didn't stop until the resources were depleted in the 1950s. With the land scarred, many people left the area.

Today new timber growth and other vegetation have healed many of the scars, leaving a wilderness of outstanding natural beauty. The dramatic changes in elevation support a rich variety of diverse forest ecosystems and plant species. Wildflowers, which constantly appear from March through October along trails and by the roadside, are exceptional.

As to wildlife, this remote wilderness has been home to bison, elk, gray and red wolves, and panthers. Now it provides habitat for white-tailed deer, beavers, muskrats, coyotes, red and gray foxes, weasels, skunks, wild pigs, river otters, and several species of small mammals. Black bears were reintroduced in 1996.

We were staying at Wildwood Lodge at the junction of State 154 and 297, near the western entrance to the Big South Fork. After one of owner Reg Johnson's "famous" breakfasts (a real treat), we turned on our fog lights and headed east toward the main visitors center at Bandy Creek. We went through farmland, then suddenly entered the NRRA and were in the forest. When we crossed over to Scott County we were on eastern time. That the Big South Fork straddles two time zones is something to keep in mind when you're visiting.

There are some 13 percent grades as the road winds through wooded hills. Soon we were at the visitors center. Most of the interpretive programs take place between Memorial Day and Labor Day, when there are regular Friday- and Saturday-night sessions on different subjects. The park is open year-round, but activity dwindles after November, except for hunting, which is allowed during the regular seasons in Tennessee and Kentucky.

The visitors center has a helpful staff and free literature about all the park activities and locations. It also has a bookshop with an excellent variety of titles for the nature enthusiast. For children 5 to 13, this is the place to sign up for the

Junior Ranger program and receive an activities book. The children write down what they've done—hiked trails, participated in programs, and visited different areas—then they talk with a ranger and answer some questions about what they've learned. Their reward is an official Junior Ranger badge.

East of Bandy Creek heading toward Oneida is a series of 10-mile-per-hour, 180-degree switchbacks as State 297 descends into the gorge of the Big South Fork. This is a preview of coming attractions for the first-time visitor. It also indicates that there is scenery to appreciate even from your automobile, although what you can see on an auto tour doesn't include the designated natural area. You get there by foot or horseback (or ATV), or by paddling a river. Those who prefer easy-access places can take advantage of lookout points like the one at the Leatherwood Ford trailhead near the eastern edge of the park, which has a paved access trail to the overlook with a view of the gorge and the river 500 feet below. Other scenic points accessible by auto are East Rim in Tennessee and Yahoo Falls and Devils Jump in Kentucky.

As you may have guessed, this is a hiker's and backpacker's paradise. Trails range from 1 mile to 50 miles in length, and they are well marked. Permits are not required, but they are recommended as a way to ensure a safer and more enjoyable experience. Be alert for seed ticks between late March and the first fall frost. Also, watch for poisonous snakes and poison ivy. Ask the rangers if there are any special problems on any trails you plan to hike. If you hike in remote places, try to avoid the dates of big-game hunting, or at the very least wear blaze orange clothing.

Your first hike might be the self-guided Oscar Blevins Trail, which starts at Bandy Creek and is a three-and-seven-tenths-mile loop. A trail booklet explains what you can observe about field succession, hardwood forests, geology, rock shelters, prehistoric Native Americans, and pioneer home-steads. Several trailside exhibits also point out interesting facts.

This NRRA is arranged into three major areas. Area I is in Kentucky; the Bandy Creek District (Area II), centrally located, contains Bandy Creek, the Leatherwood Ford Area, and some trails that begin in Pickett State Park; and Area III is the south end of the park, which includes the Honey Creek Pocket Wilderness, Burnt Mill Bridge, and parts of the Clear Fork River and White Oak Creek near Rugby.

The Bandy Creek District has 18 individual trails ranging from easy to strenuous; some of these are connected. For example, Laurel Fork is 13 miles long, a moderate hike, and connects with the John Muir Trail. It offers views of rock shelters and has numerous creek crossings.

Twin Arches Trail is a very popular destination. Drive west from the visitors center, turn right on State 154 and go about two miles, then turn right on Divide Road. Bear left at the fork and go another two and seven-tenths miles, then turn right on Twin Arches Road for two and a half miles. The walk to the arches is just over half a mile, but descending the bluff down steep stairs (and returning) will give you a work-out. You first see the north arch, more than 62 feet high, clear-ing the ground by 51 feet, and having a 93-foot span. The south arch is even more monumental: 103 feet high, with a 70-foot clearance and a span of more than 135 feet. Very few nat-ural bridges in the eastern United States are as high or as broad. If both arches are considered as a single landscape fea-ture, only a handful of natural bridges in the world can com-pare to them in size. From underneath the north arch, you can continue on a strenuous four-and-a-half-mile loop trail that takes you past waterfalls, the Jake Blevins homestead, and Charit Creek Lodge.

We mentioned the Leatherwood Ford trailhead. From here you have several choices. Do you want a four-mile easy trail that takes two hours? Head for Angel Falls Rapid along an old roadbed that follows the river. You will see tall cliffs and some very hazardous rapids. A trail guide identifies 30 different tree species seen here. Have three to six hours? Try Angel Falls Overlook, the Grand Gap Loop, or the Oneida & Western Railroad Bridge. These are moderate trails, part of the John Muir trail system, and offer exciting overlooks of the river and the rapids. The O&W railroad trestle is one of the few extant Whipple Truss bridges that were manufactured in the last half of the 19th century. How about a strenuous hike? The Leatherwood Loop Trail provides a variety of scenery, climbs 500 feet, and descends steeply into the gorge.

In Area III, the Burnt Mill Bridge Loop Trail on Clear Fork River rewards the hiker with river and bluff views and wildflowers along its four and three-tenths moderate miles. The Honey Creek Loop Trail, on the Big South Fork, is remote and difficult—five miles in five hours is the norm—but you will see overlooks, waterfalls, and perhaps some exciting paddling action on the river.

The village of Rugby on State 52 east of Jamestown is hugged by the NRRA park boundary and is well worth a visit for several reasons. It was established in 1880 by British gentry as a community where their "second sons" would live in a cultured but class-free setting. It's an authentically preserved Victorian village, with many buildings open for tours. The Harrow Road Café is open year-round, and there are historic bed-and-breakfast establishments. The town sits near the gorge of the Clear Fork and has an interesting Gentleman's Swimming Hole Trail, which makes a three-mile loop past an old cemetery to the swimming hole and a place called the Meeting of the Waters (where the Clear Fork River and White Oak Creek come together). Part of the trail is in the

NRRA. It begins on a ridge top and offers opportunity to view mixed hardwood forest, evergreen trees, shrubs such as mountain laurel, many varieties of wildflowers, and a rock shelter that early residents called Witch's Cave. Rugby is heavily visited in mid-May during its Spring Music & Crafts Festival, in early October for the annual Historic Rugby Pilgrimage, and on Thanksgiving and Christmas.

A couple of other interesting places are west of Rugby off U.S. 52. The Peters Bridge access to Clear Fork is the absolute southernmost tip of the NRRA. Turn left at the sign and go four and a half miles. To illustrate how the river's character can change: when we came here, the river was nearly dry. If paddling is your goal, it's essential to know two things: the rate of flow, which at times can exceed 40,000 cfs (cubic feet per second) and create very dangerous Class VI waters; and the features of the stretch you plan to navigate. A leaflet prepared by four white-water clubs provides run descriptions of both the Clear Fork and the Big South Fork. Pick it up at the visitors center: "A Guide to Paddling in the Big South Fork."

Guided rafting trips are also available in the area. Request an up-to-date list of outfitters from Park Service headquarters in Oneida, or from the Jamestown or Oneida Chamber of Commerce. Some outfitters, like Cumberland Rapid Transit in Jamestown, also offer canoe rental and instruction, rock-climbing instruction, rappelling, and guided mountain bike trips.

The second site we want to mention is about two miles west of the turnoff to Peters Bridge. As you are coming into Allardt from the east, look carefully for a sign pointing south to Colditz Cove State Natural Area, just a mile off State 52 on Northrup Falls Road. This is a 75-acre Tennessee Natural Area that has a one-and-a-half-mile loop trail to 60-foot Northrup Falls on Big Branch Creek, a tributary of Crooked Creek. The first part is an easy hike, just half a mile to the base of the falls. The two-tenths of a mile to the top is a strenuous stretch over wet surfaces, and you should be very careful on the bluffs of the high cliff. The rock houses you see were once inhabited by Native Americans.

In the several times we've visited this NRRA, we usually have met horseback riders when we've been near the riding trails. These trails are easy to spot, since they have a yellow horse's head on a white blaze. Riding is very popular here, and there are many miles of trails in Area II. Bandy Creek Riding Stables is a park concessionaire that boards horses and also conducts guided trips. The horse trails range from 1 mile to 40 miles in length. Some very beautiful scenery and magnificent overlooks reward riders with views not accessible by other means. Horses are not allowed on hiking trails or paved roads.

The Station Camp Horse Camp is another park concessionaire. This camp, on Station Camp Road off State 297, offers 24 developed campsites and modern rest rooms with hot showers. Each site provides water and electricity, tables, and grills and can accommodate four horses. Miles of horse trails are easily accessible.

Charit Creek Lodge, a concessionaire, is a favorite place with hikers and horseback enthusiasts, and it's accessible only by foot or horseback (we mentioned it earlier in connection with Twin Arches Trail). The lodge has rustic cabins that provide kerosene lamps and wood-burning stoves (but not electricity), rest rooms with solar-heated running water and showers, and pastures and a stable for horses. It provides full services from mid-April to mid-December, including country breakfasts and hearty dinners, and is open as a hostel the rest of the year.

The NRRA provides two mountain bike trails in Tennessee, both accessed from Bandy Creek Road near the visitors center. Collier Ridge Loop is eight miles, and Duncan Hollow

Loop is five and three-tenths miles. Both are easy to moderate. In addition, there are hundreds of miles of old dirt roads where bikes are allowed. As with horses, bikes are not allowed on hiking trails. They *are* allowed on horse trails, although the horses have priority.

Part of the fun of being in the backcountry, of course, is to do some camping. Backcountry camping is allowed almost everywhere, but you must follow guidelines and regulations. There are also campgrounds, where facilities range from primitive sites at Alum Ford in Kentucky to full service with hot showers, dump station, and swimming pool at Bandy Creek.

On the Kentucky side, a popular attraction is the Big South Fork Scenic Railway at Stearns, just a few miles north of Oneida, Tennessee. From early April through October it operates excursions to Blue Heron, where visitors learn about life in this logging and coal-mining community during the first half of the 20th century. You can pick up information at park headquarters or the Tennessee or Kentucky visitors centers.

Accommodations are limited in the Big South Fork NRRA, so travelers often look for places to stay in nearby communities. We found Wildwood Lodge to be conveniently located, and we have also enjoyed staying in a modern chalet in Pickett State Park. But new motels and resorts are opening each year, so check the latest information. Rule of thumb: to avoid disappointment, make reservations early.

*Where:* On the Cumberland Plateau of northern Tennessee and southeastern Kentucky. I-75 northbound from Knoxville: exit State 63 west to U.S. 27, go north to Oneida, then take State 297 west to the visitors center. I-40 westbound from Knoxville: exit U.S. 27 north to Oneida, then take State 297 west to the visitors center. I-40 eastbound from Nashville: exit U.S. 127 north through Jamestown, go east on State 154 and east again on State 297 to the visitors center. Closest commercial airport is Knoxville.

*When:* Year-round; Bandy Creek visitors center open 8 A.M. to 4:30 P.M. (eastern time) December through May, and until 6 P.M. June through November.

*Admission:* Free, except for some fee-use areas.

*Amenities:* Visitors center, snack bar, swimming pool, picnic grounds, scenic overlooks, trails, river access, campground with 150 sites (100 with water and electricity). Concessionaires operate stables and backcountry lodge.

*Activities:* Camping (developed and primitive), wildlife viewing, birding, hiking, backpacking, nature walks, picnicking, scenic auto tours, horseback riding, trail-bike riding, fishing, hunting, swimming, canoeing, kayaking, white-water rafting, rock climbing, photography, fishing, hunting. Rivers are Class III to Class V+.

*Special events:* Nature Photography Workshop, Competitive Trail Ride, Pioneer Camp (May and September), astronomy programs, dulcimer concerts (year-round), Craft Workshop (July), Haunting in the Hills (September), Cumberland Color Caper (October), NORBA-sanctioned mountain bike races (fall). For details, 931-879-3625.

*Other:* Caution: hunting is allowed, and visitors should inquire about season dates and regulations and take precautions accordingly. Emergencies: call park rangers, 931-879-4890, 8 A.M. to 4:30 P.M., or dial "zero" and ask the operator for the Scott County Sheriff Department, then ask for a park ranger.

*For more information:* Superintendent, Big South Fork NRRA, 4563 Leatherwood Road, Oneida, TN 37841. Park headquarters, 423-569-9778. Visitors center, 931-879-3625.

Bandy Creek Stables, PO Box 335, Robbins, TN 37852. 931-879-4013 or 423-627-2793.

Station Camp Horse Camp, PO Box 4411, Oneida, TN 37841. 423-569-3321.

Charit Creek Lodge, 250 Apple Valley Road, Sevierville, TN 37862. 423-429-5704.

Cumberland Rapid Transit Rafting Trips, Rock Creek Route, Box 200, Jamestown, TN 38556. 931-879-4818.

National Park Service Headquarters, PO Drawer 630, Oneida, TN 37841 (for Commercial Rafting Outfitters List).

Historic Rugby, PO Box 8, Highway 52, Rugby, TN 37733. 423-628-2441.

Wildwood Lodge, Highway 154, Pickett State Park Road, Jamestown, TN 38556. 931-879-9454.

Websites, http://www.nps.gov/biso/ then select, and http://www.cs.utk.edu/~dunigan/mtnbike/bsf.html.

## Pickett State Rustic Park

Before the Big South Fork NRRA was even imagined, there was Pickett State Park. It was the first state park in Tennessee, built in the 1930s, hugging the Kentucky border as if attempting to be as remote as possible. It's every bit as scenic as the Big South Fork. The difference is that Pickett, being both a state park and forest, escaped the years of logging mania in the area.

Going north on State 154 from Wildwood Lodge, we are about a mile from the forest boundary. The joe-pye weed on both sides looks regal in misty mauve, surrounded by shorter flowers of yellow and white and some asters of delicate blue growing lower to the ground.

In Pickett's 11,752 acres of mature forest are scenic botanical and geological wonders, including rock formations, natural bridges, waterfalls, and caves. It has been described as second only to the Great Smoky Mountains in botanical diversity. As in the NRRA, here you will need to take to the trails to see the backcountry. Sixty-four miles of hiking trails

*Natural bridge, Pickett State Rustic Park*

give access to some of the features we've mentioned; some connect with NRRA trails.

Pickett is really a mixture of old and new: rustic stone cottages, deluxe cabins, and modern chalets. All are fully equipped. The cabins are open April 1 through November 30, while the chalets are open year-round. There are also 40 campsites (most with electricity and water), a modern bathhouse, and a dump station. The campground is first come, first served.

A central feature of the park is the 15-acre, S-shape Arch Lake, with a shoreline of cliffs, a sandy swimming beach, and picnic areas scattered around the shore. Rent rowboats or canoes here, but motors are not allowed. Fish for mountain trout: fishermen 16 and over will need a trout stamp and a Tennessee license. The beach has a bathhouse, and lifeguards are on duty from early summer through Labor Day.

Hunting is allowed at Pickett, so during statewide hunting seasons be cautious when you are away from the park safety zones.

Summer is an active time here, with hiking, swimming, and fishing. In addition, a seasonal naturalist conducts guided tours, demonstrations, and campfire programs, and explains the natural and cultural history of the area. If you get a chance to tour Hazard Cave at night to see the glowworms, you will have an unforgettable experience. Other recreation includes archery, badminton, horseshoes, tennis, volleyball, and children's playgrounds. Borrow equipment at the park office (no charge).

This peaceful getaway place is high on our list!

---

# Julia's Hike

We were sitting on the deck at Wildwood Lodge, watching a ruby-throated hummingbird making forays to a nearby feeder that hung from a large tree. Julia Johnson hikes often, and she was talking about a favorite trail:

"The name of the hike is Rock Creek. It starts in Pickett and goes into Big South Fork for five miles along the creek. You return the same way, but it's such an interesting trail that it never bores me. I like to walk beside water, hearing the sound of it. This trail has the most wonderful display of showy orchis, which are rare around here—I counted over 50 plants in June and July—and it has wonderful wildlife.

"I usually walk it in the spring because I'm a wildflower enthusiast. My favorite months are at the end of March when the very first spring flowers come out, and then late April when the trillium are blooming and you still have some early spring flowers.

"A friend asked me to take her there in the summer. You can take a dip in the river at any point. There are lagoons, which are really pleasant, and it is well named—totally rock, with a beautiful, smooth bottom. There are little waterfalls, too. Nothing sensational, but pretty.

"You start off in a hemlock stand—so many large hemlocks that it's dark—and cross the river to begin the trail. Actually, you will cross the river several times. There are amazing numbers of snapping turtles in the water, and we saw snakes. No problems: I've never seen a poisonous snake out there, but I always take a stick with me in the summer and just knock it around.

"On this hike we allowed half an hour per mile, but it was so interesting that we took longer. There were different seed heads, different fungi. And animals. We saw pheasants [a regional term for ruffed grouse], and we both saw a gray fox. The trail goes past a lot of very interesting rock formations as well, which makes it even more beautiful."

Get to the Rock Creek Trail from State 154 in Pickett State Park. Driving north from the park entrance, cross a bridge, then just before you reach the second bridge look for a gravel road on the right. A small parking lot is down among the trees, and a short gravel road to the right leads to the trailhead.

*Where:* Pickett County, 12 miles northeast of Jamestown. Take U.S. 127 north of Jamestown; turn on State 154 north to the park entrance.

*When:* Year-round. Summer, 8 A.M. to 10 P.M.; winter, 7:30 A.M. to 4:00 P.M.

*Admission:* Free. Modest fee for camping (discount for Tennessee senior citizens).

*Amenities:* Visitors center, interpretive center, gift shop, recreation building, cabins, chalets, campsites (most have electricity and water), snack bar, nature trails, playground, beach, bathhouse, boat rental, borrow sports equipment.

*Activities:* Hiking, picnicking, backpacking, swimming, fishing, hunting, archery, badminton, tennis, volleyball, wildlife viewing, photography.

*Special events:* Summer interpretive programs, guided tours, demonstrations.

*Other:* Hunting allowed during statewide seasons; safety zones provided.

*For more information:* Park Manager's Office, Pickett State Park, Polk Creek Route, Box 174, Jamestown, TN 38556. 931-879-5821. Information packet, 800-421-6683.

Wildwood Lodge, Highway 154, Pickett State Park Road, Jamestown, TN 38556. 931-879-9454.

Website, http://www.state.tn.us/environment/parks/ then select.


## Dale Hollow Lake

Sitting some 30 miles west of Pickett State Park and surrounded by low mountain ridges of the Cumberland Plateau is Dale Hollow Lake. It has 620 miles of sprawling, forested shoreline interrupted only occasionally by recreation areas developed by the U.S. Army Corps of Engineers and by the few marinas sanctioned by that agency. Because of its unspoiled environment and clear, cold, and deep water, visitors often compare Dale Hollow to the wilderness lakes found in Canada.

We regard it as a favorite getaway place. In a boat, motoring back into one of the lake's many long, narrow coves, we are engulfed by privacy and solitude, and the workaday world quickly fades into unreality.

The superior quality of this clean-water lake and its pristine surroundings makes it a highly desirable place also for swimming, pleasure boating, skiing, and hiking. All but one of the recreation areas have campsites; all have picnic tables and comfort stations; six have drinking water; four have showers; and there are nature trails at six of the areas.

Because it holds a wide variety of both warm-water and cold-water fish, Dale Hollow is an angler's paradise. The world-record smallmouth bass came from this lake. Other species are largemouth bass, white bass, crappies, bluegills, catfish, and trophy-size lake trout, rainbow trout, muskies, and walleyes.

In winter this is an excellent place to view bald eagles, especially on the south side of the lake. In January, the U.S. Army Corps of Engineers conducts eagle-watch tours (inquire at the local office: 931-243-3136).

*Where:* North of Cookeville. From I-40, the exits to Dale Hollow are clearly marked. From the east, exit north to Livingston; from the west, exit on State 56 north to Gainesboro. Access the lake from State 53, 52, or 42. Numerous secondary roads lead to recreation areas, resorts, marinas, and launching ramps.

*When:* Year-round.

*Admission:* Lake access is free on the many U.S. Army Corps of Engineers public launching ramps.

*Amenities:* Many private marinas and resorts; Corps-provided picnicking and camping areas.

*Activities:* Fishing, boating, water sports, nature trails.

**For more information:** U.S. Army Corps of Engineers, Nashville District, Public Affairs Office, PO Box 1070, Nashville, TN 37202-1070. 615-736-7161.

## Dale Hollow National Fish Hatchery

The Dale Hollow National Fish Hatchery, located just below Dale Hollow Dam, is an interesting side trip. This cold-water hatchery is one of the nation's largest producers of trout east of the Mississippi River, supplying more than 300,000 pounds of brown, lake, and rainbow trout to Tennessee streams and lakes each year.

The hatchery's water supply is drawn from the lake at a point about 75 feet below the surface. The water varies in temperature seasonally from 38 to 60 degrees Fahrenheit. Oxygen is added to the water, which flows through the hatchery at regulated rates of 8,000 gallons per minute.

Hatchery personnel welcome questions from visitors.

*Where:* From I-40, exit north on State 56 through Gainesboro and Celina. Two miles north of Celina turn right onto Dale Hollow Dam Road, then right onto Fish Hatchery Road.

*When:* Year-round, 7 A.M. to 4 P.M.

*Admission:* Free.

*Amenities:* Visitors center, aquarium, hatch house, aeration building, 104 concrete raceways. Nearby, campgrounds, marinas, boat-launching ramps, wildlife viewing areas, trails.

*Activities:* Guided hatchery tours.

*For more information:* Hatchery Manager, National Fish Hatchery, 50 Fish Hatchery Road, Celina, TN 38551. Phone, 931-243-2443. Fax, 931-243-3962. Website, http://www.fws.gov/~r4eao/nfhdh.html.

## Standing Stone State Park

This park is midway between Celina and Livingston, five miles south of Dale Hollow Lake, and getting there can be almost as interesting as being there. We came from Jamestown, driving west on State 52 amid spectacular scenery. For the first few miles, the road follows a gorge cut by Cove Creek. As it curves and descends, we see huge rock faces and great overhangs. Bordering the highway are tall purple thistles, big daisies, and black-eyed Susans. Soon, far hills are visible, then a very narrow gorge of the East Obey River, wooded on both sides.

Later the valley widens, filled by fields of goldenrod. After we pass Livingston, it's scenic in a different way, with broad vistas opening up and distant mountains that are hazy humps on the horizon.

To enter Standing Stone State Park, turn left from State 52 onto State 136S and drive along the top of a narrow, wooded ridge for a mile to the entrance. It's always an added pleasure when the weather cooperates as it does today—overcast, breezy, and in the 70-degree range. This, in our opinion, is one of Tennessee's most beautiful parks, although others in the area have received more attention.

The original standing stone for which the park was named was an eight-foot rock placed upright on a sandstone ledge by Native Americans. Some legends say it divided Cherokee and

Shawnee territories, and others say it was a landmark used in worship and government. At any rate, it fell and is now preserved at Monterey while its name lives on in this park.

The focal point here is 69-acre Standing Stone Lake, shaped like an *X* and surrounded by high, wooded cliffs. Year-round fishing for bass and bluegills is a popular activity, and rowboats can be rented. Other features of this park are its 10 miles of hiking trails through very scenic, wooded territory and its many picnic areas. Accommodations range from rustic cabins, three-bedroom timber lodges, and luxury cabins to tent and trailer sites with full facilities and bathhouses with hot water.

Summer recreation opportunities (through Labor Day) include a swimming pool with bathhouse, concession stand, and lifeguards on duty; ball fields; a recreation building; and tennis courts.

The park is surrounded by the Standing Stone State Forest, nearly 11,000 acres where hunting is allowed during regular state seasons. However, the park and some of the adjacent forest are in safety zones where hunting is not permitted.

Standing Stone is also billed as the "Marble Capital of the United States" due to the traditional Rolley Hole National Championship, an annual September event that awards the International Marbles Festival World Cup. It was started by park ranger Bob Fulcher of Norris Dam State Park. Rolley Hole has special rules and has been played (with variations) in this part of Tennessee and in Clay County, Kentucky, for generations. This unique event includes marble trading, demonstrations of marble making and playing, bluegrass music, and square dancing.

***Where:*** From I-40 eastbound, take the third Cookeville exit to State 111, drive north and follow State 42 to Livingston, then

State 52 north; turn left and continue on State 136S for one mile. From I-40 westbound, exit at Monterey to Livingston, then follow the preceding directions to the park.

**When:** Year-round. 8 A.M. to 10 P.M. in summer (closes at sundown in winter).

**Admission:** Free. Modest fees for camping. Senior discounts.

**Amenities:** Visitors center, cabins, campsites, picnic sites, rowboat rentals, nature trails, playground, recreation building, gift shop, snack bar.

**Activities:** Fishing, hiking, camping, picnicking, wildlife viewing, photography, tennis, field games.

**Special events:** National Rolley Hole marble tournament (September).

**Other:** Interpretive specialist on premises year-round.

**For more information:** Superintendent's Office, Standing Stone State Park, 1674 Standing Stone Park Highway, Hilham, TN 38568. 931-823-6347. Website, http://www.state.tn.us/environment/parks/ then select.

## Catoosa Wildlife Management Area

The Overhill Cherokees called the Cumberland Plateau *Gatusi*, which means a hill or small mountain. As time passed, the word evolved into "Catoosa," and a tiny community once bore that name. Today the name is perpetuated in the Tennessee Wildlife Resources Agency's largest landholding, the sprawling 80,000-acre Catoosa Wildlife Management Area, which extends roughly from Clarkrange to near Wartburg. This area is located some 20 miles directly south of the Big South Fork NRRA.

This is rugged land, with steep ridges and deep valleys heavily forested with stands of mixed hardwoods, through which flow swift and tumbling streams. There is no shortage of wild country, although the woodlands occasionally give way to more moderate hilly country where small farms once existed.

Like many of the agency's other WMAs, Catoosa is operated as a multiple-use area designed to accommodate a variety of recreational activities. This has traditionally been one of the state's most popular spots for hunting white-tailed deer, wild turkey, wild boar, ruffed grouse, squirrel, rabbit, and quail. It also has appeal to fishermen. The more prominent waterways in the Catoosa are the Obed River, Daddy's Creek, Clear Creek, Fox Creek, and Otter Creek. All hold smallmouth bass, rock bass, Coosa bass, and bluegills; and Daddy's Creek and Clear Creek have a native strain of muskie.

The Obed Wild and Scenic River runs through the Catoosa but is administered by the National Park Service. It offers kayakers and canoeists some excellent white-water paddling. This river isn't for amateurs, and when it is swollen by spring rains, even experienced boaters should be wary of the dangers.

There's a bonanza of wildlife viewing and photography opportunities on the Catoosa. The area has a large variety of songbirds, hawks, owls, and various migratory and upland game birds. Eagles may also be seen. In addition to the animals listed earlier, it's possible to encounter beavers, gray and red foxes, mink, muskrats, opossums, and bobcats. Many nonpoisonous and a few poisonous snakes are present, as are many amphibians, including some unusual species of salamanders.

For hiking, there are more than 100 miles of gravel roads, 150 miles of trails, and many old logging roads that are now closed to auto traffic. Bicycling and horseback riding are allowed on roads and trails open to motorized traffic and on other trails or routes established for their use. There are no developed camping facilities on the area, but limited camping is allowed in designated places when permission is obtained from the area manager.

*Where:* Near Crossville (west of Knoxville). Exit I-40 at Genesis Road and go north for eight miles to the entrance. Access also from Wartburg: follow Catoosa Road west for six miles to Nemo Bridge and the game-checking station two miles farther.

*When:* Open all year except for February and most of March, when it is closed to all users. Closed to all except hunters during managed big-game hunts (inquire).

*Admission:* Free.

*Amenities:* Trails, gravel roads, old logging roads, river put-in and takeout points.

*Activities:* Hunting, fishing, wildlife viewing, auto tours, hiking, bicycling. (See the following location for NPS activities.)

*Other:* Dates and hunting seasons change, so ask for current information.

*For more information:* Manager, Catoosa Wildlife Management Area, 216 East Penfield, Crossville, TN 38555. 931-484-9571 or 800-262-6704.

## *Obed Wild and Scenic River National Recreational Park*

In 1976, two years after the Big South Fork NRRA was authorized, the Obed Wild and Scenic River (WSR) was added to the national park system. It is a system of nearly 50 miles of river that in winter and spring turn into some of the most challenging white water to be found anywhere. Park ranger Robert

Turan said, "White water just doesn't get any better than this!" adding that it was put on *Canoe* magazine's Top 10 list.

The Obed is the only National WSR in Tennessee, one of only three in the Southeast, and the only one in the region managed by the National Park Service. It is actually not one river but four, consisting of sections of Daddy's Creek, Clear Creek, Emory River, and the Obed. Much of its course passes through the Catoosa Wildlife Management Area. Because of this "dual ownership" situation—the WSR boundary protects just 300 feet on each side of the rim—it is jointly managed by the NPS and the Tennessee Wildlife Resources Agency.

This wild river also goes through a wild *landscape*. It has cut a narrow, steep gorge as much as 500 feet deep through country that offers only an occasional glimpse of habitation—an old mill site or homestead. What you *will* see on your ride down the river is a true wilderness. As it comes off the plateau, the river passes through several plateau ecosystems. There are numerous cliffs and overhangs, waterfalls, cascades, and huge sandstone boulders in the water at many points.

All this rugged terrain can make for some very challenging (but rewarding) hiking. Some progress has been made on the Cumberland Trail, a State Scenic Trail that, when completed, will cover 220 miles. Of the 17 trail miles through the Obed WSR, two portions can be hiked. The 4½-mile Nemo Bridge Trail and 2½-mile Devil's Breakfast Table Trail are open. The Nemo trail offers an initial stretch of moderate hiking and then a rugged 1½-mile section into and out of the Obed Gorge. The Devil's Breakfast Table Trail goes down into Daddy's Creek gorge and earns its name, "trail of a thousand steps." The goal of the Tennessee Trails Association's Cumberland Trail Conference is to complete the whole trail by 2008.

Ranger Turan came to this area after working in the Grand Canyon but calls the Obed WSR "the hidden jewel of the East." He adds: "There's such a wilderness beneath the rim. It's like a thousand years ago, but very few people ever see it."

That may change. If the current plans are implemented (read: *funded*), there will be several easily accessed overlooks and an elaborate trail system that will follow the rim of the gorge and provide some incredible views. A boardwalk will confine the foot traffic in sensitive areas to protect the landscape.

Even now the visitation is rather remarkable for such an out-of-the way place: 237,000 visitors in 1993. During the Fourth of July weekend that year, 2,000 vehicles were counted in the Nemo location alone. Among those visiting, besides white-water enthusiasts, are a considerable number of dedicated rock climbers.

The NPS visitors center is in downtown Wartburg on State 62 just west of the junction with U.S. 27. This is a well-staffed facility with displays featuring natural and cultural history and a gift shop that has field guides and books about white water and canoeing. Here you can pick up a river chart that shows the degree of difficulty for specific stretches of river according to water-flow conditions.

One of the displays at the visitors center is about the Russian wild boar, which was brought to this country and placed in hunting preserves in 1910 and 1912. These animals live in the area, but since they tend to avoid human contact, their presence is more often confirmed by tracks or upturned earth than by sightings.

The visitors center also gives slide presentations by request.

Is the river really wild? In a word, *Ohmigod!* That is the name of one spot on the Obed near the Clear Creek junction.

# Taming the Rivers

The point is, you do not tame a wild river. It may tame you, though, so it is wise to take certain precautions. The National Park Service advises:

- Always float with at least two other craft.
- Tell someone where and when you will begin and end your trip.
- Wear protective clothing for cold-water conditions (a wet suit is recommended).
- Understand how to prevent hypothermia.
- Understand the International Scale of River Difficulty and know your skill level.
- Know that river levels can change rapidly, and never paddle when the water level is in the trees.
- Always check current river conditions and know if you should portage difficult rapids. Identify how you will get off the river if necessary.
- Obtain the publication *White Water in an Open Canoe* from your local chapter of the American Red Cross.

***Where:*** North of I-40 west of Knoxville. From the west, exit north on U.S. 127 to State 62 and turn east. From Knoxville, exit north on U.S. 27 to Wartburg, then turn west on State 62. From Oak Ridge, take State 62 west past the intersection with U.S. 27. West of Wartburg, State 62 connects with several access roads.

***When:*** Visitors center, daily, 9 A.M. to 11 A.M., plus 2 P.M. to 4 P.M. Monday through Friday. Closed Christmas Day. River paddling possible usually December through April, depending on water flow; access is denied to Catoosa WMA during much of this time period.

*Admission:* Free. Guided trips available from private outfitters.

*Amenities:* Visitors center. Primitive campground in Nemo area, hiking trails.

*Activities:* Paddling (Class II to V), rock climbing, rappelling, hiking, fishing, swimming, picnicking, primitive camping, backcountry camping at Potter's Ford on the Obed when the WMA is open, hunting, fishing.

*Other:* Caution: during warm months, watch for ticks, rattlesnakes, and copperheads. Do not drink stream water without boiling or treating it. Protect your vehicle against vandalism. Do not trespass on private property. Glass bottles prohibited at all river access areas. Alcohol prohibited at all developed areas. Barrier-free access at visitors center and some backcountry sites.

*For more information:* Obed Wild and Scenic River, Park Headquarters, PO Box 429, Wartburg, TN 37887. 423-346-6294.

Flow statistics: TVA info line, 800-238-2264 (ask for the "Emory at Oakdale" reading).

Websites, http://www.nps.gov/obed/ and (Cumberland Trail) http://users.multipro.com/cumberlandtrail/obed.html.

## Frozen Head State Natural Area

Centuries ago, a major Indian trail headed west from Native American settlements on the Clinch River, over Frozen Head Mountain to the Cumberland River Valley. Tradition has it that the trail was used by early woodland tribes and then by the Cherokee. Burial mounds and indications of small communities were found along Flat Fork Creek and the Emory

River within what is now the Frozen Head State Natural Area.

The area was settled in the 1800s, then around the turn of the 20th century coal mining, logging, and sawmill operations were significant industries here. Convict labor from Brushy Mountain State Prison figured prominently in the coal-mining operations. The logging ceased in 1925. The Tennessee Forestry Division took over management and constructed fire control roads, trails, and a lookout tower on top of Frozen Head Mountain. In 1952 the entire state forest was destroyed by the worst fire in Tennessee history. In 1970 Frozen Head was designated a state park. Property transfers increased the acreage, then in 1988 all land above a 1,600-foot-elevation boundary was reclassified as a State Natural Area, leaving 11,869 acres, plus an additional 330 acres for state park development.

We drove from Oak Ridge on State 62 and turned onto Flat Fork Road, following the park sign, which warned: "Rustic Campground. No Hookups." It is four miles to the park. At first this road can be a bit unsettling, since it goes through the Brushy Mountain State Prison Honor Farm, passing various warning signs. There are fences on both sides, and guards.

At the entrance, the road crosses Flat Fork Creek. A young forest has rebounded from the disastrous fire. We see a trail marker with three blue stripes on it; just ahead on the right is the rustic-style visitors center. Most natural areas have little development, but the park part of Frozen Head allows some very nice amenities. There are playing fields opposite the center, a playground, a horseshoe pit, an amphitheater with sound system, a general store (open in summer), picnic areas, and rest rooms with showers.

Frozen Head is named for the second-highest peak in the Cumberland Mountains, at 3,324 feet one of 14 peaks in the natural area that are above 3,000 feet. Such rugged terrain sets the scene for waterfalls and huge rock shelters, making ideal habitat for wildlife of all descriptions.

With one of the best trail systems in the state (more than 50 miles), this area is ideal for hiking and backpacking. Some trails are easy, following old roads or railroad beds. Others are very difficult, having elevation changes of as much as 6,250 feet in seven miles. This list gives an idea of the variety: Lookout Tower (scenic vistas en route to the fire tower), Panther Branch (an old railroad bed, with falls and wildflowers), North Old Mac (three miles of cool and shady north slope), South Old Mac (a warm and sunny walk to the tower), Judge Branch (mountain stream, many flowers), Spicewood (steep and rocky two and a half miles), Chimney Top (giant caprock formation and long vistas, difficult four hours), Emory Gap (easy walk to a 20-foot waterfall), Lookout Tower (road passing near old prison mines), Bird Mountain (scenic, geologic formations, difficult), and Kelly Mountain (difficult one-and-a-half-mile mining road).

These remote hikes provide outstanding opportunities for wildlife watching, and the 360-degree view from the Frozen Head Mountain fire tower gives you a revealing orientation to the area. Frozen Head is also considered second only to the Smokies as a place to enjoy spring wildflowers. A detailed trail map available at the visitors center describes the trails and restrictions and gives useful safety tips.

Two types of camping are permitted. Backcountry camping is available in 10 designated sites. There is no fee, but a permit is required. Primitive campgrounds offer sites for tents, pop-ups, pickups, and small trailers, and bathhouses with hot showers but no electricity or electrical hookups. One campground has 20 sites, with overflow tent camping available in a primitive group camping area.

Since camping is so limited in the Catoosa WMA, one solution is to use Frozen Head as a base camp while visiting Catoosa and the Obed just a few miles away.

*Where:* Just east of Wartburg off State 62. Turn north on Flat Fork Road (two miles east of the intersection with U.S. 27) and continue for four miles to the park entrance.

*When:* Year-round. Visitors center open 8 A.M. to 4:30 P.M.

*Admission:* Free. Modest campground fee (50 percent discount for Tennessee senior citizens).

*Amenities:* Visitors center, playgrounds, general store, amphitheater, picnic shelters.

*Activities:* Hiking, backpacking, camping, horseback riding, mountain biking (limited), fishing (trout fishing April and May), field games, picnicking, interpretive programs, movies.

*Special events:* Junior trout tournament (April); Spring Wildflower Pilgrimage (April); Foothills Gospel Music Festival (May); Folklife Festival (August); Christmas in the Mountains (December).

*Other:* USGS Fork Mountain quadrangle and other maps available at visitors center.

*For more information:* Frozen Head State Natural Area, 924 Flat Fork Road, Wartburg, TN 37887. 423-346-3318. Website, http://www.state.tn.us/environment/parks/ then select.

# Along the I-40 Corridor: Six Easy-Access Sites

Sometimes people prefer to experience the outdoors (or learn about it) in places where access is easy. Along I-40 between

Knoxville and just west of Cookeville are six sites that meet this criterion and are definitely worth a visit. They are Mount Roosevelt State Forest, Ozone Falls, Cumberland Mountain State Park, Wilson's North American Wildlife Museum, the Garden Inn at Bee Rock, and Burgess Falls.

## Mount Roosevelt State Forest and Wildlife Management Area

Actually, we were on U.S. 70, which roughly parallels I-40 from Knoxville to Crossville. Just a mile west of Rockwood we suddenly saw the familiar binoculars sign. We turned to the right in the Mount Roosevelt Forest and drove to the top of Mount Roosevelt at the edge of Cumberland Escarpment. We surprised two white-tailed deer on the way up. They were quite shy and bounded off the road.

We found picnic tables at the top and a parking area, but no rest rooms. There is, however, a 360-degree view of Watts Bar Lake, the city of Rockwood, and high mountains many miles distant. You may climb the fire tower for a better view. A trailhead leads to the Walden Ridge Trail in the state forest. The picnic tables were full, and people were surveying the area with binoculars. In September and October this is a favorite vantage point for viewing migrating birds and butterflies—monarchs and other butterflies that also migrate southward at this time of year.

*Where:* U.S. 70, two miles west of the 70 and U.S. 27 junction west of Rockwood. Going west, turn right at the sign and drive one and a half miles to the overlook.
*When:* Year-round, but September and October are the best months to view migrations.
*Admission:* Free.

*Amenities:* Fire tower, picnic tables, trailhead, no rest rooms.
*Activities:* Wildlife viewing, picnicking, hiking.
*Other:* Caution on trails during state hunting seasons.
*For more information:* Tennessee Wildlife Resources Agency, 216 East Penfield, Crossville, TN 38555. 931-484-9571 or 800-262-6704.

## Ozone Falls State Natural Area

In the spring when plateau rivers have good water flow, this 80-foot falls in a 75-acre natural area can be spectacular. It is on the south side of U.S. 70 adjacent to the roadside about five miles east of Crab Orchard.

This is definitely not the place for unsupervised small children, since there are very high cliffs at the parking area overlook and no protective barriers. Even adults have been injured after slipping on the rocks overlooking the falls, as when a Sparta man who had been rappelling fell to the bottom of the cliff. Fortunately, his safety line engaged, breaking his free fall. Even so, he was hospitalized with injuries to both legs. This was reported in the *Crossville Chronicle*.

There is a trail to the bottom of the falls—a short but steep descent into a small canyon. You could get a good photograph there in early afternoon with the proper light.

We've seen these falls at their roaring best and also when they were simply a trickle.

*Where:* Roadside on U.S. 70 between Rockwood and Crab Orchard.
*When:* Year-round, but best during good water flow in winter and spring.
*Admission:* Free.
*Amenities:* Scenic views, short trail to bottom of falls.

*Activities:* Hiking, photography, nature appreciation.
*Other:* Hazardous precipices.
*For more information:* Cumberland County Chamber of Commerce, PO Box 453, Crossville, TN 38555. 931-484-8444.

## Cumberland Mountain State Park

In this 1,562-acre park just south of Crossville, Crab Orchard stone is everywhere—stone walls, stone buildings, stone columns incorporated into wooden fences. Even a large dam and bridge are constructed of this distinctive sandstone that was quarried nearby. The dam, which impounds the water of Byrd Creek, is the largest masonry structure ever built by the Civilian Conservation Corps during the 1930s.

Correction: the stone isn't *everywhere*. You will also see a mature hardwood forest; 50-acre Byrd Lake, where fishing for bass and bluegills is a popular sport; 15 miles of hiking and nature trails, including one that circles the lake; and abundant wildlife and remarkable botanical diversity. The day-use trails, strictly for foot traffic, attract many hikers in summer.

In addition to the park trails, 11³⁄₁₀ miles of the Cumberland Trail—the Grassy Cove Segment—are complete basically from Cumberland Mountain State Park to near Crab Orchard. This trail is usually hiked as two separate day hikes (the Brady Mountain and Black Mountain portions).

As to cabins, you'll find a mix of rustic, modern, duplex, and timber lodge types. The campground has 147 sites and water, electricity, grills, tables, a camp store, and a dump station. A feature that's a bit unusual is the group lodge: Mill House accommodates 16 people and is open year-round.

A modern 250-seat restaurant overlooks Byrd Lake. It serves two meals daily year-round, except when it is closed during the Christmas holidays.

For water activities, there is an Olympic-size swimming pool with lifeguards on duty and a bathhouse, open in summer. And rowboats, paddleboats, and canoes can be rented at the lake.

Picnic tables and pavilions are scattered throughout the park, which offers the usual types of outdoor recreation. In summer—the busy season—daily programs are conducted by recreation and interpretive specialists.

You may enjoy the National Fitness Campaign Walking Course at a large parking lot by the recreation lodge. Various stations are placed around the perimeter where you perform stretches, squats, twists, and the like, and a walking phase is incorporated into the program.

The recreation hall is open to the public all summer, but after Labor Day it can be reserved. That was the case on the September day we were there. People were busily putting up red, white, and blue balloons and spreading tablecloths. One of them explained, "Tonight we are going to honor a man who is 90 years old. He's a Democrat."

"It looks like you're going to have a band?" Ardi asked.

"Oh, yes. We'll have a full band and everything."

*Nice*, we thought, *and so American!*

*Where:* U.S. 127, four miles south of Crossville (10 minutes from I-40 at exit 317).

*When:* Year-round. 8 A.M. to 10 P.M. in summer (closes at sundown in winter).

*Admission:* Free. Fees for campsite use (senior-citizen discount).

*Amenities:* Cabins, campground, camp store, snack bars, nature trails, hiking trails, fitness circuit course, group lodge, restaurant, swimming pool, canoe and paddleboat rentals, recreation building, picnic sites (and four pavilions), playgrounds, stables, basketball and other outdoor courts, 18-hole Jack Nicklaus championship golf course.

*Activities:* Hiking, backpacking, fishing, tennis, swimming (and swimming lessons), camping, canoeing, picnicking, interpretive programs, guided tours, movies, outdoor games.

*Special events:* Inquire about special summer events.

*Other:* Barrier-free access.

*For more information:* Superintendent, Cumberland Mountain State Park, Route 8, Box 322, Crossville, TN 38555. 931-484-6138. Reservations, 800-250-8618.

Cumberland Trail Conference, Route 1, Box 219A, Pikeville, TN 37367.

E-mail, cumberlandtrail@rocketmail.com (for trail maps).

Websites, http://www.state.tn.us/environment/parks/ then select, also http://www.users.multipro.com/cumberlandtrail/ (Cumberland Trail).

## *Wilson's North American Wildlife Museum*

On the Cumberland Plateau just off I-40 between Crossville and Cookeville is the little town of Monterey. Early in the 20th century, it was a popular destination for vacationers. Then Gatlinburg developed into Tennessee's prime vacation mecca, and the traffic started passing by. Since 1995, though, a compelling reason to stop here is to visit Wilson's North American Wildlife Museum where you can see an outstanding collection of mounted specimens in naturalistic settings. All are the work of taxidermist Grady Wilson, whose wife, Janet, helped design the displays.

The museum's collection has more than 300 animals in 160 scenes behind large glass windows, and more are added each year. The museum self-guided tour conducts you along passageways resembling cave tunnels as it winds through the 8,000-square-foot building. Each scene places the animals in settings indicating their natural habitats.

Look at a winter landscape where large tufts of dried grasses protrude from the snow. No, that one isn't a clump of grass; it's a sleeping coyote, all curled up and perfectly camouflaged.

In another winter scene, a white-tailed buck is completing a jump over a fence, and a doe is following.

Realism helps put across the message of how the animals interact and survive. A fall scene shows a bobcat stalking a gray squirrel. In a western setting, a cougar is attacking a mule deer. Another vignette shows two wild boars fighting in front of a rocky cliff, from which a little waterfall tumbles into a stream, with ferns growing alongside it. Other displays have lighter moods, as in one depicting an evergreen forest where a bobcat and two kittens are playing. (The bobcat kittens, as with all of the immature animals in the museum, had died of natural causes.)

In others, a mountain lion grabs for a porcupine as a young lion watches from a small hillock; bobwhite quail wander among some old farm implements, inspecting the ground outside the barn; a river otter jumps into a pool while another watches, obviously waiting its turn.

The big ones are here, too: a grizzly, a 1,600-pound moose, a 10-foot alligator, and a 2,000-pound bison.

One of the newest scenes shows a mountain man who has come down to a stream to fish for salmon, while a large bear with the same thought in mind approaches in the background.

Wilson's taxidermy work is highly respected by clients, including the Big South Fork NRRA and several Tennessee state parks, and by schoolteachers, who bring students on nature study field trips. The museum is also rated by AAA as a highly recommended location, and we have to agree.

First you have to find it, though. The easy way is to "just think Dairy Queen." In Monterey, it's the only landmark you need to consider. I-40's two Monterey exits, 300 and 301, both connect with U.S. 70N. Coming from the west, take exit 300, then go north toward Monterey. The highway makes a sharp turn to the right (heading back toward the interstate), and the Dairy Queen is on the left a block after the turn. Turn left there onto Chestnut and continue for about a mile to the museum, which will be on your right. From the east, take exit 301 toward Monterey, turn right on Chestnut just past the Dairy Queen, and continue to the museum.

Antique buffs will find a bonus: in the museum is Janet's shop, Fox Hunt Antiques, stocked with a wide array of large and small items for sale.

*Where:* From I-40 between Crossville and Cookeville, take exit 300 or 301 and go north to Monterey. Turn onto Chestnut at the Dairy Queen and go to 914. See details in the preceding text.
*When:* Year-round. Monday through Saturday, 9 A.M. to 5 P.M.
*Admission:* Adults, $5.00; ages 3 to 12, $3.00.
*Amenities:* Museum, antique shop.
*Activities:* Viewing exhibits, nature study, educational tours.
*Other:* Barrier-free access.
*For more information:* Wilson's North American Wildlife Museum, 914 North Chestnut, Monterey, TN 38574. 931-839-3230.

## The Garden Inn at Bee Rock

From Bee Rock near Monterey, we looked far down Stamps Hollow nearly a thousand feet below us at its deepest point, enjoying playful gusts of a fickle wind while the morning sky shifted from dusky red to a warm golden hue. In certain places, like this one, the world becomes surreal. Is it the wind we hear or voices from the past? Have we entered a time warp, or has time simply suspended, leaving us to fully enjoy the moment? This effect is what prompts us to search out unspoiled places, although with populations exploding and industries expanding, finding them becomes increasingly more difficult.

Maybe elsewhere on the planet, but not so much on the Cumberland Plateau.

Actually, this "wilderness" experience was not all that remote. We had been staying at the Garden Inn, a bed-and-breakfast where hospitality, comfort, and superb cuisine are hallmarks, thanks to innkeepers Dickie and Stephanie Hinton. They offer 11 inn rooms, all with private baths, and some cabins. A unique feature of the inn's design took its cue from a wet-weather spring on the property, which is diverted through the building. Visible through an interior glass wall of the inn's lower level, the flowing water simulates a mountain brook in a natural setting of rocks and vegetation. Outside, beside a stone terrace, the water collects momentarily in a shallow pool, then spills over the edge of the huge rock overhang on which the inn was built, creating its own little waterfall.

Stamps Hollow, from which the Calfkiller River originates in its journey past Sparta to the Caney Fork, was a "truce zone" in days before white men came. By joint agreement it was used as a winter encampment for more than one Indian tribe. The Native Americans named Bee Rock after bees that swarmed around "honey holes" in crevices of the rock face.

The walk to Bee Rock from here is a five-minute stroll mostly along an old roadbed, with one rocky (but not difficult) portion. This rock is the most imposing natural feature among other prominent stone formations and caves along the cliffs that frame the valley. Providing a sheer drop of more than 100 feet, it is an ideal (and popular) rappelling site. Guests of the Garden Inn also have access to miles of old logging roads doubling as hiking trails around the plateau and down into the 4,500-acre forested valley.

On the inn's 15 acres the outdoor attractions include theme gardens (berries, ferns, azaleas, water plants, bulbs, and several others); an outdoor grassy activities court; a pavilion; and a waterfall, cave, and natural bridge. Indoor recreation areas offer large-screen TV, Ping-Pong, and a collection of gardening and other books, plus a deck for enjoying a sweeping panoramic view.

This inn offers "the best of the best" in the way of accommodations for those who like life's little luxuries along with an outdoor experience. Nevertheless, it is not so much a single destination as a base for exploring the nearby natural, cultural, and historic attractions.

Consider where you can go—on some of Tennessee's most scenic highways and byways—within an hour's drive: the Big South Fork NRRA, Fall Creek Falls and other nearby state parks, the Catoosa WMA, Dale Hollow and Center Hill Lakes, and cultural niches such as the unique and historic town of Rugby and the Muddy Pond Mennonite community, where you can watch sorghum molasses being made and buy fine quilts and other home-cooked and handcrafted items.

***Where:*** From I-40, take Monterey exit 300, then State 70 west for 100 yards; turn left on Bee Rock Road by the Garden Inn sign.

***When:*** Year-round.

***For more information:*** The Garden Inn at Bee Rock, 1400 Bee Rock Road, Monterey, TN 38574. 931-839-1400.

E-mail, hinton@multipro.com.

Website, http://www.bbonline.com/tn/gardeninn/.

## Burgess Falls State Natural Area

To get to Burgess Falls, exit south from I-40 at State 135 in Cookeville and follow the signs (about eight miles). This is a scenic recreational area created in 1971 and managed by the Department of Conservation. Actually, there are three falls on Falling Water River—the upper, middle (a wide falls), and lower (with a 130-foot fall, the tallest of the three). This stream is on its way to Center Hill Lake on the Caney Fork River.

At the parking lot are rest rooms and a large picnic shelter, which can be reserved. You'll also find a volleyball court and a playground. The trail starts out high above the river, with views of the rapids below. There are rock overhangs, and some have benches underneath them beside the trail. It's an easy seven-tenths-mile walk to the upper falls. You can nearly always count on a good water flow, and you'll have superb views of all three falls.

Take the right fork at the middle falls to go on down to the lower falls. The trail goes through a very old forest of giant beech trees that look about 100 feet tall, plus huge hemlocks, white oaks, and big-leaf magnolias.

At the head of the lower falls is an area of flat rocks with some little pools: a clearing in the forest that is idyllic. From there a metal stairway goes steeply down to the foot of the falls. It's not a place to let little children loose.

Another noteworthy feature on the trail is the remains of an old aqueduct that was used in the past to bring water to the city of Cookeville. Only some pillars and some vestiges of the pipe remain.

For a view of Center Hill Lake, walk a ridge top trail to an overlook. This trail then loops back to an old gravel road that leads back to the parking lot.

Pick a beautiful day, pack a lunch, and spend a morning or

afternoon here hiking, viewing wildlife, and picnicking. But don't go in December, January, or February. It's closed then!

*Where:* State 135, eight miles south of I-40 at Cookeville (exit 286).
*When:* March 1 to December 1, 8 A.M. until 30 minutes before sunset.
*Admission:* Free.
*Amenities:* Trails, rest rooms, picnic shelter (by reservation).
*Activities:* Hiking, picnicking, photography, wildlife viewing.
*Other:* Beware of dangerous cliffs.
*For more information:* Burgess Falls State Natural Area, Route 6, Box 380, 4000 Burgess Falls Road, Sparta, TN 38583-8456. 931-432-5312. Website, http://www.state.tn.us/environment/parks/ then select.

# South Cumberland and Sequatchie

As we mentioned in the Introduction, the Cumberland Plateau is shaped like an inverted wedge. Not only does it narrow in its southern part, but it is also divided by the Sequatchie Valley. The part west of the valley is still called the Cumberland Plateau, but the part east of the valley goes by the name of Walden Ridge. What this means to the traveler is that as you drive around the area, you will probably find many of the roads climbing or descending several hundred feet within a few miles. This describes the approach to Fall Creek Falls State Park from any direction.

## *Fall Creek Falls State Park*

This is without a doubt "everybody's favorite state park" (except possibly for Tennesseans who live in the far east or west portions of the state). We know this because of the visitation figures and the very real difficulty in getting lodging reservations even a year ahead. Also, people often have a dreamy-eyed look and speak in a hushed tone when they pronounce the name. How many times we have heard the excited comment, "Guess what—we have a room at *Fall Creek Falls!*"

We solved the housing question by staying at a favorite place, the Fall Creek Falls Bed and Breakfast just one mile from the north park entrance. It's a deluxe eight-room facility owned by Doug and Rita Pruett. We were fed well and pampered, and the location couldn't have been more perfect. The inn offers a backdrop of rolling hills and fields where deer often graze. Acres of wildlife food plots enhance the viewing potential, while herb and vegetable gardens assure fresh table fare in season. It is also the home of Silverbrook Stables, a boarding, training, and show facility.

Some vacation destinations have so much to offer that one hardly knows where to start either exploring or describing them. That's certainly true here. The nearly 17,000 acres at the top of the plateau (elevation 1,819 feet) have an abundance of natural beauty, including steep sandstone cliffs, lush virgin forests, and natural waterfalls. The recreational opportunities for everyone from small children to seniors is truly mind-boggling. Feel like a moonlight canoe trip? A creek safari? Rappelling instruction? Macramé? Square dancing? Some bass fishing in the 375-acre lake? Maybe just a swim in the Olympic-size pool? The list goes on.

Of course, Fall Creek Falls is the main attraction, and with its 256-foot free fall it's the tallest waterfall east of the Rocky Mountains. The water flow is usually decent, but during winter and spring the greater water volume creates a true spectacle. A hike to the bottom of the falls is a must for many visitors young and old. From the falls parking lot on the park's scenic auto tour, head toward the overlook, then go left from there down a terraced gravel path to a second, lower overlook. The half-mile trail to the base is difficult, with high steps and boulders. If the water flow is moderate, you will be able to navigate around under the falls to enjoy the view from behind the mist, but watch for slippery rocks.

Six other day-use hiking trails in the park wind through the ever-present rhododendron, hemlocks, and poplars. They range from easy to difficult, and there is an overnight trail that has 25 miles of loops and requires a permit. There are also bicycle and equestrian trails. Walking, bicycling, and horseback riding are very popular, and hikers take to the main roads as well as the trails.

Our first stop is the nature center near the north entrance. We have already seen several deer, many squirrels, and a crow. Some of the leaves have turned, and some have fallen. We walk toward the building, noticing the polka dots of sunshine on the woodland floor. Inside are displays that educate visitors about Tennessee geology, animals and plants of the area, and the makeup of a forest. A small viewing room shows films on request about wetlands, snakes, the Smoky Mountains, Fall Creek Falls, and other subjects. And there's a gift shop.

We decide to take the self-guided auto tour. After we leave the Fall Creek Falls overlook, we continue on a one-way loop by the Cane Creek Gorge, stopping at all the overlooks, not wanting to miss a single spectacular scene. High above the gorge, we listen to the sounds of the wind through the trees and the water below. A sign reminds us that this rugged forest is a fragile place that needs protection.

A much-photographed spot, and one of the most inspiring vistas at Fall Creek Falls State Park, is Buzzard's Roost. It's just a short walk to this secluded rock promontory overlooking the gorge. A stiff wind blows in our faces as we gaze toward the bluffs opposite, looking for the hawks or buzzards that are often soaring there. Soon we are rewarded by not one but three majestic birds. The gorge below is a wilderness that holds dense, old-growth forest. This is in contrast to the rest of the park, which was logged extensively back in the 1930s but has grown back.

We think one reason for the great popularity of this park is that it offers truly scenic and wild places but also ultra-modern accommodations at the inn and cabins on Fall Creek Lake, and almost every type of outdoor recreation and program possible. There's even a modern laundromat in the Village Green area. So, if your taste is for backpacking and camping or tends toward golf on one of the top public golf courses in the United States (according to *Golf Digest*), you can be satisfied right here. Everything is first class.

*Where:* State 284 south of State 30, halfway between Spencer and Pikeville. From I-40 eastbound, exit south on State 111 at Cookeville, then go east on State 30 at Spencer. From I-40 westbound, exit south on State 127 west of Crossville, then go west on State 30 at Pikeville. From I-24, exit east on State 55 at Manchester, join U.S. 70S at McMinnville and drive toward Sparta, then exit east on State 30 to Spencer and on to State 284.

*When:* Year-round. 8 A.M. to 10 P.M. in summer (closes at sundown in winter). Stables are open April 1 through late October. Olympic-size pool open in summer only.

*Admission:* Park is free. Fees for camping, golf, swimming, bicycle and horse rental, and some special events.

*Amenities:* Inn; restaurant; cabins; campsites (three campgrounds); group lodges; nature center; "village green" with camp store, laundromat, craft center, visitor lounge, public pool and bathhouse, recreation center, amphitheater, snack bar, information center, lighted tennis courts and ball fields, and picnic grounds; 18-hole golf course with pro shop, snack bar, dressing rooms, rental clubs, gasoline and pull carts, driving range, and practice green; canoes, pedal boats, fishing boats with electric trolling motors for rent; bait shop; hiking and backpacking trails, self-guided walking trails, motor nature trail, paved bicycle path; stables.

*Activities:* Every activity imaginable as indicated by the amenities list, plus full summer schedule of interpretive programs, and Friday-through-Sunday programs in other seasons.

*Special events:* Fall Creek Thaw (April); Senior Capers (April and November); backpacking weekends (March and November); Spring Wildflower Pilgrimage (May); rock-climbing workshops (May and October); bicycle tours (June and September); Mountaineer Folk Festival (September); Fall Colors Weekend (October); Elderhostel, Christmas on the Mountain (December).

*Other:* Barrier-free access. Reserve accommodations well in advance. Large RVs should use State 111 rather than State 30.

*For more information:* Fall Creek Falls State Park, Route 3, Pikeville, TN 37367. Office, 423-881-5298; inn and cabin reservations, 800-250-8610; Fall Creek Inn, 423-881-5241; nature center, 423-881-5708; picnic shelter reservations, 423-881-3297; campsite reservations, 800-250-8611; camper check-in station, 423-881-5569; golf pro shop, 423-881-5706. Website, http://www.state.tn.us/environment/parks/ then select.

Fall Creek Falls Bed and Breakfast, Attention: Doug and Rita Pruett, Route 3, Box 298B, Pikeville, TN 37367. 423-881-5494. Website, http://www.bbmtview.com/~bbonline/tn/fall creek/.

## Rock Island State Park

Located on State 287S (also called Great Falls Road) just off U.S. 70S, halfway between Sparta and McMinnville, this park is not far from Fall Creek Falls. In some respects it has been overshadowed by its neighbor: it's half the size and is a young park, begun in 1969.

What it has to offer, though, is impressive. The Caney Fork and Collins Rivers join here, and Tennessee Valley Authority's Great Falls Dam and hydroelectric plant just below that point has created the Great Falls Reservoir with 125 miles of shoreline. The generators control the river flow below the dam, where the river runs for a short distance to the upper end of Center Hill Lake (created by the Center Hill Dam near I-40 several miles north).

But what a run! Right out of the gate, so to speak, is the Great Falls. As you enter the park, you'll see a historic cotton mill on the right, and the falls is directly behind it. An overlook, a picnic area, and rest rooms are here. A foot trail descends the gorge, where you can walk right up to the sparkling rush of the twin falls and even under them when TVA isn't generating. A caution about that: the generating schedule is subject to change at a moment's notice and without warning. You'll have to climb out of the gorge, but take a look around and have an exit plan.

Besides the falls, this park has several other attractions. It's one of the best "fishing holes" in the state, with several boat-launching areas both on the Great Falls Reservoir and on the Caney Fork below the dam. Fishing is most productive in spring (though enjoyed in other seasons, too), while boating and waterskiing are popular in spring, summer, and fall. In summer the launching ramps have heavy use, and parking areas fill up early, so plan to arrive before noon. At one of the launching ramps is a sandy swimming beach that was created by natural sand deposits. It has a playground and bathhouse.

This is one of the few parks in the state where reservations can be made for campsites (and are in fact recommended). There are 50 sites, all equipped with electrical and water hookups, grills, picnic tables, bathhouses with hot showers, and a dump station. Although the campground is open year-round for self-contained units, water is turned off from December through February and sometimes in March, depending on the weather.

This park also has an interpretive specialist on duty year-round. You can sometimes arrange a tour to Big Bone Cave in the nearby Bone Cave State Natural Area. The cave is protected and is open only for interpretive tours. Discoveries there include fossils of Pleistocene-era mammals—a jaguar and a giant ground sloth, to name two.

There are four picnicking areas in the park, some linked by trails or logging roads. There are also playgrounds, basketball and tennis courts, horseshoe pits, and fields for other outdoor games. We recommend the Collins Nature Trail, a one-and-a-half-mile loop following a bend of the Great Falls Reservoir. You might see wild turkeys and white-tailed deer here.

As part of the ongoing park development, 10 modern cabins were completed in 1994, each fully equipped to sleep 10 people. Their Victorian architecture echoes the early development of the area in the 1910s and 1920s clapboard siding, metal roofs, and front and rear porches.

We talked with park ranger Joe Moore, who gave us an excellent tip: "If you'd like to know where to eat around here, the best plate lunch in the area is at Bright's Grocery in Walling. They offer real country cooking, and they're very friendly folks. But get there before noon."

We decided to check it out, going left on 70S after leaving the park. In a couple of miles we saw the sign: "Grocery, Game Room, Deli, Tanning Bed, Arts, Crafts and Curiosities, Country Home Cooking, Homemade Pies. Open Monday–Friday."

He was right on both scores. We were too late for lunch, but they *were* friendly!

*Where:* Exit I-40 south onto State III at Cookeville. Drive south to Sparta, then take U.S. 70S for about 12 miles. Turn right (west) on State 287S to the park entrance.

*When:* Year-round. Campground closed in winter to all but self-contained units.

*Admission:* Free. Fee for camping and cabins.

*Amenities:* Visitors center, campsites, picnic grounds and pavilions, general store, archery range, cabins, boat-launching ramps, tennis courts, swimming beach with bathhouse, hiking and nature trails.

*Activities:* Fishing, swimming, boating, picnicking, camping, hiking, wildlife viewing, scenic views, photography, outdoor games, tennis, kite flying, Frisbee tossing, guided tours.

*Special events:* Walleye tournament (April); Arts & Crafts Fair, Bluegrass Jam, Autumn Colors Celebration (October).

*Other:* Reservations accepted for campsites; year-round interpretive specialist.

*For more information:* Superintendent, Rock Island State Park, 82 Beach Road, Route 2, Box 20, Rock Island, TN 38581. 931-686-2471. Website, http://www.state.tn.us/environment/parks/ then select.


## Cumberland Caverns

More than 5,000 of the 39,000 known caves in the United States are in Tennessee! Most caves are never seen except by *cavers*, a term that describes those who explore and map caves, understand safe caving techniques, and show proper respect for the cave and the property owner. Caving can be very dangerous and requires training and experience. The recommended way to become a caver is to join an organized local caving group (called a *grotto*), and then gradually learn caving skills. A majority of the avid cavers are members of the National Speleological Society (NSS).

Commercial caves, on the other hand, offer a way for the general public to become acquainted with cave features, geology, and history. Tours led by knowledgeable guides take you through winding passageways to underground streams and waterfalls, soaring rooms, and curious formations that took shape over millions of years.

Cumberland Caverns, near McMinnville, is one of the best-known commercial caves in Tennessee. It has about 32 miles of explored passageways and advertises itself as the most extensive mapped cave in the state and the second-largest cave system in the country.

The standard tour lasts an hour and a half. Tour guides explain the different cave formations in an interesting way. Because of the many stair steps, taking the tour can be somewhat of a workout. The most impressive room is called the Hall of the Mountain King, a large breakdown chamber (so-called because of the boulders and slabs on the cave floor that have fallen from the ceiling). It is said to be the largest single cave room in the eastern United States—600 feet long, 150 feet wide, and 140 feet high.

Visitors learn to identify stalactites, stalagmites, columns, helictites, flowstone, cave coral (also called popcorn), and other formations. They also learn how saltpeter, an essential ingredient of gunpowder, was made in the 1800s in the cave. Blind albino crayfish live in streams in the cave, but bats are rarely present here.

Some of the most impressive features of this cave, such as the Crystal Palace with its rare and beautiful pure white gypsum flowers, and the Monument Pillar (a 15-foot pure white stalagmite with a green pool of water at its base and diamondlike calcite crystals embedded in its surface), are not shown on the commercial tour.

But there is glitter of another sort. Deep within the cave, a sound-and-light show, God of the Mountain, interprets the Biblical account of creation. Then, in an underground dining room the mood changes as a theater organ plays and a three-quarter-ton crystal chandelier suspended from the ceiling glows with 160 lights in red, white, blue, and gold, chasing shadows and dramatizing the immensity of the cave. It came from the Loew's Metropolitan Theater in Brooklyn.

The history of the cave is told in *Cumberland Caverns* by Larry E. Matthews, published by the NSS. More than just the story of a cave, it relates the fascinating account of explorations, the thrill of discoveries such as the Crystal Palace, accidents and rescues, and for Roy Davis (who operates the cave under a lease agreement) the fulfillment of his dream.

Cumberland Caverns is not far from Fall Creek Falls and Rock Island State Parks and makes an ideal side trip or rainy-day alternative when you're at these parks.

*Where:* From McMinnville, take State 8 southeast for seven miles and follow the signs; turn left on Dark Hollow Road, then left again to the caverns.
*When:* Daily from May 1 through October 31, 9 A.M. to 5 P.M.; by appointment November through April.
*Admission:* Fee for guided tours.
*Amenities:* Gift shop, rest rooms, snack bar.
*Activities:* Commercial tours, historic tours, wild tours.
*Other:* Dress for 56-degree temperature. Underground dinner theater available by reservation.
*For more information:* Cumberland Caverns, 1437 Cumberland Caverns Road, McMinnville, TN 37110. 931-668-4396.

National Speleological Society, 2813 Cave Avenue, Huntsville, AL 35810-4431. 205-852-1300. (For general caving information and addresses of local grottos.)

## South Cumberland Recreation Area

Savage Gulf, Great Stone Door, Fiery Gizzard Trail, Lost Cove Cave, Sewanee Natural Bridge—seductive names that for decades have called adventurers to some of the wildest country on the plateau. Ten areas, including a visitors center, in four counties are grouped together and managed by the Tennessee Department of Environment and Conservation as the South Cumberland Recreation Area (SCRA). The visitors center, on U.S. 41 between Monteagle and Tracy City (3 miles from I-24 exit 134, 42 miles northwest of Chattanooga), should be everyone's first stop. It is open seven days a week.

Inside is a large 3-D map showing the whole area, with ranger stations, trails, campsites, and natural and cultural features pinpointed. There are four distinct ecological zones— plateau top, bluff, gulf (a regional term for gorge), and aquatic—providing exceptional recreation opportunities. Ranger naturalist Randy Hedgepath talked about some of these:

"For floating, the Duck River from Normandy Dam and the Elk River from Tims Ford Dam are designated by TVA a National Recreational Waterway for weekend use. There's 20 or 30 miles of each that are really good Class I to Class IV floats, good for seeing wildlife such as kingfishers, ducks, herons, and ospreys. The Collins River is also a nice Class I pastoral float from Big Springs down to Rock Island State Park. For white-water canoeing, there's the Little Sequatchie just north of Jasper. It takes a four-wheel-drive access.

"For stream recreation, trout fishing is available in several streams around here where rainbow trout are stocked: the Elk,

Duck, Little Sequatchie, Crow Creek, Battle Creek, Sweden Creek, and the Collins River.

"As for hiking, we have a heaven for hikers—lots of trails of our own, plus many private trails around the area, such as the Bowater Company pocket wilderness trails, and there are state forest trails. We have a regular schedule of guided hikes on Saturdays and Sundays. In fall we walk along the bluff tops to get views of fall color from all the overlooks. In spring we take wildflower hikes. Around here, every stream that comes off the mountain has waterfalls, so when the flowers start waning we take waterfall hikes. A lot of the gorges—like the upper part of the Fiery Gizzard, with its Canadian hemlocks and northern maples—are cool in summer, and many of the little waterfalls have natural swimming holes, so we have gorge trail hikes and swimming hole hikes. Most of our streams dry up from July to October. In winter we take ice and snow hikes.

"Our trails offer a choice: the maximum reward for minimum effort, or the maximum challenge. You can walk flat country all day and see view after view, or you can go down in the gorges across miles of rock gardens. Name a great outdoor experience and the plateau has it: caves, waterfalls, unbroken forest for miles and miles, and wildlife!

"We tell people to dress appropriately for the weather when hiking: rain gear if it's raining, shorts and a light shirt when it's hot. A good hat is advisable, and so is sunscreen. In all seasons you need high-top hiking boots, and you always need drinking water.

"If you're going on a cave tour, you need lights and a helmet and clothes that you don't mind getting dirty. Our cave tours are first come, first served. We meet at the Carter Natural Area parking lot, our southernmost unit outside Sewanee. We are one of the most cave-rich regions in the world, so caving is optimal around the SCRA."

Randy related to us a curious experience involving a waterfall.

"I was going up a dry streambed one day in a part of the park that was virtually unexplored, and as I went around a curve, there was a beautiful waterfall 30 or 40 feet wide going over a 20-foot cliff. After it went over the cliff, it disappeared into a sink. It has a name, Ranger Creek Falls, and it's a seven-mile round-trip hike from the Stone Door Ranger Station. When there's a lot of rain, the sink will fill up and the water goes on down the riverbed."

About the wildlife: often seen are white-tailed deer, turkeys, raccoons, opossums, squirrels, coyotes, red and gray foxes, beavers, otters (stocked on some of the streams), and migratory birds. Beavers are in lower elevations near Crow Creek and have been seen at the Carter Natural Area's Lost Cove Cave and on the plateau near the Franklin State Forest.

Turkeys can be shy, but once when Randy was resting on a stretch of remote trail, he looked up to find 40 or 50 wild turkeys walking all around him!

Hunting is allowed on the plateau, but not in the Grundy Forest State Natural Area at Tracy City or on some 18 miles of trails in the Great Stone Door area that are safety zones (although the trail goes near the boundary at some points). All hunting conforms to regular statewide season dates—periods from September to January—so, check these if you plan to be in the area.

Wildflower watching, from mid-March to October, is very popular. "Animals can be very hard to see," Randy explained, "but we have tons of wildflowers. The common kinds are some of the most beautiful, and every month except in winter you have a different set of flowers. But we also have some very rare wildflowers like the pink lady's slipper orchid and a very rare white fringeless orchid.

"Then there's the Hawkins Cove Natural Area, a 244-acre

tract with no trails or development, which has been set aside to protect a rare August-blooming wildflower called the Cumberland rosinweed. The property is sandwiched between the highway and the old Mountain Goat railroad grade that went from Cowan up to Sewanee. It is marked with a red triangle of paint on the rocks and trees alongside U.S. 64."

Randy also explained the popularity of rock-based activities:

"In the limestone you can find sea creatures such as crinoids and brachiopods. The sandstone layers yield weird alligator-skin-looking fossils that are actually the bark off tree ferns of ancient ages. Among all the rock types, probably the most fossil-rich is shale, a swamp deposit of mud from sandy clay. There you'll find fern leaves, grass, worms, and all sorts of different things.

"As for climbing and rappelling, we have perfect rock here. The sandstone on the cliffs is hard and stable. You can start at the top and rappel, or you can climb up first. Nearby, the Prentice Cooper State Forest has some highly prized areas. One called the T Wall (Tennessee Wall) is very famous. We have the Great Stone Door, which is getting a little bit overcrowded but is still excellent. [Stone Door is] the only place in the park where rock climbing and rappelling are allowed."

For rappelling instruction, Randy recommends the Adventure Guild in Chattanooga, located at the Rock Creek Outfitters. "That's a great organization," he said, "and they have a training wall at the north end of the Walnut Street Bridge."

The SCRA locations are scattered over a fairly wide area. For easy access to all (and—we admit it—*comfort*) we like to stay at Jim Oliver's Smoke House Resort at Monteagle. On nicely landscaped grounds with trees and a duck pond are modern cabins with fireplaces, hot tubs, and screened porches; RV hookups; 96 motel rooms; the Smoke House Restaurant and Trading Post; and playgrounds, a swimming pool, tennis courts, and a picnic pavilion. Exit I-24 at the Smoke House billboard, and you're there.

## Grundy Forest, Fiery Gizzard, Foster Falls

There are two ways to get to Foster Falls, a 60-foot waterfall on Little Gizzard Creek (a tributary of the Big Fiery Gizzard) in a TVA "small wild area." Be advised: it is often a dry creek in summer.

One approach is to start at the Grundy Forest State Natural Area two miles west of Tracy City on State 56 and hike from the northern terminus of Fiery Gizzard Trail. This can be an all-day or two-day affair.

In just the first two miles you'll pass a monster hemlock half a century old beside a huge rock shelter (Cave Spring is underneath), 10-foot Blue Hole Falls and swimming hole, the Black Canyon, a 20-foot columnar Chimney Rock monolith, a 2⁸/10-mile side trip past the Dog Hole Coal Mine to Raven Point Campsite, and the Fruit Bowl of huge boulders.

After 12⁷/10 miles of main trail (plus your side trips) you reach the Foster Falls parking lot. Along the way you've visited Raven Point, an overlook 1,800 feet in elevation. You have seen the double Anderson Falls that drop a total of 80 feet, have had a difficult descent-and-climb into and out of Laurel Branch Gorge, and have been rewarded with views of Foster Falls from two sides. A second camping spot, Small Wilds Campsite, is 3½ miles from the southern end of the trail. Camping is free, but you need to get a permit from the SCRA visitors center.

One other caution: the trail is on private land, so be sure to respect the property and the generosity of the owners in allowing public access.

The other way to see the falls is by auto. Drive to Tracy City, continue on U.S. 41 for eight miles, and turn right at the sign. TVA provides a picnic area and seasonal campground for overnight visitors. It's 125 yards to the falls from the parking area, an easy walk that crosses a footbridge along the way. The gorge is a sheer drop here, but a protective cable makes viewing a little safer.

In Tracy City, we recommend a stop at the Dutch Maid Bakery. It is Tennessee's oldest family-owned bakery, started in 1902 by a master chef from Switzerland, and open ever since. We sat at a table with a cheery, red-checkered cloth and talked with owner F. Lynn Craig while we decided what to have with coffee. A fresh-baked specialty bread or a fruit-filled turnover? Jams and jellies, mountain honey, relishes? We decided on a sugar-plum-filled jelly roll. Mr. Craig said they used to make them long and skinny, then decided the filling should be emphasized and so fattened them up. We also took some pull-apart bread, a Dutch Maid invention.

The bakery still does it the old-fashioned way. Their Hobart mixer was built in 1929, and when the shaft needed replacing, they had one made locally. Their slicer is even older. It dates back to 1915 and works perfectly.

## Savage Gulf State Natural Area

The Savage Gulf State Natural Area has been described as a giant crow's foot carved into the Cumberland Plateau, which is easy to visualize from the maps provided. It is 11,500 acres of true wilderness with tumbling creeks, narrow gulfs, and sandstone cliffs. The gulf has 55 miles of trails and 10 primitive campgrounds. Because it is a Class II Natural Scientific Area, the only kinds of development allowed are foot trails, footbridges, and overlooks.

The eastern access point is the Savage Gulf Ranger Station. From Tracy City, take State 56 north toward Altamont, turn right on State 108 and go through Gruetli-Lager, then turn left on State 399 and follow the signs.

Thirteen trails make up the system: six accessed from each ranger station, plus a Connector Trail that is very challenging. Half of the trails are easy and range in length from a four-mile loop to a long interconnected system. The difficult Collins Gulf Trail is the longest (nine and nine-tenths miles). The Stagecoach Historic Trail follows one and six-tenths miles of a stagecoach route that was used through the area from 1843 to 1900. Both day hikers and campers have to register before using the trails.

## The Great Stone Door

The Great Stone Door is a giant crevice in the rock at the plateau edge in the Savage Gulf State Natural Area. One hundred fifty feet deep and 10 feet wide, it allows access to the gorge below. For centuries, Native Americans used it as a passageway.

The Stone Door Ranger Station is the western access point to the Savage Gulf. From Tracy City, take State 56 north to Beersheba Springs, then turn right at the sign and follow a one-way road to the check-in station. You will find modern rest rooms and a signboard showing the trails. There is also a shady grove with benches surrounded by tall maple, pine, oak, and hickory trees. Nearby is the Stone Door Camping Area.

What may be unexpected is the wide blacktop path that provides barrier-free access to an overlook three-tenths of a mile away. From there it is seven-tenths of a mile to the Stone Door, where you stand on sheer precipices for breathtaking views of raptors riding thermals and miles of unending cliffs across a giant chasm. In this short walk are rock ledges to sit on, great vistas, and wildlife to watch through binoculars. The wind whistles up the canyon, and it's hard to leave. The forest looked healthy: we saw only one dead tree in the entire landscape and surmised that it probably had been hit by lightning.

The trip down the "door" can be treacherous when footing is slippery. Rocks provide handholds, but it's a steep descent nevertheless.

Near the overlook you can access two other trails. The Big Creek Rim Trail is easy. It follows the edge of the plateau past several overlooks and ends at the Alum Gap Camp Area three and two-tenths miles away. The Big Creek Gulf Trail goes down through the door and descends steeply into the gulf, then comes back up near Alum Gap Camp. It is challenging, so many people prefer to make this an overnight hike. Another way to return to the ranger station from Alum Gap Camp is via Laurel Trail. From the junction of Big Creek and Laurel Trails an interesting short trail, Greeter Trail, goes to Greeter Falls. It is an easy mile to the Boardtree Creek suspension bridge overlooking the double Boardtree Falls, then a moderate three-tenths of a mile to a split. Go left to see the 50-foot-high Lower Falls and plunge pool, or go right to the 15-foot Upper Falls.

## Sewanee Natural Bridge, Buggytop Trail, Lost Cove Cave

These locations are at the southern end of the SCRA. From I-24, take U.S. 64 and 41A southwest toward Cowan. Turn left (south) in Sewanee onto State 56.

To see the Sewanee Natural Bridge, turn left again on Natural Bridge Road. In less than a mile you will come to a paved parking lot. The University of the South donated the bridge to the state in 1976. A gravel walk takes you down to the arch.

Weathered from solid sandstone, this arch is 27 feet high and has a 50-foot span. You can walk on top or climb down underneath it. Behind it is a rock overhang that gives a "cave" feeling and produces a constant trickle of water from a seep at its base.

We came early in the day on a cool and cloudy morning threatening rain, but to the east we saw a pale peach sunrise under the clouds as we looked toward Lost Cove.

Continue on State 56 about four miles past Natural Bridge Road and look on the left for the parking lot for the trailhead of Buggytop Trail. It is often a good idea when you will be in remote places to have someone drop you off and pick you up instead of leaving your car unattended. We were reminded of this when we saw a lot of broken car-window glass in the parking lot.

The two-mile Buggytop Trail leads to the Carter State Natural Area of the SCRA and the Buggytop entrance to Lost Cove Cave. The name is appropriate because Lost Creek flows into the cave, gets "lost," then emerges as Crow Creek. The trail climbs to the top of a ridge, then follows the ridge top north. You may see some of the rare Cumberland rosinweed, a variety of compass plant in the sunflower family, along this stretch. Be sure to register at the booth where the trail starts to descend into Lost Cove. You'll be going through private property until you come to two large beech trees with red blazes indicating that you have reached the natural area. Continue descending through boulder fields, cross the Old Lost Cove–Sherwood Road, then you will soon reach a junction. Take the right fork to the Buggytop entrance (the left fork leads to an overlook and a sinkhole).

Seeing the immense cave mouth is worth the hike. It's an opening 100 feet wide and 80 feet high at the base of an overhang 150 feet high. This is a protected cave that contains rare and endangered species of salamanders and bats. Only experienced cavers should explore it, and never alone. If you're interested in a guided cave tour that explains the cave environment, check with the rangers at the visitors center about schedules and safety instructions.

## Grundy Lakes State Park

It's not all wilderness in the SCRA. For a pleasant and interesting day trip this state park offers a lakeside walk, swimming, and historic coke ovens that were built in 1883 and used until 1896.

Follow U.S. 41 to Tracy City. It will turn a sharp right. After that, watch for the signs where you will exit left. The road enters a forest, then less than a mile farther you see Grundy Lake on the left. Igloo-shape coke ovens sit in a neat row on the opposite shore, and more of them are beside the road on the right, covered now with a blanket of sod and even an occasional tree. The lake has a man-made sandy beach held by a concrete retaining wall at the water's edge. Nearby, a small island is reached by a footbridge. It is a steep hillock with young pine and dogwood trees growing on it, and the view from the top is nice. A bathhouse, a large parking area, and a wooden raft in the water complete the picture.

A two-mile, one-way drive follows the shore, with picnic tables alongside in picturesque spots. A recreation area provides a basketball court, an exercise course, and a larger picnic area with many tables.

On a cool and breezy day we walked the Lone Rock Trail, starting at the far right end of the parking lot where the ground was covered with black and crunchy slag from the coke ovens. The trail begins by following the water's edge. We saw nice patches of orange-flowered jewelweed, and Lea saw a crawfish claw, evidence that a raccoon had been feeding there. We surprised some young blue-winged teal, which flew away when we were about 20 feet from them.

The trail leads across an earthen dam that has created an upper pond above the lake. We thought we were approaching a field of butterflies, but they turned out to be flying grasshoppers. After we crossed the dam, wooden steps led back down toward the water, and a footbridge took us across a small ravine. Lea picked up some hickory nuts and acorns on which squirrels had been feeding and then photographed them on a rock (ever the photographer at work!). The trail went on past the exercise area and beside a bank fragrant with pine needles.

After we returned, we drove around again for a picnic by the lake. The breeze was still with us, and white clouds floated by. A teenage boy stopped his car across the lake, fished awhile from the bank, then drove on.

It had been a good day. Scenic, historic, easy to walk, and we had seen waterfowl and squirrels and evidence of a raccoon. We also had seen fish jumping in the water and a little tree toad.

*Where:* For all SCRA locations, the visitors center is on U.S. 41 between Monteagle and Tracy City, three miles from I-24, exit 134. Obtain directions here for nine other locations.
*When:* Daily. Visitors center open 8 A.M. to 4:30 P.M. Day-use areas open 8 A.M. until dark.
*Admission:* Free.
*Amenities:* Nature trails, interpretive center, museum, backcountry campsites, picnic sites, ranger stations, cave, playgrounds, canoe access sites.
*Activities:* Hiking, guided hikes, rock climbing, rappelling, rockhounding, wildlife viewing, wildflower viewing, photography, picnicking, guided cave tours, backpacking, camping, swimming, fishing, paddling.

**Special events:** Fall Color Overnighter, Fall Colors Weekend (both October).

**Other:** Barrier-free access to overlook at Stone Door Ranger Station. Caution advised during state hunting seasons except in safety zones.

**For more information:** South Cumberland State Recreation Area, Route 1, Box 2196, Monteagle, TN 37356. 931-924-2980 or 931-924-2956. Website, http://www.state.tn.us/environment /parks/ then select.

Jim Oliver's Smoke House Resort, PO Box 579, Monteagle, TN 37356. Reservations, 800-489-2091.

Dutch Maid Bakery (mail order), Main Street, PO Box 487, Tracy City, TN 37387. 931-592-3171.

## Sequatchie Valley and Walden Ridge

Scenic U.S. 127 follows the Sequatchie Valley from Crossville to Dunlap, then ascends Walden Ridge, skirts east of the Prentice Cooper State Forest, follows the Cumberland Escarpment, and descends to Chattanooga from Signal Mountain. From the South Cumberland, an equally scenic "back road" to Chattanooga is on State 108 through Gruetli-Lager, then following that road south instead of turning off to Savage Gulf. Descend the escarpment at Whitwell, pick up State 28 momentarily, then turn left on State 27 across the valley to Powells Crossroads, climb Walden Ridge and go through Prentice Cooper, then down again, following the Tennessee River Gorge beside Raccoon Mountain and on to Chattanooga. These are definitely roads less traveled.

Information about different loop tours, including the Sequatchie County Loop, is available at the SCRA visitors center. You'll find breathtaking scenery and many other things to see and do. We'll mention just a few.

***Canoeing the Sequatchie.*** This is a pastoral Class I river good for beginners, but with the added element of spectacular scenery. At Dunlap, check out "Canoe the Sequatchie" owned by Scott and Ernestine Pilkington. Look for a beached house-boat (their office) on the north side of the Sequatchie bridge just south of Dunlap on U.S. 127 (423-949-4400 or 423-855-4961).

***Hang Gliding.*** We are told that the Sequatchie near Whitwell is one of the three best spots in the nation for hang gliding. Contact Sequatchie Soar and Flight (423-949-2301), which offers training and equipment.

***Pocket Wilderness Hikes.*** Bowater Company owns several pocket wilderness areas that are open to hikers. Most are on the eastern escarpment of Walden Ridge, roughly between Dayton and Spring City off U.S. 27. A booklet, *Take a Hike*, available at the SCRA visitors center, gives addresses, directions, and descriptions. Laurel-Snow Pocket Wilderness leads to two scenic waterfalls; Piney River Trail is for backpackers and has a camping area; Twin Rocks Nature Trail offers gorge overlooks; and Stinging Fork Trail leads to a falls. Another outstanding location is the Virgin Falls Pocket Wilderness near Sparta. You can also request the booklet from Bowater (address follows).

***Prentice Cooper State Forest (and WMA) and Cumberland Scenic Trail.*** We had hoped to walk parts of the Cumberland Trail while we were in the Prentice Cooper neighborhood, but the "Do Not Enter" sign stopped us. An archery hunt was going on in this 24,000-acre forest, which closes periodically for various hunts. It is advisable to call the WMA manager (423-658-9201) before planning a visit.

The Cumberland Scenic Trail is 13⁷/₁₀ miles. You can park

overnight at the forest, or at Signal Point Park on Signal Mountain. The trail follows the magnificent "Grand Canyon of the Tennessee River" from a high vantage point of giant rock bluffs. It passes through ancient Indian rock houses, descends to cross two creeks, then climbs again to its destination on Signal Mountain.

There are also two forest loop trails. Mullen's Cove Loop is 10 miles and offers equally outstanding views; Pot Point Loop is a 12-mile trail that leads to overlooks and interesting rock formations, including a 30-foot high natural bridge. Miles of forest roads provide some challenging terrain for mountain bikers, though foot trails are off-limits to bicycles.

*For more information:* South Cumberland State Recreation Area, Route 1, Box 2196, Monteagle, TN 37356. 931-924-2980 or 931-924-2956.

Chattanooga Area Convention and Visitors Bureau, 1001 Market Street, Chattanooga, TN 37402. 800-322-3344 or 423-756-8687.

Bowater Newsprint Calhoun Operations, Attention: Sally Lee, 5020 Highway 11S, Calhoun, TN 37309-5249. 423-336-7301.

Mountain biking Website, http://www.cs.utk.edu/~dunigan /mtnbike/.

# Chattanooga and the Tennessee River Gorge

Chattanooga is like a prized jewel—impossible to describe without considering all the facets. For us, it's always an exciting place because it offers so much. It is a unique combination of desirable location, easy access, premier outdoor environment, historic significance, mild climate, and spectacular attractions.

This city is on direct interstate routes between Atlanta and Nashville and Birmingham and Knoxville. It is at the southernmost tip of the Cumberland Plateau, and it is a gateway to the Cherokee National Forest to the east and the Great Smoky Mountains beyond.

Surrounding Chattanooga is a never-ending scenic backdrop. Three mountains—Signal Mountain, Raccoon Mountain, and Lookout Mountain—border it from the northwest to the southwest. Chickamauga Lake, impounded by Chickamauga Dam on the Tennessee River within the city limits, is a major water recreation area that extends for miles to the north. To the east is a series of ridges. The Tennessee-Georgia state line, from which you see more mountains beyond, is the southern city limit.

With this backdrop, nature enthusiasts have many choices either in the city or just a few minutes away: fishing, boating, swimming, riverboat cruises, hiking, skydiving, white-water rafting, horseback riding, hang gliding, rappelling, cave tours, scenic auto tours, guided interpretive outings, steam locomotive tours, and visits to nature centers and the world-class Tennessee Aquarium.

The mountains to the west share a common feature: the Tennessee River Gorge which, eons ago, cut deeply into Walden Ridge. Today, as the river leaves Walden Ridge, it becomes Nickajack Lake, impounded by Nickajack Dam south of Jasper. By some miracle much of the gorge and the surrounding mountain escaped development while the area was being settled. Thanks to concerned citizens, corporations, and government agencies, it is being preserved as a premier biosphere environment.

We met James C. Brown, executive director for land stewardship of the Tennessee River Gorge Trust, at a hawk watch on Raccoon Mountain sponsored by the Tennessee Ornithological Society (TOS). We scanned the skies over the gorge, looking for raptors. The trust has brought at least 56 percent of the 25,000 acres in the "viewshed"—the sight line—along the 18-mile gorge under its protection. This grassroots organization has been active since 1981.

*Protection* means keeping development out of the area by easements or by ownership and property management. Restoration, education, and scientific research are part of the effort, too.

This land provides a high-quality, diverse habitat that supports many threatened and endangered species of plants and animals. Among the animals are ospreys, bald eagles, and peregrine falcons. In 1980 there were only five active osprey nests in Tennessee, but they have been reintroduced in the gorge. As for rare plants, an example is the rose gentian, which had not been seen in the state since 1895 but now has been discovered here. Masses of trout lilies bloom in one of the locations, and another has the largest population of endangered mountain skullcap plants. The trees in the gorge are intact and healthy, especially on one parcel that is a prized example of mixed mesophytic forest land. Evidently, some of the environmental degradation affecting the higher elevations is simply passing overhead at this altitude.

It's worthwhile to visit the gorge. Several annual events such as the Spring Gorge Ramble, Raccoon Mountain Hawk Watch, Tennessee River Rescue, Williams Island Tour, Fall Foliage Week, and a volunteer work day help keep the gorge project before the public. If you're in the area, be sure to check these out.

*For more information:* Chattanooga Area Convention and Visitors Bureau, 1001 Market Street, Chattanooga, TN 37402. 800-322-3344 or 423-756-8687. Website, http://virtual.chatta nooga.net/cvb/.

Tennessee River Gorge Trust, 300 James Building, Chattanooga, TN 37402. 423-266-0314. Website, http://www.trgt .org/ (information updates and calendar).

## Tennessee Aquarium

"We just got here and we're going *downtown?*" We imagine that children might ask their parents something like this when, on arriving in Chattanooga, their first stop is not the lake or the mountaintop but the middle of the city! More likely, though, they'll be excited about visiting the magnificent Tennessee Aquarium at Ross's Landing Park on the Tennessee River.

Aquarium, park, and river meet at this place. The river is a dominant feature of the city, providing miles of fishing, pleasure boating, and river walks along the banks. Ross's Landing Park, surrounding the aquarium, is part of a park-and-trail system that will ultimately provide a continuous stretch for 20 miles, from Chickamauga Dam to the Tennessee River Gorge. The landing is an environmental art piece that celebrates the history and culture of the area from pre-1600 through 1992. A series of paved bands, plantings, art, and artifacts depicts historic periods that go back in time as they retreat from the river. Man-made arches landscaped with trees and other plants provide panoramic river views when climbed, while fountains spew walls of water that reflect the silhouettes of mountains.

Rising in the midst, high as a 12-story building, is the aquarium, unsurpassed in the world as a living demonstration of freshwater life. It reveals mysteries of river, lake, and stream ecosystems by duplicating real environments. There are more than 40 exhibits, a spectacular 60-foot canyon, forests, and about two dozen tanks. The natural habitats show life both underwater and above, including the fish, birds, reptiles, and other animals that inhabit each place.

The adventure begins with a four-story ride up an escalator to the top. Take time to look outside at the Tennessee River, a powerful waterway flowing around wide bends. You'll probably see both commercial and pleasure craft, and you may even see the *Southern Belle* riverboat taking up to 500 passengers on one of its popular cruises. When you leave the aquarium, you will know much more about the life-giving force of this 652-mile-long river, which has more species of fish in its upper streams than are found in comparable areas anywhere else in the United States.

The next step is the self-guided tour. As you wander through the different areas, you gradually descend to ground level. Each habitat area is like a piece of nature taken up and set down again intact. Because these are living habitats, the events taking place will be different in the morning, at midday, and when afternoon shadows take over—just as they are in nature.

The Tennessee River starts as a small and quiet mountain stream, with clear water that gurgles and tumbles, depending on the seasonal rains. Songbirds and wildflowers and a forest are its companions. The Cove Forest area of the aquarium recreates this lush environment. Sounds of little waterfalls and birdsongs fill the area.

As the brook grows into a mountain stream, brook trout maneuver in the fast currents, looking upstream for a caddis fly or other tasty morsel to float by. Nearby, sleek river otters show off their entertaining swimming tricks.

At Discovery Falls the world underneath the falls is revealed. Constantly moving darters flash by, and salamanders blend with the river bottom. The Tennessee River Gallery display shows a full-fledged river. Giant catfish lurk among gigantic rocks in the deep water, lying motionless during the day, then shaking off their sluggishness for an evening feeding.

Downriver, the Nickajack Lake display is the largest freshwater tank in the world, 25 feet deep and holding 138,000 gallons of water. This is largemouth bass country, and on a lower viewing level are carp, flathead catfish, and freshwater drums. Nickajack Lake still holds the world record—54 pounds, 8 ounces (1972)—for freshwater drums.

Farther along its journey, the Tennessee River joins the Mississippi and passes close by Reelfoot Lake in west Tennessee. There is a display about Reelfoot, an area described in Chapter 1. This is an excellent place to get a preview or a reminder about that earthquake-created sunken cypress forest.

The river finally reaches Delta Country, where we see cypress and mangrove swamps and many kinds of snakes, turtles, and fish. This is also the land of Spanish moss, humming insects, and steamy humidity. And yes, there are alligators, the great reptiles that often inspire dread. Called "the master of the swamp," they are well adapted to this environment. A visit to the aquarium reveals many fascinating facts about this animal. Cypress swamps are also a paradise for bird-watchers, and this display rewards its visitors with both plumage and song.

At the end, the great Mississippi waterway dumps itself into the Gulf of Mexico. It takes an 88,000-gallon tank—the only saltwater tank in the aquarium—to show the various features of the Delta and Gulf. At the edge of the sea, young fish, shrimps, crabs, sponges, and mollusks collect among submerged roots of mangrove trees. Farther out, the seawater becomes a vivid turquoise where colorful ocean fish swim among coral reefs. Stingrays, bonnethead sharks, and porkfish provide some interesting activity to watch.

It's hard to pick an area of the aquarium to rave about the most, but Rivers of the World might get our vote. Six rivers are featured. The 800-mile Saint Lawrence River flows east from the Great Lakes to the Atlantic. In it are found salmon and sturgeons, but the water quality has deteriorated so that it no longer supports the traditional numbers. The mysterious Amazon is a watershed that harbors many strange creatures (including dangerous piranhas and freshwater stingrays) and more wildlife species than anywhere else in the world. The Zaire, which used to be the Congo, tantalizes with sound and color. Native drums beat messages while pythons, monkeys, chameleons, tiger fish, and colorful birds go about their usual activities. The Shimanto River of Japan literally dives from snowcapped peaks to the Philippine Sea, staying clean and unspoiled on its journey. Notice the silvery fish that populate this environment. Then there is the Yenisei River of Siberia, clear and very cold, flowing north across the tundra to the Kara Sea. In the forests along its 2,500-mile path are animals that exist nowhere else in the world. The final exhibit is that of tropical Asian rivers that originate in the Himalayan mountains. These rivers support many fish that we would consider unusual.

The last stop is a well-stocked gift shop. A commemorative guide to the aquarium (for sale here) is well written and very informative. As we exit, we both agree: for adult or child, this place should not be missed.

Here's a tip: an easy way to get to the aquarium without parking hassles is by trolley. At the Chattanooga Choo Choo complex, just 14 blocks up Market Street from the river, is a restored railroad terminal in the best Victorian tradition. It has gardens, restaurants, shops, accommodations, and a model railroad museum. Antique trolley cars provide free shuttle service between the Choo Choo and the museum every few minutes seven days a week (Monday through Friday 6 A.M. until 9:30 P.M., Saturday 9 A.M. until 9:30 P.M., Sunday 9 A.M. until 8 P.M.). You can also catch the trolley anywhere along the route.

*Where:* In Chattanooga, take I-24 to exit 178, then follow the signs (about two miles).
*When:* Year-round, 10 A.M. to 6 P.M. (last ticket sold). Closed Thanksgiving and Christmas Day.
*Admission:* Adults, $10.25; ages 3 to 12, $5.50.
*Amenities:* Gift shop. Restaurants and visitors center at adjacent Ross's Landing.
*Activities:* Viewing of exhibits.
*Special events:* Inquire.
*Other:* Barrier-free access, free use of wheelchairs. Strollers not allowed, but loaner backpacks provided for small children. FM Assistive Listening System and TDD pay telephone for people with hearing difficulties.
*For more information:* Tennessee Aquarium, One Broad Street, PO Box 11048, Chattanooga, TN 37401-2048. 800-262-0695. TDD, 423-265-4498. Website, http://www.tennis.org/.

*Southern Belle*, Chattanooga Riverboat Company, 201 Riverfront Parkway, Pier 2, Chattanooga TN 37402-1616. 423-266-4488 or 800-766-2784.

Chattanooga Choo Choo Holiday Inn, 1400 Market Street, Chattanooga, TN 37402. 423-266-5000 or 800-872-2529. Website, http://www.choochoo.com.

## Three Mountains: Lookout, Raccoon, and Signal

In Chattanooga we sometimes stay overnight on Lookout Mountain at Herman and Judy Haecker's Chanticleer Inn in a 1920s-style cottage where we can open a window for views of azaleas in spring and hear trilling birdsongs in many seasons. It's a block from Rock City Gardens, only 10 minutes from the heart of downtown, and just a few minutes from anywhere else we'd like to visit.

Lookout Mountain, towering 1,716 feet above the city at an altitude of 2,391 feet, deserves its name. From at least one site—Lover's Leap in Rock City—it is possible on a clear day to see seven states. Because it was such a vantage point, Lookout Mountain played an important role in Civil War battles. The Union army's plan was to gain control of the mountain and then take Chattanooga, which was strategically important as a railroad center.

The most famous of this area's Civil War battles was fought on Lookout Mountain. It is depicted in a painting, *The Battle Above the Clouds*, by James Walker, which is on display at the Point Park visitors center, located near the Lookout Mountain Incline Railway. The incline makes several trips an hour up and down the mountain. Point Park is part of the Chickamauga/Chattanooga National Military Park. On view here are three gun batteries that hint at the siege lines of the battle. Also, the Ochs Museum and Overlook has exhibits that tell how the Battle of Chattanooga figured in the outcome of the Civil War. In summer there are daily tours, historical talks, and demonstrations in the park. Check at the visitors center for schedules.

Point Park gives access to an elaborate trail system. The four-and-a-half-mile Bluff Trail, rated moderate, goes from the park to Sunset Rock (where people often gather to watch sunsets) and on to Covenant College, whose silhouette on top of the mountain can be seen for miles. Trail hikers will find parking areas at the park, the rock, and the college. Down the mountain is Cravens House, where a fierce Civil War battle took place. An easy four-mile trail loop starts here (Cravens House, Gum Springs, and Bluff Trails) and gives access to interesting natural, historical, and archaeological features. The park trails also connect with others that begin at the Chattanooga Nature Center below.

An earlier Lookout Mountain battle in 1782 is not so well known. In September that year, the militia of Tennessee's first governor, John Sevier, fought and won "the last battle of the Revolutionary War" on the mountain slopes. Their foe was Chief Dragging Canoe and his Indian warriors.

Native Americans occupied this area long before the first white man, Hernando de Soto, set foot here in 1540. *Chattanooga* is an Indian word that means "rock coming to a point," an accurate description of Lookout Mountain. The area was a seat of government and culture of the great Cherokee Nation and was its last capital. It was also the home of Sequoyah, who invented the Cherokee alphabet. A lot of interest in and appreciation of Native American culture is expressed here, perhaps in part to make up for the cruel removal of the Cherokees to Oklahoma on the well-known "Trail of Tears." A group departed from Chattanooga in 1836, and the forced removal was in 1838. Four thousand men, women, and children—nearly a third of the 13,149 people forced to march—died along the way.

The northwest face of Lookout Mountain is ideal for hang gliding: it's a sheer drop that provides some of the best thermal and ridge soaring in America. Georgia's State 189 goes southwest from Lookout Mountain along the edge of the precipice. We took that route to Lookout Mountain Hang Gliding, a USHGA-certified school that offers training 365 days a year. The flight park is a complete facility with a campground, swimming pool, and volleyball court. Every spring it is home of "The Great Race" launched from a 13-mile-long ridge boasting an altitude gain of 10,400 feet and a cross-country record of 154 miles. The facility also has beginner and novice hills and gives certification in these categories. We looked over their pro shop and were about to watch some takeoffs when a sudden storm came up with lightning, torrential rain, and wicked gusty winds. On mountaintops, weather activity is often intense, so this was not surprising or unusual.

OK, the weather was being uncooperative. On to Plan B. We knew a place just off U.S. 41 on Lookout Mountain Road where we'd be hidden far away from the elements. Destination: Ruby Falls, the deepest and highest underground waterfall in America. An elevator takes us down 260 feet through solid limestone and deposits us inside the mountain. We'll be taking a quarter-mile walk past natural rock formations and fossils to a circular waterfall chamber 1,120 feet underground. We hear the roaring of the falls long before we see it. (The effect is most dramatic in winter and spring when rains increase the volume of water flow.)

Ruby Falls was not named for its color—though colored lights do enhance the appearance—but for Ruby Lambert, wife of Leo Lambert, who discovered the falls. Some 400,000 people visit this unique spot each year, making it one of the most popular attractions in the Chattanooga area. Even visitors who use wheelchairs can ascend to a tower and view the panorama of river and city below. They can also descend into the first part of the cave, where a recorded and projected presentation tells about the cave's history and features.

The drive to Raccoon Mountain Caverns and then to TVA's

Raccoon Mountain Pumped Storage Plant is one of the most scenic in the immediate area. Take U.S. 41 west from downtown, go a mile past the I-24 access point, and look for the Raccoon Mountain Caverns sign on the left. This attraction has a Crystal Palace Tour lasting 45 minutes during which visitors walk about a half mile and see many different kinds of rock formations, which are explained by knowledgeable guides. Wild Cave Tours—lasting two, four, or six hours—are available by reservation (although on most days a two-hour "adventure" tour is also available without advance reservations). All equipment is provided, but you will need to inquire about the proper clothing and shoes to wear. The cavern gift shop has food, supplies, and other items. On the wild and adventure tours, you will see many more of the passageways, beautiful rock formations, waterfalls, and unique underground scenery for which this cave is noted. The cave extends three miles into the mountain. To get to the more remote areas, you will be scrambling over boulders, wading in three inches of water, slogging through mud, and sometimes stooping or crawling.

Raccoon Mountain Caverns offers other amenities in a very pleasant valley setting: a campground, an alpine slide, and hiking trails. It's worth considering as a base of operations.

Back on U.S. 41 we continue west for another mile, then see the sign announcing the TVA Raccoon Mountain Pumped Storage Project and turn right. We are going to circle the mountain and the lake at its summit and meet Ken Dubke, Chattanooga's "bird man," a retired National Park Service ranger and the education committee chairman for the TOS. Locally, he organizes hawk watches and other activities.

The drive is exhilarating. No houses, hardly a sign of civilization to mar our view of the Tennessee River Gorge and the river itself. No switchbacks here, just a nice, circular drive winding up the mountain. We come to a fantastic overlook: a wide concrete walk, benches, a wooden rail fence, tables, and trees providing shade. The air is so clear that we see every detail of the river and the city below.

We stop to watch a doe and fawn feeding. They pay no attention to us but keep on eating and finally cross the road and disappear into the shade of the forest.

We drive on a one-way road on top of the dam, looking way below at Nickajack Lake, then turn off to the Laurel Point picnic area. Everything is barrier free here: there are paved trails and ramps where needed. We leave the pavement and follow a loop trail through the woods. The wind is rustling through the trees. Then, a warning sign: "Rock Bluff Ahead." Naturally, we have to investigate; it's almost like the Stone Door all over again, with a rock that is split apart and a trail below—except this sheer drop is only about 30 feet. Below is a beautiful view of the river.

Ken is outside the pumping station at the top of the mountain, watching for hawks.

"Smoky Mountains doesn't stand a chance against us for migration of birds of prey," he says. "Even Yellowstone doesn't stand a chance against our five acres over there at Signal Point on Signal Mountain."

We are intrigued. "Over 20 years of hawk watches, have the birds been decreasing?"

"Well, some hawks decreased for a while. DDT nearly wiped them out in this area, but now what I'm really excited about is the number of hawks that are actually nesting in people's yards in Chattanooga."

When we left, we promised we'd try to make the Sandhill Crane Weekend in late February, a two-day TOS-sponsored event that watches for the thousands of cranes that stop over at the Blythe Ferry/Hiwassee Wildlife Refuge area (north of Chattanooga off State 60 near Birchwood) during their annual northward migration.

*Signal Point*

Signal Point (directions follow) is a premier site for watching raptors, accessing the Cumberland Scenic Trail, and viewing the city and the Tennessee River 1,000 feet below.

**Where:** Lookout Mountain: from U.S. 41 west of Chattanooga, exit on State 318 and follow signs.

Raccoon Mountain: U.S. 41 west of Chattanooga (Pumped Storage Plant exit is to the right, one and one-tenth miles past the billboard announcing the exit to Raccoon Mountain Caverns).

Signal Point Park: take U.S. 27 north across the Tennessee River and exit on U.S. 127, turn left on Signal Mountain Boulevard and follow signs (seven miles from the 127 exit).

**When:** Most attractions are year-round. Cravens House tours 9 A.M. to 5 P.M., April through November.

**Admission:** Free at Covenant College, Lookout Mountain Flight Park, Raccoon Mountain Pumped Storage Facility, and Signal Point. All other locations have modest admission fees.

*Amenities:* Many (inquire). For Chickamauga and Chattanooga National Military Park events, 706-866-9241.

*Other:* Barrier-free access, except limited at Ruby Falls.

*For more information:* Chanticleer Inn, 1300 Mockingbird Lane, Lookout Mountain, TN 37350. 706-820-2015.

Cravens House, 423-821-7786.

Lookout Mountain Hang Gliding (Flight Park), Route 2, Box 215-H, Rising Fawn, GA 30738. 800-688-5637 or 706-398-3541.

Lookout Mountain Incline Railway, 827 East Brow Road, Lookout Mountain, TN 37350. 423-821-4224.

Point Park, Chattanooga/Chickamauga National Military Park, 110 East Brow Road, Lookout Mountain, TN 37350. 423-821-7786. Website, http://www.nps.gov/chch/.

Raccoon Mountain Caverns, 319 West Hills Drive, Chattanooga, TN 37419. 423-821-9403. Website, http://www.raccoonmountain.com.

Raccoon Mountain Pumped Storage Station, U.S. Highway 41W, Chattanooga, TN 37419. 423-751-8096.

Rock City Gardens, 1400 Patten Road, Lookout Mountain, GA 30750. 706-820-2531.

Ruby Falls, Lookout Mountain Scenic Highway, Chattanooga, TN 37409. 423-821-2544.

Tennessee Ornithological Society, Chattanooga Chapter, 423-238-4969. Website, http://funnelweb.utcc.utk.edu/~awjones/TOS.html.

## Reflection Riding Botanical Garden and Chattanooga Nature Center

Everyone we've met who has visited this place has given it rave reviews. After all the testimonials, we *had* to see for ourselves; and we weren't disappointed.

Reflection Riding is a scenic 300-acre historic site, nature preserve, and botanical garden at the foot of the western face of Lookout Mountain, just below Point Park. The Chattanooga Nature Center (on the property) sponsors outdoor activities and provides educational opportunities in its complex of buildings. Inside are exhibits, a children's discovery center, a library, an auditorium, a gift shop, and a wildlife rehabilitation laboratory. One modest fee allows access to both. Outside are trails, Lookout Creek, and a 1,700-foot wetland boardwalk.

More than 14 miles of trails crisscross up the mountain, connecting with National Park Service trails in the 2,000-acre Point Park. They go through oak forests and scattered groves of pines where deep gorges and moss-covered boulders attract birds and other wildlife. The "Great Stone Face" of Point Rock atop the mountain is visible for miles below.

In times past, *riding* meant "a path of pleasure," probably a reference to horseback or carriage travel. The Reflection Riding self-guided auto tour delivers handsomely on that promise with its combination of outstanding scenic beauty, abundant plant specimens, wildlife, and remnants of a rich local history.

This place is home to more than 1,000 species of plant life, including more than 300 wildflower species. Spring blooms include shooting star, trillium, lady's slipper, blue phlox, fire pink, Virginia bluebells, and wild geranium. One of the most spectacular displays in February and March is the blue-and-white carpet of blue-eyed Mary in the fields. Summer fields have lyre-leaved sage, buttercups, golden alexanders, and daisy fleabane. Autumn offers vivid foliage and gold and purple asters. Winter is the time to view evergreens, rocks, lichens, and late-winter blossoms such as hepatica.

The auto tour is a three-mile, one-way lane. Much of it is shaded by trees, each variety marked: red maple, white pine, black cherry, huge oaks that form a canopy overhead, dogwood, beech—trees that are found in the southern Appalachians. The road passes meadows, woodlands, and ponds. (In one pond we see about 30 Canada geese.) It goes near Lookout Creek, no longer free flowing because of water control at Chickamauga and Nickajack Dams. In earlier times it was an excellent spring that provided good water to the Indians.

Candy Flats, where a line of 3,000 Union troops moved through during the battle of Lookout Mountain in 1863, is one of many historic sites. The Battle Above the Clouds actually started on this property! Portions of several old trails have been preserved on this land: the Great Indian Warpath (de Soto used it in 1540), the Saint Augustine Cisca Trail (ending at Manchester, Tennessee), and the Old Federal Road (Augusta to Nashville—in 1807 the first road through the Cherokee Nation). Also here is one of the oldest buildings in Tennessee: Cherokee Chief Walking Stick's log cabin.

The wetland boardwalk we mentioned starts at the visitors center. It's a shady, wide, blacktop path at the start and later is elevated above a wetland area as it goes to Lookout Creek. Along the way are benches and outdoor pavilions from which you can comfortably observe the wildlife.

The Chattanooga Nature Center has a full schedule of activities year-round and is closed only for Thanksgiving, Christmas, New Year's, and Labor Day.

Annual events are similar to these: Doris Meeker, the "eagle lady," who comes in mid-October; Over the River and Through the Woods, an old-fashioned Christmas celebration for families; Haunted Swamp for Halloween; and a Cajun-flavored event around Memorial Day. The April Wildflower Festival and plant sale is the biggest weekend of the year, with guided wildflower walks every hour. This is a sampling, since programs vary from year to year.

Among the activities are summer day camps and wilderness excursions. Some special programs take place at Greenway

Farm, an environmental education center in Hixson that is part of the Tennessee Riverpark system. Some events: Owl Prowl, planetarium shows, Walk the Greenway, Wildflower Walk, GardenFest, Winter Wonders Party.

Popular seasonal activities are weekly canoe trips on Lookout Creek in summer, owl prowls in late fall and winter, and Eagle Watch field trips to nearby Nickajack Dam in January.

There are always exhibits—either traveling ones or an interactive exhibit prepared by the staff, with furs, bones, antlers, and other things people can touch. In one room a diorama shows insect, bird, mammal, reptile, and amphibian species native to the area. A library in this rustic center has a cozy ambience—many windows, a fireplace, and books about science and nature.

A separate building is a discovery center for small children. They can crawl inside a reconstructed beaver lodge, study bird nests, watch turtles or try on a giant turtle shell, play imaginative games, make rubbings, and learn about geology and many other things.

Several people work in the rehabilitation center where injured animals are nursed back to health. Usually, they treat 300 to 600 each year, but one year when they were taking in many small animals, they had 1,500. Jimmy Newman, who heads that department, said, "We've learned that we can't take all the little guys. In one season we had 800 calls about baby squirrels. What we do is tell people how to take care of them. If medical care is needed, we'll help, but follow-up care, no."

We looked at a scoreboard of animals that had been released. A typical list: great horned owl (auto collision), Cooper's hawk (secondary poison), barred owl (auto collision), three raccoons (orphaned), sharp-shinned hawk (secondary poison), gray fox (dog attack), screech owl (secondary poison), 17 possums (mother was killed in an auto collision), two killdeers (improper human intervention), screech owl (head injury), and raccoon (attacked by dog).

*Where:* From I-24 west of Chattanooga, take exit 175 (Brown's Ferry Road) south to U.S. 41 (Cummings Highway). Go left seven-tenths of a mile, then right on Old Wauhatchie Pike and immediately right on Garden Road. Follow signs for one and one-tenth miles.

*When:* Year-round, daily. Monday through Saturday, 9 A.M. to 5 P.M.; Sunday, 1:00 P.M. to 5 P.M. Closed major holidays.

*Admission:* Adults, $2.50; ages 4 to 12 and 60 and over, $1.50.

*Amenities:* Interpretive center, educational exhibits, library, trails, auto loop.

*Activities:* Hiking, scenic auto tour, birding, photography, wildlife viewing, canoe trips, crafts, naturalist workshops.

*Special events:* Eagle Watch (January), Native Plant Sale (April and September), Wildflower Festival (April), Jambalaya Jammin' (May), Fall Wildlife Weekend (September), "Haunted Swamp" (October), Bird Seed Sale (October and November), Over the River and Through the Woods (December).

*Other:* Barrier-free access.

*For more information:* Reflection Riding Botanical Garden, 400 Garden Road, Chattanooga, TN 37419. 423-821-9582.

Chattanooga Nature Center, 400 Garden Road, Chattanooga, TN 37419. 423-821-1160.

## Tennessee Riverpark

Here's a suggestion for a day in Chattanooga, circling north and east from downtown: visit the Tennessee Riverpark at Chickamauga Dam, check out the Tennessee Valley Railroad Museum, and finish up at Audubon Acres.

This greenways system is an ongoing project that will eventually give continuous access along the river. It will make the riverfront accessible to the public for 20 miles from Chickamauga Dam to the Tennessee River Gorge, incorporating parks, trails, and historic landmarks.

Tennessee Riverpark, a two-mile-long park along the riverbank below the dam, was the first section completed. It is for all ages, with playgrounds, groves of trees, meadows where kite flying is popular, picnic pavilions, rest rooms, and parking lots.

The modern Hubert Fry Center is named for a Chattanoogan who had the vision to provide a quality outdoor experience for disabled people. The five fishing piers and wide concrete trail at riverside do just that. The center has a meeting area, bait shop, snack bar, and Native American exhibit. The grounds are landscaped with many types of native trees and other plants.

Along the Woodland Habitat Trail, look carefully for eastern bluebirds, wood ducks, frogs, monarch butterflies, and great blue herons (which nest on Maclellan Island and fly over). At dusk, look for eastern screech owls, luna moths, beavers, bats, muskrats, mink, and raccoons. A trail guide tells you where. Also, the TOS conducts bird walks throughout the year.

Another series of completed segments of this greenways system goes from Ross's Landing Plaza (at the Tennessee Aquarium) to the Walnut Street (pedestrian) Bridge, the Bluff Furnace Segment (in the Bluff View Art District), and on to the historic Battery Place neighborhood. A third segment is the North Chickamauga Creek Greenway, providing a one-and-two-tenths-mile connector to Greenway Farm.

*Where:* Off State 58 (4301 Amnicola Highway). Go north from downtown on State 58, or from I-75 exit on State 153 and go north to Chickamauga Dam.
*When:* Year-round. Open sunup to sundown.

*Admission:* Free.

*Other:* Barrier-free access.

*For more information:* Tennessee Riverpark, Hamilton County Parks and Recreation Department, 2318 North Gold Point Circle, Chattanooga, TN 37343. 423-842-0177.

Tennessee Ornithological Society, Chattanooga Chapter, 423-238-4969. Website, http://funnelweb.utcc.utk.edu/~aw jones/TOS.html.


## Tennessee Valley Railroad

While Chattanooga, like most cities in the region, grew up along navigable waterways, its importance in the mid-1800s was as a railroad center that provided a life link between the North and the South. The famous "Great Locomotive Chase" (also called "Andrews' Raid") illustrates how essential the railways were in that period. In a daring Civil War escapade, Union captain James J. Andrews conspired to take a small band of men into Confederate territory and hijack a northbound train while it idled at a breakfast stop at Big Shanty, Georgia, near Atlanta. His plan was to blow up trestles and tracks and thus destroy the Confederate supply line to battlefields in Tennessee. His raid was foiled by the train's conductor, Captain William A. Fuller, and others who pursued quickly, commandeering a series of engines along the way and all giving chase. They forced Andrews to abandon the train near Chattanooga.

The Tennessee Valley Railroad, using World War II–era steam and diesel locomotives, recalls the golden age of railroading between 1910 and 1950, when throughout our nation mournful whistles of steam trains echoed for miles in the stillness of the night. The museum is about three miles south of

Chickamauga Dam on Cromwell Road, off State 153. Trains run short trips daily (and hourly) from June 1 through Labor Day and on weekends in spring and fall, some terminating at the Chattanooga Choo Choo. The railroad line follows much of the old route, including a historic tunnel through Missionary Ridge. This is the largest operating historic railroad in the South, with many restored locomotives and railroad cars on display. Its most famous engine is the Baldwin Locomotive Works #4501 built in 1911 and formerly owned by the Southern Railway.

Details are essential to the early-20th–century atmosphere on these trains. Crew members wear overalls, bandannas, and gauntlet gloves and use authentic railroad-style pocket watches. A uniformed conductor gives the "Allll-abooooard!" traditional call to start the train, then punches tickets that are replicas of those used by the Georgia Railroad in 1932.

The railroad runs Dixie Land Excursions from April through November to Kensington, Chickamauga, LaFayette, and Summerville, Georgia, using either steam- or diesel-powered trains (some routes including "Dinner on the Diner" in the fare).

The railroad also offers Autumn Leaf steam-powered excursions through areas where vivid fall foliage is on display. Just imagine riding the rails for hours through forests flaming with color, beside gorges, up mountain grades, over trestles, and through tunnels—behind a puffing, hissing, and whistling engine. It's unforgettable!

Now, on down State 153 toward I-75 on the way to Audubon Acres.

**Where:** Grand Junction Station is at 4119 Cromwell Road, three-tenths of a mile from State 153 at the Jersey Pike exit. From I-75, exit on State 153.

*When:* April through November, with daily steam-powered local trips June 1 through Labor Day. Hours conform to train schedules (in summer, 10 A.M. to 5 P.M. Monday through Saturday, and 11:30 A.M. to 5 P.M. on Sunday).

*Admission:* Modest fee and fares.

*Amenities:* Railroad museum, dining room, gift shop, 1930s short-line passenger railroad, picnic area, free parking.

*Activities:* Exhibit viewing, rail and dinner-train excursions, charters.

*Special events:* All-day excursions to northwest Georgia (most weekends), Mileage Collector (April), Downtown Arrow trains (summer weekends), Pops in the Park (July), Autumn Steam Excursions (October), Fall Steam Specials (November).

*Other:* Barrier-free access.

*For more information:* Tennessee Valley Railroad, 4119 Cromwell Road, Chattanooga, TN 37421. 423-894-8028 or 800-397-5544. Website, http://www.chattanooga.net/rail/.

## Audubon Acres

This sanctuary belonging to the Chattanooga Audubon Society (CAS) is a busy hub of outdoor activity year-round. It has 130 acres of meadows, floodplain, woodlands, and ridge tops and 10 miles of hiking trails that provide excellent views of wildflowers, birds, and other forest inhabitants. Signs identify 60 species of trees on the property. And there's history: a swinging bridge over South Chickamauga Creek leads to the Little Owl's Village Site where pre-Cherokee Indians once lived.

Have a picnic at tables in a pine grove where nearby are some bluebird boxes. Close by is rustic Walker Hall, which has an early-pioneer exhibit. For additional historic interest, tour the Spring Frog Cabin built in 1754 and furnished in late-1800s style. It is named for a Cherokee naturalist.

We walk across the swinging bridge. A squirrel is scurrying above us along a cable. A little striped lizard crosses our path and burrows under some pine needles to escape our footsteps. The trail follows the creek for a while, which is flowing gently with hardly a ripple, mirroring the hillside perfectly. We hear several kinds of birdsongs and enjoy the tranquil setting.

Life can be exciting here. A great din of crow calls might mean that dozens of the birds are mobbing a red-tailed hawk. Muskrats swim in the creek and climb the bank to eat a "foliage salad" snack. Pileated woodpeckers have been seen walking under the chestnut trees; and many birds visit for a few days or build nests and stay for a season.

Here's a brief list of some typical events and field trips: eagle-watch day trips, museum tours, birding field trips, planting and pruning workshops, Good Earth Festival, wildflower strolls, Audubon Wildlife Festival, "As the Indians Lived" (a discovery day camp), Native American skills workshops, and "Indian Summer Days."

The first Native American day camps were so popular that the program was expanded.

As Linda Harris, a former director of this facility, explained, "Native Americans in this area look at Audubon Acres as a place where they can share their spirit. They have wonderful skills of traditional living, while we have a place where they can teach and a large, open field suitable for Native American games."

The Indian Summer Powwow attracts Apache, Navaho, Seminole, Creek, Sioux, Cherokee, Chippewa, and other tribes who demonstrate dance, drums, storytelling, arts, crafts, food, and games.

Chattanooga Audubon also owns Maclellan Island, a 22-acre wildlife sanctuary in the middle of the Tennessee River near Ross's Landing. The island supports a nesting colony of great blue herons, and migrating warblers often stop to feed. Endangered ospreys have been raised and released there, too. Other animals such as squirrels, rabbits, raccoons, possums, beavers, muskrats, and foxes call this island home. You'll find mussels and possibly see mallards, geese, and other waterfowl along the river's edge.

The *Dazzling Duck*, an amphibious vehicle formerly used by the military for building bridges, runs guided excursions to the island, where you can debark for a few hours. There, Audubon naturalists answer your questions and point the way to a self-guided tour along shady natural paths. Alternately, you can remain on the "Duck" for a tour along the river with an Audubon naturalist as your guide.

The 40-foot-long *Dazzling Duck* oper- ates seven days a week from noon until 9 P.M., making a round-trip in about an hour and a half. It first drives through a few blocks of Chattanooga's downtown area before taking to the water and going off on its river cruise.

A third property owned by CAS is the 460-acre David Gray Sanctuary on Sale Creek in north Hamilton County (known also as Audubon Mountain). Hikers enjoy the miles of trails passing through stands of hemlocks and rhododendrons and crossing streams. A favorite destination is the observation platform on Walden's Ridge, perfect for watching hawks riding thermal currents.

***Where:*** North Sanctuary Road. From I-75, take exit 3A, go east to Gunbarrel Road, then follow the signs.
***When:*** Year-round. Open 9 A.M. to 6 P.M. Monday through Saturday and 1 P.M. to 6 P.M. on Sunday (closes at 5 P.M.

December through February). *Dazzling Duck* boat cruises, daily from noon until 9 P.M.

**Admission:** Modest entrance fee. *Dazzling Duck* cruises: adults, $11.50; seniors, $9.75; under 12, $7.50 (tickets on board or at the Chattanooga visitors center next to the Tennessee Aquarium).

**Special events:** Arbor Day (March), Heritage Day (May), Spring Dulcimer Festival (May), Indian Summer Days (October).

**Other:** Barrier-free access.

**For more information:** Audubon Acres, Chattanooga Audubon Society, 900 North Sanctuary Road, Chattanooga, TN 37421. 423-892-1499.

*Dazzling Duck* information: Chattanooga Audubon Society, PO Box 245, Chattanooga, TN 37401. 423-265-4650.

# 4

# Great Valley and Blue Ridge

## Call of the High Country

A cool river passing through a parched land illustrates the drama that comes from contrast. Contrast—like conflict—enhances drama in visual art, in a suspense novel, and in nature. Would high mountains have such allure without the valleys from which we gaze longingly? And would they be worth the ascent if we, having scaled the peak (or driven to the top), were not rewarded with even grander views?

The eastern region of Tennessee is full of contrasts. The Great Valley, a wide swath going diagonally from Chattanooga through Knoxville to Kingsport in the upper eastern corner of Tennessee, takes up one-fifth of the land area of the entire state. It's called a valley because it is lower than the Cumberland Plateau to the northwest and the Blue Ridge province of the Appalachian range to the southeast, but it is actually a series of corrugated folds made up of valleys and ridges. These aren't wimpy little features: the elevation ranges from 600 to 2,600 feet. Look at the Tennessee map and you will see clearly how all major roads take a parallel track.

Next, the drama: toward the southeast and running parallel, the great spine of the Blue Ridge of the Appalachian chain forms the border between Tennessee and North Carolina. It is widest and highest in the Great Smoky Mountains National Park, the most-visited national park in the United States.

Throughout this region, wherever we may be, the high country speaks with an irresistible voice: *Come to the mountain!* We listen, and some of us think we have lived only when we have seen the view from the "top of the world."

# The Tennessee Overhill

East of Chattanooga is an area referred to as Tennessee Overhill Country. It encompasses three counties—McMinn, Polk, and Monroe—and includes the entire southern division of the Cherokee National Forest. A look at the early history of our country reveals the logic of the name, which was a term used by the British in the South Carolina low country. To them, a group of Cherokee villages in Tennessee was 24 mountains away and thus "over the hills."

The Overhill is somewhat off the beaten path (that is, the interstates), so it has retained the quiet, rural and small-community flavor of the early to mid-1900s. Even with the attention the area received during the 1996 Olympic Games (with the canoe and kayak slalom races held here on the Ocoee River), it remains surprisingly unspoiled. The pristine qualities that vacationers come here to bask in—clean air and water and a rural ambience—are still here in abundance. It's a great getaway where you can enjoy forest settings, camping, paddling for all levels of competency, fishing, horseback riding, scenic views, gliding, rappelling, caving, hunting, waterfalling, and even panning for gold. For scenic drives, take the Ocoee Scenic Byway in the Cherokee National Forest or the new

Cherohala Skyway between Tellico Plains, Tennessee, and Robbinsville, North Carolina. (Tip: ask if you'll find rest rooms on the latter stretch of highway.) This area is also rich in cultural history: of early Native Americans, the impact of industry and mining (copper and gold), and the country music that was born here.

The Olympics did inspire a host of new lodges, cabins, and bed-and-breakfast inns in the area. You'll find many new restaurants, too. Copperhill is known for excellent Mexican and Japanese restaurants, Madisonville offers Bagel Peddler with "much more than bagels" in the original dining room of the historic Kefauver Hotel, and Etowah has the new "Café Etowah," a great place to dine. Linda Caldwell, our best source for "things cuisine" in the Overhill, suggests trying their rib eye with peppercorn sauce, red potatoes, salad, and a raspberry napoleon.

The Overhill headquarters of tourism development are in the 1906 restored L&N depot in Etowah on U.S. 411. Pick up information here about rivers, the forest, museums, scenic self-guided auto tours, special events, dining, and lodging. One very special excursion has been offered in the past (and we hope will be reinstated): a vintage train that leaves from Etowah and goes for 96 miles deep into the forest to Duck-town and back, making a loop that circles Bald Mountain twice and crosses over itself atop a 62-foot-high wooden tres-tle. This is the third-longest rail loop in the world.

*For more information:* Tennessee Overhill Heritage Associa-tion, L&N Depot, 727 Tennessee Avenue, PO Box 143, Etowah, TN 37331. 423-263-7232. E-mail, cldwll@cococo.net.

Monroe Tourism Council, PO Box 37, Madisonville, TN 37354. 800-245-5428 (United States and Canada) or 423-442-4588.

## Cherokee National Forest, Southern Division

The Cherokee National Forest is Tennessee's largest public land and its only national forest. Flanking the Great Smoky Mountains National Park on both east and west, it covers nearly 630,000 acres between Chattanooga and Bristol. A good way to get an introduction to the southern division of the forest (west of the Smokies) is to stop at any of the three ranger stations.

The Hiwassee Ranger Station is on State 310 a mile east of U.S. 411 at Etowah. This district has more than 92,000 acres of streams, scenic views, and wildlife. In it are 2 designated campgrounds, 6 picnic sites, 11 trails totaling 46 miles, 13 major waterfalls, 3 fishing guide services, 4 float services, 3 horseback trails totaling 33 miles, and a shooting range. Off-road vehicles are not allowed in the Cherokee National Forest.

The Ocoee Ranger Station is on U.S. 64 opposite Lake Ocoee. In its territory are the Ocoee Scenic Byway (U.S. 64 between Parksville and Ducktown), 6 campgrounds, 1 picnic site, 2 swimming beaches, 3 boating sites, and 25 trails totaling 76 miles.

The Tellico Ranger Station in the town of Tellico Plains oversees a variety of sites that include waterfalls, camping, picnicking, boating, fishing, hiking, and swimming. Among the most scenic are Indian Boundary Lake and Bald River Falls. In 1996, the 50-mile-long Cherohala Skyway (State 165 in Tennessee), which begins at Tellico Plains and traverses some of the most breathtaking scenery in the Cherokee and Nantahala forests, opened with fanfare as our country's 20th national scenic byway. It is one of the highest roads east of the Mississippi River, gaining elevations of more than 4,000 feet for miles and in one place climbing to 5,200 feet. We used to say it was worth a trip to Tellico Plains just to eat at the Tellicafe, known far and wide for its memorable gourmet fare. Now we have another compelling reason to come here, for who could resist the magnificent Charohala?

For river information, we suggest a stop at the Hiwassee Scenic River and Ocoee White Water River visitors center on U.S. 411 south of Etowah at Maggie Mill Road. If park manager Jamie Nicholson is in, you'll enjoy talking with him.

Tennessee State Parks manages the rivers that are classified as State Scenic Rivers and the 43-site Gee Creek Wilderness primitive campground at the foot of Chestnut Mountain, just a mile off U.S. 411 across from the visitors center. The campground sits just south of the entrance to the Gee Creek Wilderness, which has excellent native trout fishing, spectacular hiking trails, and guided horseback trips to the top of Starr Mountain.

The Hiwassee River is one of Jamie's favorites. "We have the first 23½ miles of the Hiwassee after it enters Tennessee," he said. "Along that stretch there's a great variety of aquatic wildlife, and the river differs a lot. For the first few miles— down to the Appalachian powerhouse—the water is channeled through a nine-mile-long tunnel. Because of this, the upper section is basically dry except for a little inflow from streams, but it's accessible all the way down to the powerhouse. We've found several varieties of endangered mussels there.

"At the powerhouse the water is dumped back into the riverbed, and the stream becomes wetter again. From there to the town of Reliance is the middle section. It's the most popular for paddling, with Class I, II, and III white water— good for beginners and intermediate paddlers. We have over 100,000 visitors annually that do the Hiwassee River. The John Muir Trail follows beside it from the Childers Creek parking area near Reliance all the way to the North Carolina line.

"Then the flat-water section goes down-river from Reliance. A lot of folks like to fish and flat-water canoe in that area."

Jamie said there are 56 species of fish in the Hiwassee, although it's managed mostly for rainbow and brown trout, with 150,000 of these fish stocked annually. The watershed is 90 percent forested, and water quality is excellent. Due to U.S. Forest Service restrictions, the Hiwassee has a limited number of outfitters, who rent funyaks, tubes, and rafts. "You just don't find rivers that are used as much as this one that are as clean and pretty," he said. "Until you get to Reliance, there's no habitation along it and no agricultural or industrial runoffs."

The magnificent Ocoee River gets a lot of publicity for its excellent white water in a five-and-a-half-mile section of Class III and IV. There are 24 outfitters on this river, which normally plays host to upward of 250,000 paddlers. It has been the site of both World Cup and Olympic events.

"We host a leg of the team trials every year on the Ocoee," said Jamie, "which is helpful in the selection of the U.S. canoe and kayak teams. We've hosted the World Rodeo competition—championships for the canoe and kayak acrobatic skills. During such events a shuttle bus runs every 30 minutes between Ducktown and Parksville to make it easier for the public to view the action."

The Ocoee Scenic Byway is part of a main route from Chattanooga to Asheville, North Carolina, and the Smokies, so it is quite well traveled. We wondered how many people simply drive through and never discover some of the sensational backcountry. For example, State Forest Road 77 goes up Chilhowee Mountain to a campground, continues on top of the ridge to the Oswald Dome Lookout six miles beyond on Bean Mountain, then descends to State 30 just south of Reliance. It's a ride on top of the world (well, this part of the world), with views of the lake below and too many far hills to count. In October it can be one of the best places to see fall color.

We spent a few nights in Reliance at a cottage in a meadow at the edge of Spring Creek, where we knew that resident trout were just waiting for a fly to be cast their direction. Talk about Shangri-la! To us, this was the middle of everywhere that counted. Nearby were the Hiwassee River and the John Muir Trail. Bald River Falls and Indian Boundary Lake near Tellico Plains were a few miles north. And the great Ocoee was a few miles south.

Ardi joined forest rangers Mary Jane Burnette and Tammy Rowe for a hike one morning. The John Muir National Recreation Trail, like this whole area, had been damaged extensively in a freak spring storm that year and so was open for only 3 of its 20 miles—from Childers Creek near the Webb Bros. store in Reliance to the Big Bend parking lot.

The memory of the day comes in a montage, with little scenes flashing—a sort of video of the mind: an old logging road going through a stand of poplar; Tammy finding a recent beaver-cut on a tree; a view of Hood Mountain; cardinal flowers and asters along the trail; mature hemlocks and big rocks; the rush of rapids and a clearing where rafters stop for lunch.

Mary Jane said she had seen raccoons here at dusk and after dark. "It's nice to walk at night," she said. "You tend to really listen for sounds."

The vegetation keeps changing; and some of the names, like dog hobble, have interesting beginnings. Reportedly, when hunters were out with their dogs, the bears would lead the dogs into the dog hobble. The bears, being large and bulky, could get through it, but the dogs would get caught in the tangle.

Goldenrod—but what kind? Tammy produced a book and riffled through the pages: "Rough-stemmed goldenrod.

*National Audubon Society Field Guide to North American Wild-flowers/Eastern Region*, photo 344. Never go on a hike without it," she said triumphantly.

More videos: little green partridgeberry, wild ginger, mint, trillium, yucca. More pages riffling. More triumphant shouts.

Back at Spring Creek, Willie Freeman, a neighbor, has brought a bouquet of wildflowers of extraordinary beauty. Each stem has a solitary white flower that is striped with green veins and has a single, rounded leaf halfway up the stem. "I planted these in my garden after I found them on a mountain," she says. "They're called grass-of-Parnassus."

*Where:* McMinn, Monroe, and Polk Counties east of Chattanooga and Cleveland, Tennessee.

*When:* Year-round (some activities are seasonal).

*Admission:* Free. Campground and some day-use fees.

*Amenities:* Modern and primitive campgrounds, picnic sites, swimming beaches, trails, fishing guide services, river outfitters, old-time country stores, restaurants, motels, lodges, cabins, bed-and-breakfast hosts.

*Activities:* Camping, hiking, wildlife viewing, scenic drives, photography, waterfalling, picnicking, paddling (canoe, kayak, raft), horseback riding, llama trekking, mountain biking, rockhounding, rappelling, swimming, boating, fishing, hunting, gold panning, museum tours.

*Special events:* Inquire at individual locations.

*For more information:* Cherokee National Forest, PO Box 2010, Cleveland, TN 37320. 423-476-9700.

Hiwassee Ranger District, Highway 310, PO Drawer D, Etowah, TN 37331. 423-263-5486.

Ocoee Ranger District, Route 1, Box 348D, Benton, TN 37307. 423-338-5201.

Tellicafe, 128 Bank Street, Tellico Plains, TN 37385-4901. 423-253-2880.

Tellico Ranger District, 250 Ranger Station Road, Tellico Plains, TN 37385. 423-253-2520.

Hiwassee Scenic River State Park, PO Box 255, Delano, TN 37325. 423-338-4133. Website, http://www.state.tn.us/envi ronment/parks/ then select.

## Ducktown Basin Museum

It seems that wherever several states meet along Tennessee's borders, the places turn out to have some kind of special character. We're not sure why this is, but we can pretty much guarantee that if you go to any of these spots, you will find something very interesting.

Ducktown, in the middle of the Copper Basin in the southeastern corner of the state, is no exception. For years the basin was a 50-square-mile moonscape of bizarre, barren hills carved into raw gullies from erosion. It didn't get that way naturally but came from 137 years of mining and forestry, from 1850 through July 1987.

Until a few years ago, motorists traveling through the forested Ocoee Scenic Byway toward the North Carolina line were in for a jolt when they suddenly reached the stark landscape of the basin. But a dramatic turnabout was in the making. Today the land is almost totally revegetated, thanks to herculean efforts by TVA, the mining corporations, Bowater Company (which furnished seedlings), the U.S. Forest Service, and the USDA Soil Conservation Service.

The Ducktown Basin Museum on the site of the old Burra Burra Mine has the whole story. Exhibits tell the history of the area from ancient times, the development of the Cherokee culture (trading, daily life, games, some early families), Cherokee forced removal and the Trail of Tears, a replica of Fort Marr (1814), "discovery" of copper in 1843 (the Cherokee extracted copper much earlier), mine memorabilia, a display of minerals and ores, and old photographs from mining days.

The story of what the mining did to the environment is as fascinating as the results were dramatic. The museum library has information collected from the mining companies and agencies involved.

Next to the museum on the Burra Burra mine site is an acreage left purposely barren so that visitors can see what the whole area looked like before reclamation. The mine was underground, and underground workings came up close to the surface here.

How could the area have become so totally devastated? And why? Didn't the people who lived here *care*? Here are some explanations given by museum curator Ken Rush:

"In 1850, when mining began, the area had no inhabitants because the Cherokee had been driven out 12 years earlier. There were no real roads or railroads, so mining communities grew up at the mine sites. Because there were no rail lines to bring in coal to smelt the ore, the standing timber had to be used for fuel. It was burned in ricks to make charcoal for firing steam engines that ran the mining equipment.

"The ore was in sulfide deposits—copper sulfide, iron sulfide (fool's gold), and zinc sulfide—meaning there was more sulfur in the ore than anything else. This ore is also a pyritic ore because of the fool's gold it contains.

"To extract metal, a metal smelter heats the ore to a temperature where it will burn on its own and melt. Afterward, the slag is poured off and the metal is left behind. However, in the 1800s the state-of-the-art way to extract a pyritic ore was to heap-roast it. The first step was to pile timber about waist high, pile the ore material on top, then light the wood. When the wood burned hot enough, the sulfur would burn off. The rock that was left could then be put in a furnace and smelted.

"With all this activity going on, by 1878 some 30,000 acres had been cleared of every adult tree standing," Ken said. "The sulfur that was liberated from the roasting process was forming sulfur dioxide, which did not go up in smoke as it would have from a smokestack, but settled on the ground next to the roast yards. It created an acid condition that killed the young vegetation and prevented any new growth."

In 1878 the mining stopped. It resumed in 1890 when a railroad line came into the basin, allowing importation of coal to fuel the furnaces and timber for heap-roasting (remember, no mature timber was left here). Larger furnaces were built, and so were larger and more numerous roast yards. More sulfur was emitted. In this barren and mountainous terrain, every time it rained, some of the soil washed away. Eventually, four to five feet of it had disappeared. Starting in the 1930s, some effort was made to revegetate, but without much success.

The basin's "denuded forest" nightmare has a happy ending. The rest of the story, including reclamation techniques used, can be learned at the museum.

One thing we should point out: unlike today when we hear about companies dumping toxins with a purposeful disregard for the environment, the adverse effects of early mining operations were mainly because of lack of technology to deal with the problems. The reason the Copper Basin saw such drastic impact—and a NASA photograph from space shows that impact clearly—was its unique combination of terrain, soil makeup, and weather patterns.

***Where:*** Burra Burra Hill, downtown Ducktown. Exit U.S. 64 at State 68, go north and watch for a sign pointing right.
***When:*** Year-round. Monday through Saturday, 10:00 A.M. to 4:00 P.M. Closed Thanksgiving, Christmas, New Year's.
***Admission:*** Modest fee.
***Amenities:*** Exhibits, library, gift shop, old mine buildings.

*Activities:* Slide shows, historical research, photography, tours of mine shops and change house.

*Special events:* Halloween Ghost Stories (October).

*For more information:* Ducktown Basin Museum, Burra Burra Hill, PO Box 458, Ducktown, TN 37326. 423-496-5778.

## The Lost Sea

The billboards proclaim: "World's Largest Underground Lake." They refer to the Lost Sea, located inside Craighead Caverns, between Sweetwater and Madisonville on State 68 in the northern part of Tennessee Overhill Country. In 1976 it was declared a Registered Natural Landmark by the National Park Service. Easy to find, it is just 6 miles off I-75, 60 miles from Chattanooga and 40 miles from Knoxville.

This was one of the most interesting cave tours we took because it had many elements: large rooms, a waterfall, cave formations, prehistoric and historic use, and a ride on the lake in a glass-bottom boat. Our guide, John Hooper, a student at Tennessee Tech University, was very knowledgeable about the cave and about caving in general. He made the tour informative and enjoyable.

Besides the expected stalactites, stalagmites, and columns, we saw some complex and unusual formations.

One, "The Cascades" was enormous and included three types of formations—*draperies*, formed by water dripping through a crack in the rock and depositing calcium carbonate; *flowstone*, created on the cave floor from flowing water that has dripped from the draperies; and *bacon rind*, black and orange columns (the orange color is from iron oxide).

At another place on the ceiling of the cave were several examples of very rare white *anthodites* (a Greek name for "cave flower"). According to our guide, the cavern contains half of the known anthodites in the world.

John explained that Civil War activities took place throughout the cave. One was the making of gunpowder. The dirt of the cave floor was rich in nitrates and phosphates, which were leached out with water and collected in a kettle. The "mother liquor" was mixed with sulfuric charcoal, making the black powder needed to fire rifles and cannons.

In earlier times, a secluded area at the back of the cave was the site of Cherokee council meetings. The cave was owned by Chief Craighead during the early 1800s, ceded to him by a land grant. In the council chamber a great many artifacts were found.

The Cat Chamber goes even further back in time. It is a large pit in which skeletons and footprints of a giant Pleistocene-era jaguar were found. The reassembled skeleton measured eight feet long, not including the tail. The animal is estimated to have weighed 500 pounds. The skeleton is now in New York's American Museum of Natural History, but a plaster cast was made for display at the Lost Sea.

The third-largest room—600 feet long—is called the Kiln Room because of the red kiln clay that lines the floors. Farmers used to create a durable red paint for their barns by mixing the clay with buttermilk. There are still barns in the area that have been painted with "buttermilk barn red."

As the tour approached the lake, the ground level dropped and followed the Little Grand Canyon, formed by an underground stream. The tour passed a waterfall—Crystal Falls—and a disassembled moonshine still.

The story of the Lost Sea is this:

In 1905 a great drought caused the water level in the cave to drop. This revealed a three-foot crack in the rock, which was discovered by a little boy who was exploring the cave. He crawled through 40 feet of mud and water and found the lake room and the underground lake. People scoffed at his claim of the discovery, but a year later his father agreed to come and see for himself. By that time, the water had risen and covered the crack, so the lake was again lost.

Rumors circulated for years, though; finally in the 1960s a tunnel was blasted through to the lake chamber, rediscovering the Lost Sea. The lake is now stocked with large rainbow trout which can be seen (and are fed) during a boat ride.

The 4½-acre lake available to the tour is only one of the underwater caverns. More than 13 acres of water have been mapped, but there are known to be even more.

*Where:* From I-75 north of Chattanooga, take exit 60 and go east on State 68 past Sweetwater for six miles and follow the signs.

*When:* Daily, 9 A.M. until sundown. Closed Christmas Day.

*Admission:* Modest fee.

*Amenities:* Cave, underground lake, restaurant, sweet shop, nature trail, picnic area, trading post, general store. Camping and lodging nearby.

*Activities:* Cave tours, picnicking, hiking, photography.

*For more information:* Lost Sea, 140 Lost Sea Road, Sweetwater, TN 37874. 423-337-6616.

# In and Around Knoxville and Oak Ridge

Knoxville can make a boast that any vice president of marketing would envy—*location, location, location!* Sitting in the midst of the Great Valley, it is surrounded by many great vacation spots. Within striking distance—two hours, more or less—are, going clockwise from a 12:00 position, the Norris Lake area parks, Cumberland Gap National Historic Park,

Cherokee Lake, Douglas Lake, the Foothills Parkway, Great Smoky Mountains National Park, the Tennessee Overhill, Fort Loudoun and Watts Bar Lakes, Oak Ridge, the Obed, and the Big South Fork NRRA.

It makes sense, then, to use Knoxville as a base if you intend to take in a wide territory on your vacation. We discovered the Wayside Manor Bed & Breakfast on an eight-acre estate just south of Knoxville at Rockford (it's also near the airport) and found that it fits this vacation style very nicely—giving excellent access in every direction while providing all sorts of amenities.

***For more information:*** Knoxville Convention & Visitors Bureau, 810 Clinch Avenue, Knoxville, TN 37902. 423-523-7263 or 800-727-8045. Website, http://knoxville.org/default_index.html.

Wayside Manor Bed & Breakfast, 4009 Old Knoxville Highway, Rockford, TN 37853. 800-675-4823 or 423-970-4823. Website, http://the-mid-west-web.com/wayside.htm.

## Oak Ridge: Working at Being Green

On August 2, 1939, Albert Einstein wrote a letter to President Franklin D. Roosevelt that contained a warning. He knew of experiments taking place in Berlin under Adolf Hitler that might produce some extremely powerful uranium weapons. That letter triggered a scramble by our government to develop the technology that led to production of the first atomic bomb. Everything about the "Manhattan Project" was top secret. In those days Oak Ridge, which grew quickly but silently among the ridges and valleys less than 20 miles west of Knoxville, was a hidden city without a name or an official post office address. It "didn't exist."

Looking back, many lessons had to be learned. Just as the

early settlers in the Natchez Trace State Park area of west Tennessee hadn't realized how their farming mismanagement would deface the land, and just as the mining companies in the Copper Basin couldn't predict that they would create a great barren area that would stand for more than a hundred years, so the early developers of nuclear technology had to learn how to deal with radioactivity and nuclear waste.

The sprawling 35,000-acre Oak Ridge Reservation (ORR) is a Department of Energy property that includes eight registered State Natural Areas. On these lands, scientific research projects are conducted by the Oak Ridge National Laboratory (ORNL) and by other specialized federally funded projects. One of these, the National Environmental Research Park, uses 12,400 acres of protected land to conduct studies on wetlands, wildlife, and vegetation. The research park is included in the Southern Appalachian Man and Biosphere Reserve. In the ORR, the major natural communities include barrens, river and creek bluffs, and floodplains and wetlands. Acre by acre, the ORR has more plant and animal species than the Great Smoky Mountains National Park, and many of these are rare, endangered, or unique.

Oak Ridge has worked hard to become a truly green city. No one knows yet how detrimental the developing days were to the environment and the people who worked and lived here or the extent of residual effects, but today's "greenness" is certainly visible. In this beautiful valley with its tree-lined ridges and tree-lined streets are parks, Melton Hill Lake, the Clinch River, picnic areas, hiking trails, and other pleasant recreation facilities.

This city is also the headquarters of Tennessee Citizens for Wilderness Planning (TCWP), an activist organization that informs its members about pending legislation, holds public meetings, conducts extensive research, sponsors field trips, and offers service opportunities. In Oak Ridge, it maintains two trails for the public—the North Ridge Trail and the Haw Ridge Canoe Trail—and provides films to the Oak Ridge Public Library that may be borrowed (out-of-state rental fee is $5.00). The films, from the Harvey Broome Memorial Film Series, include *So Little Time* narrated by Roger Tory Peterson (about threatened waterfowl habitats), *No Room for Wilderness* (about vanishing South African wildlife), and others just as provocative.

The North Ridge Trail is a seven-and-a-half-mile National Recreation Trail that passes through a city-owned wooded greenbelt along the northern city limits. Eight short trails give access to it (ask for a description and map provided by the Environmental Quality Advisory Board of Oak Ridge).

The Haw Ridge Canoe Trail is a four-mile loop in a large, shallow flat-water canoeing area along the shoreline and coves of the Clinch River/Melton Hill reservoir. Enjoy a morning or afternoon gliding among cattails, reeds, and sedges in a serene environment that attracts wildlife such as herons, ospreys, kingfishers, geese, ducks, and muskrats. Fish are abundant among logs and stumps and milfoil beds. Access is at Solway Park on Edgemoor Road near the Solway Bridge on State 62 (from Oak Ridge, take the second entrance into Solway Park after passing the entrance to the boat-launching ramp). A descriptive map is available from TCWP.

TCWP has a pretty impressive record of achievements, which visitors now benefit from. The organization's efforts contributed to these successful results:

Plans were abandoned to build another highway through the Great Smoky Mountains National Park. The Tennessee Scenic Rivers Act—the first of its kind in the nation—passed. Plans for Devil's Jump Dam on the Big South Fork were scrapped, and the Big South Fork NRRA was established. The Obed River was included in the National Wild and Scenic Rivers System. Strip-mine-control legislation was strengthened. The Tennessee Natural Areas Preservation Act and the Tennessee Trails System Act were passed.

Efforts continue in the Big South Fork, the Cherokee National Forest, the Great Smoky Mountains National Park, urban greenbelts, and State Natural Areas. Tcwp also supports national efforts protecting parklands, wildlife refuges, free-flowing streams, wetlands, and air and water quality.

One scenic drive that we enjoyed took us eight miles west on Bethel Valley Road to the ORNL and an overlook and trail above the Graphite Reactor, a National Historic Landmark where scientists were first able to control atomic power in late 1943. It was the world's first continuously operated research reactor and functioned for more than 20 years.

A gravel road leads to a parking lot at the trailhead. We are in cedar barrens—dry sites where eastern red cedars, oaks, pines, and redbuds grow in the open glades that often occur on shallow, shaley limestone soils. Walking the trail from the parking lot to the overlook, you can read signs and plaques along the way that describe the history of the area and the vegetation that you see. Pines, cedars, and conifer needles on the forest floor are fragrant. At the overlook, a panoramic view unfolds of the entire ORNL. There, at an open pavilion, you can push a button to start a 13-minute-long slide show focusing on energy. Displays explain some ORNL research projects: acid rain, atmospheric carbon dioxide, and management of fast-growing tree species as agricultural crops. The overlook is open daily from 9 A.M. until dusk.

***Where:*** Visitors welcome center on Tulane Avenue off State 62 (Illinois Avenue). From I-75 in Knoxville, exit on State 62 west to Oak Ridge, then turn right on Tulane (next door to the American Museum of Science and Energy). From I-40 west of Knoxville, exit on State 58 north to State 95, take 95 north to Oak Ridge, then turn right on State 62 (Illinois Avenue) and left on Tulane.

***When:*** Oak Ridge welcome center open year-round, Monday through Friday, 9 A.M. to 5 P.M. ORNL facilities (self-guided tour) open year-round, Monday through Saturday, 9 A.M. to 4 P.M.; closed Sundays and holidays (overlook open daily).

***Admission:*** Free.

***Other:*** Barrier-free access or ORNL.

***For more information:*** Visitors Welcome Center, 302 South Tulane Avenue, Oak Ridge, TN 37830-6726. 423-482-7821 or 800-887-3429.

National Environmental Research Park, Building 1506, Oak Ridge National Laboratory, PO Box 2008, Oak Ridge, TN 37831-6034. Phone, 423-576-8123. Fax, 423-576-9939. Website, http://www.esd.ornl.gov/facilities/nerp.html.

Tennessee Citizens for Wilderness Planning, 130 Tabor Road, Oak Ridge, TN 37830. 423-482-2153.

## *American Museum of Science and Energy*

"Everything a museum should be" is here at the two-story American Museum of Science and Energy, one of the world's largest energy exhibitions, located in downtown Oak Ridge. This is an impressive place where adults and children participate in interactive exhibits, play computer-assisted learning games, and discover facts about all kinds of energy. Best of all, it's open daily year-round except Thanksgiving, Christmas Day, and New Year's Day and is free to the public.

The museum has two focuses. First is the Oak Ridge story that recalls the turbulent World War II years and our country's rush to the atomic age. The second track educates visitors about all types of energy in ways that leave indelible impressions.

The Energy Curve is a dramatic 3-D standing display. Square columns with multicolored horizontal bands stand like monumental, fat dominoes, each representing a decade. Starting in 1800, they rise slowly at first and then shoot up toward the ceiling as they approach the 1990s. Each color represents a certain type of energy, so it is easy to see where the energy use is coming from. Signs explain the related lifestyle and population changes.

Several times a day, live demonstrations are given in the auditorium. One that is always a hit is the "hair raising" experience (in which energy causes a volunteer's hair to stand on end). Videos and lectures (usually 30 to 45 minutes long) are also regularly scheduled. A multimedia show tells the fascinating Oak Ridge story, bringing that episode of the '40s to life. In no other place could the story be told with such impact, because here (and open to visitors) are the Graphite Reactor, the Oak Ridge National Laboratory, and other locations that recall this city's past.

Lissa Clarke was our guide for a complete tour. Upstairs are many exhibit halls where learning is fun. At the Exploration Station we weighed and measured ourselves—hand span, lung capacity, strength, temperature, and other things—in metric equivalents. A very loud and large perpetual-motion machine converted five types of energy with exciting crashing noises. We whispered in a "whisper dish": no secrets here! Simple machines. Colors in light. Can we balance 14 nails on the head of just one nail? Lissa did it! This place really takes the textbook out of the learning experience. Individual schools don't have the resources to do this, so busloads of students come from all over the United States and from Canada. It's a very popular place.

Other exhibit halls are: The American Experience (how homes were equipped before electricity), The Age of the Automobile (and how petroleum demand was affected),

Earth's Energy Resources (all types and comparisons), The World of the Atom (the pioneers and industrial uses), the Y-12 plant (one of the three main plants of the Oak Ridge National Laboratory), and National Defense (missiles, bombs, and the Apollo space program), and more addressing the question of hazardous waste and practical advice about saving energy. All in all, more than 200 displays and exhibits are housed in this large facility.

Want to take home a reminder? Unique energy- and science-related toys, books, and games are available in the Discovery Shop just inside the entrance.

Lissa made the point that information about our energy resources helps the public make wiser decisions about using and conserving them. Nature enthusiasts will find food for thought here. Some will conclude that to appreciate nature, something more is called for than simply going out *in it*! How each person responds to that awareness can make a difference.

*Where:* South Tulane Avenue at State 62 in downtown Oak Ridge, 20 miles northwest of Knoxville.
*When:* Daily, 9 A.M. to 5 P.M. (until 6 P.M. June through August). Closed Thanksgiving, Christmas Day, New Year's Day.
*Admission:* Parking and admission are free.
*Amenities:* Interactive exhibits and multimedia presentations, gift shop, auditorium, lecture rooms, picnic area.
*Activities:* Self-guided tours, films, live demonstrations.
*Special events:* Group events available by reservation (scavenger hunts, building bluebird nesting boxes, annual Paper Airplane Contest, and the like).
*Other:* Barrier-free access.
*For more information:* American Museum of Science and Energy, 300 South Tulane Avenue, Oak Ridge, TN 37830. 423-576-3200. Website, http://www.korrnet.org/amse/.

## University of Tennessee Arboretum

Even on short nature walks it's easy to look like itinerant ped-dlers of outdoor paraphernalia: camera, binoculars, backpack or fanny pack, and canteen, all dangling from various body parts, plus pen and notebook in hand and pockets full of film and other photography supplies. However, when we got to the UT Arboretum in Oak Ridge and decided to explore a short trail for half an hour, we weren't keen on being loaded down with all that stuff.

We should have remembered the first rule of the nature writer: "As sure as you don't bring your camera, you'll see something you'd die to photograph."

The UT Arboretum is in the 2,260-acre Oak Ridge Forest three miles from the heart of town. This is the headquarters for the university's forestry experiment station overseeing 12,000 acres in four forests in east and middle Tennessee. The other three are Friendship Forest (north of Chattanooga), Cumberland Forest (south of Frozen Head), and Highland Rim Forest (south of Tullahoma).

Technically, an arboretum is a place where an extensive variety of woody plants are cultivated for scientific, educa-tional, and ornamental purposes. At this arboretum there are also 250 acres open to the public, with more than 2,500 woody plant specimens and more than 800 species. Around the vis-itors center are display beds of native wildflowers and other plants and a rock garden of endangered and unusual plants. Three self-guided walking trails from half a mile to one and four-tenths miles long are part of the Tennessee Scenic Trails system.

We decided to walk the Tulip Poplar Trail. The first part goes through a pine-oak forest. The area had been damaged by fire and was in the process of secondary plant succession where pine, tulip poplar, sassafras, and other fast-growing pioneer tree species quickly reforest the clearings. All along the trail are clues that tell of disturbances such as fire, southern pine beetle damage, timber cutting, and farming.

As we approached a stand of stately, tall tulip poplars (Tennessee's state tree), we walked up on two does and a fawn who quietly nibbled on leaves until we were just a few feet from them. (Oh, for that camera!) The trail continued through a field of blooming joe-pye and other weeds to a grassy area of many shrubs, junipers, and eastern and western conifers in shades of blue and green. The specimens are all marked. Some, such as a honeysuckle from China, are exotics. We were pleased to see bluebird boxes on some of the trees in this clearing. Our return trip took us through the Heath Cove Trail, where we enjoyed the plant specimens along the trail and a scenic spot that overlooks a little gorge.

The longest trail is a combination of the Oak-Hickory and Lost Chestnut Trails, one leading to the other. It passes white oak, sourwood, black gum, sassafras, papaw, tulip poplar, wild black cherry, red maple, and hickory trees, and some American chestnut stumps. UT is working to breed American chestnuts that are resistant to the blight that virtually destroyed all specimens of this species early in the 1900s. (Since pucker brush still grows up for a time around the stumps, these trees are not actually dead. Also, some still grow out West where they had been planted before the blight came—and the blight did not travel to that part of the United States.) Shrubs and other specimens on this trail include bursting-heart, pipsissewa, ebony spleenwort, Christmas fern, maidenhair fern, and bracken fern.

The White Pine Trail is a half-mile walk that starts near a marsh where willows, alders, and bald cypress grow and ends at the visitors center, crossing the point of a ridge along the way and going through mature pines. Depending on the season, blooms and fruits include pinxter flowers (pink azalea), blueberries, muscadines, rattlesnake orchids, pink lady's slipper, and wild ginger.

Conservation education is an important part of the arboretum according to Superintendent Richard Evans. The forest is a show-and-tell example from which people can notice clues to its past and learn to interpret them. Most of the forest popped up after being disturbed during the turn of the century and on through the 1950s. A much more recent disaster was a tornado that came through in 1993. The history of natural disturbances—old and new—in a forest stand, and how the forest recovered is very useful in making forestry decisions today.

"We have an ongoing program that covers land-use history here, the ecology, and how it was developed, and what the impacts have been," said Richard. "These stories all have a conservation theme, and we want them to teach."

All the publications in the visitors center are free. Most are produced by the University of Tennessee Agricultural Extension Service. We picked up one about nematode control in the home garden, another about the Chinese chestnut in Tennessee, and a third about growing hydrangeas. Some bulletins were about prominent insect and disease problems. For more information about the arboretum, you can view a slide-and-tape program. Also, maps and trail guides are available.

Some 30,000 people come here each year, with spring and fall being the busiest seasons. If you want to view wildlife look for deer, wild turkeys, squirrels, rabbits, gray foxes, coyotes, and hawks and other birds.

Don't forget your camera!

**Where:** State 62, three miles southeast of downtown Oak Ridge. Coming from downtown, look for the entrance on the left.

***When:*** Grounds are open year-round from 8 A.M. until sunset. When the gate is closed, park outside. Visitors center open Monday through Friday, 8 A.M. to 4:30 P.M. (closed on major holidays).

***Admission:*** Free.

***Amenities:*** Visitors center, walking trails, wildflower garden, trail guides, information kiosk.

***Activities:*** Walking, plant and wildlife viewing, photography.

***Special events:*** UTAS (UT Arboretum Society), a volunteer organization that supports the UT Forestry Experiment Station, offers tours, plant sales, and a newsletter.

***Other:*** Elderly and disabled people may request permission to drive maintenance roads. Pets and picnicking are not permitted.

***For more information:*** University of Tennessee Arboretum, 901 Kerr Hollow Road, Oak Ridge, TN 37830. 423-483-3571.

UTAS, PO Box 5382, Oak Ridge, TN 37831-5382 (for arboretum society membership application).

## Ijams Nature Center

It's a quiet and serene 80 acres bordering the Tennessee River (here, called Fort Loudoun Lake) in Knoxville. You'll find woods, a spring-fed pond, a cave, meadows teeming with wildlife and flowers, and trails that wander over most of the area on both hilly and flat terrain. Some wildlife activities are not surprising: bees working on flowers, squirrels compulsively gathering whatever mast they can find. And then—as is always the case in nature—you can discover a great amount of hidden activity that changes with the seasons. Ijams Nature Center is very accessible, since it's practically downtown. Getting back to nature could hardly be easier.

Children, adults, seniors, and families are equally enchanted with what they find here. The new Nature Center facility, which opened in 1997, houses a 2,000-square-foot exhibit hall, a nature store, a children's loft, and a combination classroom and laboratory. The exhibits focus on geology, living things, and the environment in interactive and entertaining ways.

When we visited, we saw reptiles that are indigenous to the area, a working beehive, turtles, snakes, and frogs. The "Ijams Motel" is a cage for little creatures such as praying mantises or spiders that stay awhile and then are turned loose. A pond ecosystem display holds a loggerhead musk turtle and a catfish, and on a lower level is a "stream" where small kids can see the fish that are inside. Another display identifies nests that might be found outside and the animals that make them. There are nature books to read, too. The displays change from time to time, so what you see on a visit could be different from what we are describing.

Look over the grounds, and what you see is surely a paradise. All the abundant plant life, animals to discover, ponds, meadows, bluffs, woods, and the lakeshore provide ever-changing views as you walk along or engage in activities.

Regularly scheduled outings are very popular. Monthly adventures include canoe trips, owl-watching expeditions, workshops, and weekend special events. Sessions are geared for age groups, beginning with two-year-olds. Spring and summer are active seasons, but fall is the busiest time of year. An October plant sale—one of the fall highlights—brings speakers from different nurseries who give talks on perennials.

According to Ijams's executive director, Bo Townsend, probably the biggest event of the year is the Enchanted Forest on the weekend before Halloween. "Instead of vampires jumping out and scaring people," he said, "we take children down the trail to meet with Tree and Raccoon, Deer, Mushroom, and Spider—people dressed up as these characters. It's a great hit. One year the theme was Robin Hood and His Merry Men. About a thousand people showed up. It was great fun and an educational opportunity to dispel some myths about bats and snakes."

It's also fun just to wander around the parklike property. This was a private estate until 1964, and an English cottage–style garden, an herb garden, and a butterfly garden remain as reminders. The woodlands encircle the meadows and overlook the lake and Dickinson Island. Bo described some of the things that visitors might see on the trail:

"At the pond, green herons, large snapping turtles, and wood ducks may be feeding. A family of screech owls occupies the wood-duck box in spring. Usually, some nonpoisonous water snakes are out in the pond hunting tadpoles. Large bullfrogs are all over the place. This is a great place for birding because of the diversity of habitat and the many birds that come here. Then at the lake you can see great blue herons, wood ducks, coots, and occasionally some mallards. We've seen muskrats and signs of beavers, but we don't 'have' any beavers in here."

The Discovery Trail is a nature stroll that has markers and a trail guide and takes about 30 minutes, depending on how engrossed you are in what you see. It goes up a hill to a clearing surrounded by hemlocks, then toward the pond where the Fern Walk loops around it as a side trip. From there, it leads to the lake overlook. A little farther on, another side trip goes to a sinkhole. Soon the trail enters a meadow and passes the gardens mentioned earlier. The paved Serendipity Trail is in this area, too. And in another corner of the property is the Pine Succession Trail through a recovering forest.

Learning and having fun combine so well in the outdoors. We're always glad to find something that gives a little extra information. Ijams published an illustrated brochure that describes some of the common herbs found there, their origins, range, flowers and fruit, and cooking tips. It even gives sage advice (no pun!), as in this saying: "When a man gives a woman a sprig of basil, she will fall in love with him and never leave him."

We hold that the reverse is certainly true: when a woman cooks with basil, her basil-lovin' man will never leave *her*.

It pays to come here often to check out what's new. Within the last few years, Ijams has expanded dramatically, but this is an ongoing project. Come and discover!

*Where:* Traveling east on I-40 entering the downtown Knoxville area, take the James White Parkway exit (388A, also State 158), then take the second exit (Cumberland Avenue/ U.S. 441) and keep left. Turn left at the second light (Gay Street). Go over the Gay Street bridge, past the light (watch for a green Ijams Nature Center sign at the light) and onto Sevier Avenue. Go past two lights on Sevier and continue for two-tenths of a mile. When Sevier curves to the right, make a left onto Island Home Avenue. Island Home makes a turn to the right and then to the left, so watch for the Ijams signs. The entrance is on the left (about five miles from the I-40 exit).

*When:* Grounds are open year-round, 8 A.M. to sundown. Museum open 9 A.M. to 4 P.M. Monday through Friday, noon to 4 P.M. on Saturday, and 1 P.M. to 5 P.M. on Sunday.

*Admission:* Free.

*Amenities:* Nature center, museum, gift shop, trails, cave.

*Activities:* Naturalist-led walks, workshops, slide talks, canoe trips, owl prowls, wildlife viewing, photography, weekend and night programs.

*Special events:* Earth Day Celebration, Wildflower Walks, Not So Far A-field Trips, Fall Festival and Plant Sale, The Enchanted Forest, Down to Earth Holiday Party.

*Other:* Barrier-free access, quarter-mile paved trail for disabled patrons.

*For more information:* Ijams Nature Center, 2915 Island Home Avenue, Knoxville, TN 37920. 423-577-4717. Website, http://www.ijams.org/.

## Knoxville Zoo

Celebrating a 50th birthday is a milestone, even for a zoo, but when the anniversary ties in with the opening of two new major habitat areas, we're talking party, party, party. The "50th" came in 1998 for the Knoxville Zoo, and this inspired a community birthday party that began on March 28, with the two habitat openings occurring soon afterward. Chimp Ridge emulates an African forest home for the zoo's chimpanzee population, and a prairie dog exhibit invites kids to test their tunneling abilities while they "burrow" through child-size tunnels and pop up in plastic bubbles to come eyeball to eyeball with some real prairie dogs.

These two newest habitat areas follow closely on the heels of Gorilla Valley, Big Cat Country, and an award-winning North American river otter exhibit which were added in the mid-1990s. More than a face-lift, the new look of the zoo, along with its work on various species-survival projects, has earned it a solid place among highly rated zoos of the Southeast.

Gorilla Valley, with its great ape building, courtyards, and a naturalistic outdoor setting that includes massive rocks, tropical plantings, and a waterfall, is typical of the realism portrayed throughout the new habitats. You can watch these large but gentle animals from within a simulated cave or from afar, overlooking the valley. Next to this area is Big Cat Country where you will see Bengal, Siberian, and South China tigers, snow leopards, and lions. All are in woodland habitats or grassy areas with trees and boulders to make life interesting for the occupants. A Cheetah savanna is a hilly, one-acre natural habitat for these swift and gentle cats. Pridelands, the African lion exhibit new in 1997, created quite a stir by giving up-close views from several vantage points of Sara and Duma, a young lion pair which (like many of the animals on display) are being helped by the zoo's participation in the internationally recognized Species Survival Plan.

The African Plains habitat has giraffes, zebras, ostriches, sable antelope, and Thompson's gazelles. We were taken by the Arabian oryx, from Arabian Oman, living in a shady area with much vegetation. It was saved from extinction by a captive breeding program that started at the Phoenix Zoo. These are quiet, handsome animals with black markings on the face, long vertical horns, and some brown on the tail and legs. The young are the coloration of palomino horses.

The zoo houses more than a thousand animals, including polar bears, sea lions, seals, gibbons, lion-tailed macaques, Australian kookaburras, Bali mynahs, the very endangered red pandas, hippos, and one of the most extensive reptile collections in the United States. Penguin Rock, an enclosed space with a large pool where some endangered penguins reside, provides bi-level views of these interesting birds. Watch them swim, play, stand like regal maîtres d'hôtel, and then turn comical with their distinctive waddling walk.

Try to catch one of the animal shows when you visit (featuring elephants, marine mammals, birds, and others). The bird show we saw was impressive. At the start, a flock of birds flies over the audience and onto the stage where, one by one, the birds disappear into a hollow log. Then, for 25 minutes different birds appear onstage with the trainer and perform various tricks. We learn about the birds as well as their habitats and habits, and find out why we should care that their natural habitats do not disappear. It's a polished performance that is very entertaining and makes its points well. Afterward, the audience can go down to look at the birds and ask questions. Sharon Collins conducted the show we saw, but there are several trainers who take turns doing that.

Everyone has his or her favorites at a zoo. Would yours be the elegant giraffes with their measured movements and towering presence? The playful river otters indulging in inventive water games? Or do those jungle tigers simply mesmerize you? You'll have plenty of animals to consider here if you want to play "That's My Favorite."

Favorites or not, revisiting the Knoxville Zoo left us decidedly impressed. If you haven't visited lately, check it out.

*Where:* Going east on I-40 in Knoxville, take exit 392 south (Rutledge Pike/State 11W) and follow the signs.

*When:* Year-round, daily, except Christmas Day. 10 A.M. to 4:30 P.M. (ask about extended hours in summer).

*Admission:* Adults, $6.95; ages 3 to 12 and over 62, $3.95. Half price December through February. Parking, $2.00 per car. Extra fees for tram rides, camel rides, and Kid's Zoo.

*Amenities:* Animal habitats, Zoo Shop, Tiger Tops Café, tram, concessions, picnic areas.

*Activities:* Wildlife viewing, animal shows, keeper chats, picnicking, photography, "Zoo Choo" (train) rides, elephant and camel rides.

*Special events:* March through October, December (schedule changes).

*Other:* Barrier-free access. Stroller and wheelchair rentals. Group rates available.

*For more information:* Knoxville Zoological Gardens, PO Box 6040, Knoxville, TN 37914. 423-637-5331. Website, http://www.knoxville-zoo.org/.

# A String of Pearls

With the Great Smoky Mountains just south of Knoxville, is it possible to look in another direction? The answer, surprisingly, is yes. Think about it: when it's summertime and the fishin' is easy—and the walleyes, white bass, crappies, striped bass, rainbow trout, brown trout, catfish, bluegills, largemouth bass, smallmouth bass, and spotted bass are waiting for your hook—and the lakes are surrounded by wooded hills, and the campgrounds and trails beckon—just *maybe*, you gotta go and dip that hook, walk that trail, and light that fire. It's time to head up to the Norris Lake Recreation Area.

We think of a particular series of locations as a "string of pearls" because several prime destinations are close together and lined up in a semicircular configuration. From Caryville to Maynardville they are Cove Lake State Park, Norris Dam State Park, TVA's Norris Dam Reservation, the Museum of Appalachia, and Big Ridge State Park.

*For more information:* Anderson County Tourism Council, PO Box 147, Clinton, TN 37717. 423-457-4542 or 800-524-3602. Ask for the "Norris Lake brochure."

## Cove Lake State Park

Cove Lake State Park is at Caryville in a valley surrounded by peaks. It sits under the western tip of long Cumberland Mountain, which goes northeast all the way to Kentucky and beyond. If you drive north of Caryville on I-75 for five or six miles, Short Mountain is on the right. Cross Mountain and Brushy Mountain are west of town. Beyond them but out of sight is an area that has been heavily strip-mined.

The park restaurant is one of our favorite lunch places whenever we have a hankering for good country cooking with lots of well-prepared vegetables. We can look out the windows and watch wildlife while we eat. Siltation has made the lake mostly a large freshwater marsh habitat that attracts many kinds of migrating birds and other animals. Several places, including trails and an overlook at the lake, offer viewing opportunities. This lake is recognized for the Canada geese that are present year-round, but visitors will usually see other animals as well.

In addition to the expected recreational facilities and the other amenities we've mentioned, Cove Lake offers boat rentals, fishing, swimming, and guided excursions in summer. Just north of the park boundary is the terminus of a 10-mile segment of the Cumberland Trail that extends from Big Creek Gap near LaFollette to this park. The trail has a very difficult six-mile section and so is best hiked in the recommended direction (beginning at Big Creek Gap).

*Where:* From I-75 north of Knoxville, take exit 134 (U.S. 25W) to Caryville and follow signs to the park.
*When:* Year-round. Swimming pool, early summer through Labor Day.
*Admission:* Free.
*Amenities:* Lake, campground, restaurant, Olympic-size swimming pool, lake, picnic areas and pavilions, playgrounds, recreation lodge, trails, lighted tennis courts, rowboat rentals.
*Activities:* Camping, boating, fishing, swimming, hiking, bicycling, picnicking, wildlife viewing, guided walks, bicycle tours, float trips, archery lessons, organized games, campfire programs, movies, slide shows.
*Special events:* Inquire.
*Other:* Barrier-free access.

*For more information:* Cove Lake State Recreational Park, 100 Cove Lake Lane, Caryville, TN 37714. 423-566-9701. Website, http://www.state.tn.us/environment/parks/ then select.

Cumberland Trail Conference, Route 1, Box 219A, Pikeville, TN 37367 (trail maps for Cumberland Mountain segment of Cumberland Trail).

E-mail, cumberlandtrail@rocketmail.com.

Website, http://users.multipro.com/cumberlandtrail/.

## Norris Dam State Park

The whole Lake Norris area is immense, so encountering the name in several places might be confusing. The dam impounds both the Clinch and the Powell Rivers, which back up in two directions, forming 800 miles of shoreline. At some places it's more than a mile from shore to shore. When the Tennessee Valley Authority was created in 1933, Norris Dam was its first project. The dam was completed three years later; since then TVA has gone on to impound a whole series of lakes that are so extensive that they're referred to as the Great Lakes of the South.

Norris Dam State Park, on the shore of Norris Lake, has 4,000 acres of old-growth forest, caves, clear streams, and scenic valleys. The park has property both west and east of the dam—property that was a gift from TVA to the state. The western part has modern cabins, a modern campground, and a village green area with an Olympic-size swimming pool, a recreation building and outdoor sports courts, and a laundromat and other amenities; the eastern part has rustic cabins and a rustic campground. There are many miles of trails, some through the forest, and spectacular views of the lake. During the summer, naturalists conduct guided walks, lake floats, and cave tours. East of the dam are the Lenoir Pioneer Museum, a threshing barn, and an 18th-century gristmill that grinds meal in summer. Admission to these places is free.

Mountain bikers can park across from the museum and get on the gravel-surfaced Lower Clear Creek Road by the mill and from there continue on a 20-mile series of jeep roads that are open also for hiking and horseback riding.

At the dam is the Norris Dam Marina, a large full-service commercial marina open year-round that rents houseboats, pontoon boats, runabouts, and WaveRunners and has a gift shop and snack bar. There are many commercial resorts, charter services, and campgrounds around this lake.

When TVA gave the lakeshore property on both sides of the dam to the state, it retained a parcel of land below the dam. From there, a prime 13-mile scenic float on the Clinch River goes all the way to the backwaters of Melton Hill Lake near Oak Ridge. It is a renowned trout fishery. Rainbow trout in the three- to five-pound range are plentiful, and the state-record brown trout (28 pounds, 12 ounces) was caught here in 1988. Fishermen know all about the opportunities in tailwaters: when TVA is generating, float fishermen cast for the big browns with plugs and spinners; when the dam is not releasing, the waders and fly fishermen take over. For floaters and boaters, a good place to launch is 1²⁄10 miles below the dam because from that point on there is a controlled flow.

Hikers can pick up trail maps at the dam information center. The quarter-mile paved Edge Path, perfect for wheelchairs or anyone who doesn't like to stumble, starts at the dam and joins the Songbird Trail, which goes through woodlands along the east side of the Clinch River. West of the river is the River Bluff Small Wild Area, nearly 300 acres, containing a three-and-two-tenths-mile loop trail. This is a premier site to look at wildflowers in spring. Mallards, Canada geese, great blue herons, and great numbers of songbirds will likely be present. If you'd rather see four-footed species, watch for deer, groundhogs, rabbits, chipmunks, squirrels, mink, and foxes.

From the dam, U.S. 441 goes south under a canopy of big trees, following the Clinch River, which at this point is at the bottom of a gorge and flanked by wooded hillsides. The Clinch is wide and tree lined all the way to Oak Ridge and beyond. People driving west on I-40 get a view of it again at Kingston, where it flows into the Tennessee River.

From here to Big Ridge State Park, go south on U.S. 441 to State 61, then east.

*Where:* From I-75, take exit 128 at Lake City and go east for about two and a half miles on U.S. 441.

*When:* Year-round.

*Admission:* Free.

*Amenities:* Extensive lake access, historical sites, caves, forest, cabins, campgrounds, picnic sites, trails, swimming pool, village green, recreation center, marina, Lenoir Museum and cultural complex.

*Activities:* Camping, swimming (and swimming lessons), picnicking, hiking, mountain biking, archery, tennis, Ping-Pong, volleyball, boating, waterskiing, fishing, wildlife viewing, guided walks, float and cave tours.

*Special events:* Inquire.

*Other:* Barrier-free access.

*For more information:* Norris Dam State Park, 125 Village Green Circle, Lake City, TN 37769. 423-426-7461. Reservations, 800-543-9335. Website, http://www.state.tn.us/environ ment/parks/ then select.

Tva Norris Dam Reservation, Highway 441, Norris, TN 37828. 423-632-1825. For Clinch River generation schedule: 423-632-2264 (24 hours).

Norris Dam Marina, PO Box N, Norris, TN 37828. 423-494-8138.

Website for east Tennessee mountain bike trail information, http://www.cs.utk.edu/~dunigan/mtnbike/.

## Museum of Appalachia

A mile from I-75 exit 122 is the 65-acre Museum of Appalachia, a fascinating place if you're curious about aspects of pioneer life. Its owner, John Rice Irwin, was a schoolteacher who had a great interest in the culture and heritage of pioneers in the southern Appalachian hills and hollows. He started collecting authentic relics. One thing led to another, until 25 years later he had amassed thousands of items. His museum is a complex that has more than 30 log structures—smokehouses, barns, corncribs, blacksmith shops, a school, a church, and more—and a three-story Hall of Fame dedicated to the men, women, and children of Appalachia.

For a refreshing change from commercialization, there is no better place to stop and visit. Some of the activities you'll see: spinning and weaving, riving red oak shingles, making Kentucky rifles, early spring plowing, and examples of life in a dirt-floored cabin.

The museum also hosts an annual Homecoming Weekend each October from Thursday through Sunday. This internationally heralded event is the ultimate "old-timey" experience. It goes on from 9 A.M. until dark, with nonstop mountain music and lots of activities celebrating Appalachian traditions. It brings 150 craftspeople, 250 professional and amateur musicians, dozens of authors of regional books, genealogists, historians, and numerous country cooks. They'll fire up the woodstoves and serve generous portions of pinto beans, fried pies, chicken and dumplings, country ham and biscuits, pit barbecue, and other Appalachian specialties.

*Where:* From I-75 north of Knoxville, take exit 122 and go one mile east on State 61.
*When:* Year-round, daylight hours. Closed Christmas Day.
*Admission:* Adults, $7.00; 6 through 15, $4.00; under 6 with parents, free. AAA and senior discounts. Group rates available.
*Amenities:* Mountain farm and homestead complex with dozens of log structures, display building, craft and gift shop, auditorium, Appalachian Hall of Fame.
*Activities:* Self-guided tours, pioneer lifestyle demonstrations.
*Special events:* July 4th Celebration, Tennessee Fall Homecoming Weekend (four days, October), Christmas in Old Appalachia.
*Other:* Barrier-free access.
*For more information:* Museum of Appalachia, PO Box 1189, Norris, TN 37828. 423-494-7680 or 423-494-0514.

## Big Ridge State Park

Big Ridge State Park is 18 miles from Norris Dam but on the same lake. As we approach on State 61, we drive over Bluebird Ridge, then drop down into a cove where the park sits on a heavily wooded 3,687-acre tract. To say it's idyllic is an understatement.

This is a rustic park built in the 1930s but recently renovated, with 19 cabins, 56 campsites on the lake, a snack bar, an interpretive center, playgrounds, and an old gristmill. It also has three picnic areas with tables and grills and three pavilions that may be reserved. Lake activities include boating and fishing (canoes, paddleboats, and flat-bottomed rowboats can be rented). Swimmers enjoy a sandy beach and an enclosed kiddie pool. Park interpretive specialists conduct guided hikes, nature programs, and other activities in summer.

The park has 15 miles of trails (trail guides are available at the park office). Big Valley Trail is six miles long and rated moderate. It starts at the Old Mill, climbs and descends several times, and in spring rewards hikers with blooms of pink lady's slipper. The Ghost House Trail ascends Pinnacle Ridge to 1,400 feet, where it overlooks a deep valley. Yellow star grass and dwarf irises bloom along the trail at certain places. Dark Hollow Trail goes up steeply to Big Ridge and later climbs farther, passing by an old cemetery. Other trails go to Rock Point (1,520 feet altitude), Sharp's Station (one of the first two settlements west of the Appalachians), and Indian Rock, where a settler was scalped in 1794. The highest point in the park is 1,540 feet, but trails go up and down the hills many times, making up to 400-foot changes in elevation. Another series of trails includes Lake Trail, Dark Hollow, and Big Valley Loop. It is about five miles long, starts at the group camp, and changes 350 feet in elevation. Along it are footbridges, marshes, hills and valleys, and the lakeshore. In the right season, blueberries are ripe and tantalizing.

It's off the beaten path, which may be just what you're looking for!

**Where:** From I-75 north of Knoxville, take exit 122 (State 61) and go 12 miles east.
**When:** Year-round.
**Admission:** Free.
**Amenities:** Cabins, campground, group camp, lakes, snack bar, launching ramps, beach, lifeguards (seasonal), picnic sites and pavilions, outdoor recreation courts and fields, hiking trails.
**Activities:** Camping, hiking, swimming, fishing, boating, picnicking, birding, nature study, wildlife viewing, guided hikes, naturalist-led programs, organized sports activities.

*Special events:* Inquire.

*Other:* Barrier-free access.

*For more information:* Big Ridge State Park, 1015 Big Ridge Road, Maynardville, TN 37807. 423-992-5523. Website, http://www.state.tn.us/environment/parks/ then select.

# Cumberland Gap National Historical Park

Often, what is historic about our country is forever connected with the challenges that explorers and settlers faced in getting past seemingly insurmountable barriers in the movement west. The search for passes over the Rockies we all know about; and the Mississippi and other rivers were a challenge.

Before 1750, Europeans knew of no way to cross the daunting Appalachians in the area of Kentucky and Tennessee. That year, explorer Thomas Walker discovered a route that Indians had been taking for generations to hunting grounds in Kentucky and were using as a warrior's path for their raiding parties. This was the Cumberland Gap. In 1767, Daniel Boone crossed the gap to explore the West. He marked the trail that became the Wilderness Road and later settled in Kentucky. The gap was critically important in commerce until the 1820s when railroads, canals, and steamboats began providing better transportation.

Most of this 20,000-acre national park straddles the Kentucky-Virginia line, but its southernmost tip sits west and south of Cumberland Gap, Tennessee. All three states have a share in its historic significance and outstanding natural beauty.

From Caryville it is only an hour's drive to the gap, and a very scenic one! Wooded hills and mountains surround I-75 from Knoxville to Caryville, then the granite escarpments of Cumberland Mountain appear on the left as U.S. 25W goes toward LaFollette. Along the State 63 scenic highway, the valley widens and the mountains recede on both sides for some 25 miles. If you make this trip in the fall, you'll see trucks pulling loads of tobacco and smell the smoke wafting from the curing barns. Suddenly, though, you are in the mountains again: the valley is gone, while evergreen trees and rocky cliffs take over. The gap is near.

Harrogate, just a couple of miles south of the gap, is the home of Lincoln Memorial University, whose Abraham Lincoln Museum has one of the world's finest Lincoln and Civil War collections, with more than 25,000 artifacts on display. It's open to the public every day from 9 A.M. until 4 P.M. (afternoons only on Saturday and Sunday) for a very modest admission fee.

The Towne of Cumberland Gap (it prefers its historical name) sits just off the highway at the foot of the gap. It's down in a deep hollow that nestles among the mountains, through which passed the historic Wilderness Road. A quaint place, it offers tearooms, craft shops, a 1920s drugstore, the "towne hall" in an old schoolhouse, and a trading company. At the edge of town is a trailhead for the Wilderness Road Trail and the remains of an iron furnace that began operation in the early 1820s, producing 150-pound pigs (ingots) that were sold to local blacksmiths or shipped to Chattanooga. The bellows were powered by a waterwheel, and the pigs were shaped by a 500-pound hammer. Information about this is on a plaque at the site.

The Cumberland Gap twin tunnel opened in 1997, creating two lanes of traffic in each direction under the gap and making travel between Tennessee and Kentucky much quicker and safer. This state-of-the-art engineering feat goes through nearly a mile of solid rock to reroute traffic from the overmountain highway (U.S. 25E). Computerized technology creates lighting transitions from daylight to artificial light and controls a sophisticated exhaust system that maintains air quality in the tunnel. The tunnel project incorporates new four-lane approaches and highway interchanges, repair of an abandoned railroad tunnel, two new pedestrian bridges on hiking trails, and three new parking areas.

The old gap highway is being restored to a primitive pathway landscaped with native plants and closely resembling the one that the pioneers traveled. From this old highway, you can access the Daniel Boone Heritage Trail and the Wilderness Road Trail. Tri-State Peak, 1,990 feet in elevation, is on the trail less than half a mile off the road.

Pinnacle Point offers an authentic "high place"—2,440 feet in elevation—and views that go on forever, it seems. To get there, start at the park headquarters in Middlesboro, Kentucky, on U.S. 25E and take Pinnacle Road to the point, where you'll be on the Kentucky-Virginia state line on the backbone of Cumberland Mountain. The road does a lot of climbing, with tight switchbacks, so don't plan to go in your stretch limo (no vehicles more than 20 feet long allowed). There is a large, paved parking lot and a blacktop trail for handicapped access to the overlook at the point. Is it our imagination, or is the air really cleaner here? We take deep breaths, just in case. Far below, looking toward Tennessee, are the valleys and towns from which we just came.

Back at the visitors center, we watch a film that shows the grandeur of nature in this place and tells about its fascinating history. It makes us want to see more, and we make a mental note to return. One especially interesting tour goes to the historic Hensley Settlement of farmsteads in Kentucky that were abandoned in the 1950s and now are operated as three demonstration farms. You can read about this in the companion book, *Natural Wonders of Kentucky*.

Park personnel are very friendly here and eager to answer questions and help us get information. Their brochure points out that this is a wild area and cautions people not to hike alone. We believe a visit to the center is an appropriate beginning for a vacation here. There's something comforting about being armed with facts when in unfamiliar territory!

*Where:* From Knoxville, exit I-75 at Caryville, take U.S. 25W to LaFollette, then State 63 to U.S. 25E just south of Harrogate and turn left (north) to Cumberland Gap. The visitors center is on U.S. 25E at Middlesboro, Kentucky (access through the new tunnel).

*When:* Year-round. Park gates open 8 A.M. to 6 P.M. in summer; close at 5 P.M. from September to mid-June. Closed December 25 and January 1.

*Admission:* Free (museum has donation box). Wilderness Road Campground $10.00 per night.

*Amenities:* Visitors center and museum, auditorium, exhibits, gift shop, bookstore, 160-site campground, primitive campgrounds, 50 miles of hiking trails, caves (some accessible only by trails), Hensley Settlement, overlooks, Iron Furnace.

*Activities:* Sight-seeing, wildlife viewing, nature appreciation, hiking, bicycling, camping, picnicking, interpretive programs, photography. Shuttle tours on summer weekends to Hensley Settlement (three hours, reservations required), other tours, guided walks, campfire programs, living-history demonstrations in summer.

*Special events:* Owl prowls, star watches, quilt festivals, pioneer camps. Inquire.

*Other:* Barrier-free access (visitors center, Iron Furnace, Pinnacle Overlook). Inquire about road and trail conditions.

*For more information:* Cumberland Gap National Historical Park, PO Box 1848, Middlesboro, KY 40965. 606-248-2817. Website, http://www.nps.gov/cuga/.

Abraham Lincoln Museum, Lincoln Memorial University, Cumberland Gap Parkway, Harrogate, TN 37752. 423-869-6235. Website, http://www.lmunet.edu/.

# Great Smoky Mountains National Park

Without a doubt, the Great Smoky Mountains National Park (GSMNP) is the region's prize wilderness—an 800-square-mile tract that has more visitors than any other park (topping out at around 9 million each year). It has more species of plants than anywhere else in the United States, more than 800 miles of trails, the last large protected eastern habitat for black bears, and many preserved pioneer homesteads dating back as early as the 1820s. Yes, it allows outstanding scenic views from the highways and byways, but it reserves its inner secrets for the hiker and backpacker while its caretaker, the National Park Service, struggles valiantly to protect the fragile ecosystem, which is an official biosphere reserve.

Half in Tennessee, half in North Carolina, the park's dividing line takes the high road (which is also the Appalachian Trail, or AT), following the backbone of the Smokies from the eastern boundary near Big Creek past some romantic-sounding places: Mount Cammerer, Mount Guyot, Charlies Bunion, Newfound Gap (where U.S. 441 crosses), Clingmans Dome (the highest point in Tennessee at 6,642 feet), Silers Bald, Thunderhead Mountain, and Spence Field. The mountains here are well defined—they are not the corrugated ridges of the Great Valley. The AT departs from the state line near the park's western border, going into North Carolina to Shuckstack and on to Fontana Dam.

Most of the traffic comes from the Tennessee side and flows through Gatlinburg. This predictably causes slowdowns on almost any weekend and especially during spring and fall. Probably the one miscalculation first-time visitors make is not allowing for this problem. "After all, we're leaving the big city and going to the wilderness, right?" Well, yes and no.

There are some ways to avoid the heaviest traffic. The most-used corridor starts either in Knoxville or a few miles east at the Sevierville exit of I-40 (at State 66), then goes through Sevierville and Pigeon Forge. Coming from the east, you could just as easily take I-40 toward Asheville and then take exit 435 at Newport or 440 or 443 south of Newport—all of which connect with U.S. 321, go through Cosby, and follow the northern park boundary west to Gatlinburg. If you're approaching Gatlinburg from the west, exit I-40 onto U.S. 321 (Lamar Alexander Parkway) a few miles east of Kingston. You can follow U.S. 321 through Maryville and Townsend and all the way to Pigeon Forge. You can also leave U.S. 321 east of Townsend at State 73 and go directly into the park, turning left onto Little River Road, which takes you to the Sugarlands visitors center. This last alternative is very scenic, but traffic often runs 30 miles an hour or slower in the park. Also, you should check current road conditions, since flooding can close park roads, sometimes requiring major repairs.

*Why* people visit may have to be answered by 9 million different voices each year—the individuals themselves. We do have clues, of course. Many people come to drive along scenic roadways, to shop, to visit museums and attractions, to attend conferences and workshops, and to take short hikes and learn about nature. A smaller percentage are avid hikers, backpackers, and campers (but in actual count, they are many).

We come for the magnificent scenery, the lure of the mountains, the crisp air, the friendliness of the people, to walk trails and discover wildflowers, to photograph, or to gaze upon undulating hills miles away and feel the sun and wind from a mountaintop. Whether we are staying in a chalet above Gatlinburg or in a cottage beside an ever-gurgling stream, the mountains feel like home and we are at peace.

## A Look Around

Let's say you are coming to the Smokies from the Tennessee side. You may drive through Knoxville, Newport, Cosby, Maryville, Townsend, or Pigeon Forge, but your route will eventually take you to Gatlinburg.

Both Gatlinburg and Pigeon Forge are resort towns that cater to families. Pigeon Forge is noted for tourist attractions, including the Dollywood theme park (named for its founder, Dolly Parton), motels, and large factory-outlet complexes. Gatlinburg presents a combination of Bavarian ambience and Appalachian culture in its different motels, chalets, and commercial enterprises. Since the late 1920s, it has grown from a tiny hamlet that had only a post office, the Greystone Hotel, the Mountain View Hotel, and Ogle's General Store into a sophisticated small city with a convention center, high-rise hotels, and businesses that cater to tourism year-round.

It hasn't forgotten its beginnings. For instance, Wiley Oakley Drive, which winds among chalet-dotted hills northwest of the downtown area, is named for a colorful character called the "Roamin' Man of the Smoky Mountains" who was born at the foot of Mount LeConte and lived in the area for 70 years, operating most of the time as a mountain guide. *Roamin' & Restin'*, Oakley's autobiographical account, gives insight into the character of the area's mountain people.

*Mount LeConte, Great Smoky Mountains National Park*

The Gatlinburg welcome center is on State 441 just north of town. Exit to the right into a large parking lot. Here you will find displays about the area, a comfortable place to relax, a bookstore with an excellent selection about the Smokies, and lots of information about the immediate area. If you are headed next for the Sugarlands visitors center, the Gatlinburg bypass will allow you to avoid the city traffic.

Sugarlands is just inside the park on the main corridor, 33-mile-long Newfound Gap Road (U.S. 441), going through the park from Gatlinburg to Cherokee, North Carolina. There are other roads near the edges of the park (some are gravel and one-way), but the great interior is truly protected and traversed only by the Appalachian Trail and other horse and hiking trails.

Expect more than a visitors center at Sugarlands: it's a museum and a theater, too. This is really *the place* to go to plan your Smoky Mountains vacation itinerary (unless, of course, you've preplanned everything). Even if your plans are already made, the things you will learn here will help you have a better appreciation for this park and catch the excitement over what you're about to experience (and, who knows, you may even make some changes!). Every few minutes, movies about the park are shown or rangers give talks and hold question-and-answer sessions. Also, the books, pamphlets, self-guiding booklets, tapes, and maps that are sold here are full of useful information.

The displays at Sugarlands relate to specific kinds of forests. This is logical, because the GSMNP is working to preserve the world's finest examples of temperate deciduous forest. Each display shows actual examples and illustrations of animals and plants that are found in that type of location. In the beech gaps, for instance, are found pink turtlehead flowers, American beech trees, burying beetles, carrion beetles, common shrews, wild hogs, southern lady ferns, lichens, the solitary vireo, rose-breasted grosbeaks, dark-eyed juncos, yellow birches, tulip poplars, painted trillium, spring beauty—and the list goes on.

At the other end of Newfound Gap Road in North Carolina is the Oconaluftee visitors center, which is next to the Cherokee Indian Reservation and near the western terminus of the Blue Ridge Parkway.

## Auto Tours

Here's another confession: occasionally we just drive and gaze and think we're having an out-of-the-(car)door experience. That's not what we recommend, though. More often—and especially in the Smokies—we like to investigate what's out there by taking walks and enjoying all the features of the forest. We take along *Mountain Roads and Quiet Places*, a book that describes more than a dozen scenic drives within and alongside the park. We also rely on the inexpensive auto tour guides that are sold at the Sugarlands visitors center.

Newfound Gap Road has an auto tour guide and a cassette tape that includes recorded interviews with rangers, biologists, and people who lived there in the past. The road climbs nearly 3,600 feet from Sugarlands Valley to the 5,048-foot gap at the state line, where a seven-mile spur road to Clingmans Dome takes you to that "must-see" spot. Along the way are many pull-offs and small parking lots. At some of these are paths called "quiet walkways" that provide short strolls into the forest. Others are observation points where you can see Mount LeConte, the Chimney Tops, Sugarland Mountain, and Mount Mingus. Still others give access to longer park trails.

Because of the dramatic change in elevation on this road, it passes through a number of climate zones and forest types: tulip trees, oaks, and maples in the valley; mixed oak, cove hardwoods, pine-oak, and hemlock in higher elevations; and heath-bald, northern hardwoods, and spruce-fir at the top of the range. If you stopped at Sugarlands, you may have learned to recognize the features of different zones.

One of the most popular auto tours goes to Cades Cove, an isolated valley where about 500 people were farming the land at the time the park was established in the early 1930s. Getting there involves taking Little River Road from Sugarlands to its turnoff to Townsend and continuing on Laurel Creek Road to the Cades Cove Loop. You can loop around and return the same way, or exit from the cove onto a one-way road: choose Rich Mountain Road, which leads to Townsend, or Parson Branch Road, which ends on U.S. 129 south of the park. From there, turn left toward Twentymile and Fontana Dam in North Carolina or turn right and return to Townsend along the western section of the Foothills Parkway. Both Rich

Mountain and Parson Branch Roads are closed in winter. In fact, Parson Branch Road was heavily damaged in a massive local flood early in 1994 and was not completely rebuilt until 1998.

Our most recent visit to Cades Cove was in October—always a time of heavy visitation—so we were there midweek to escape the heaviest traffic. Dogwoods were turning red, and tulip poplars were showing yellow leaves. The road passes the trail to Laurel Falls, a paved walkway that gently rises to these pretty 60-foot-high falls in a two-and-a-half-mile round-trip. No time to stop on this trip, though, since a Cades Cove tour is usually an all-day one. We also passed by the Metcalf Bottoms picnic area which has dozens of tables among the trees and where Wear Cove Gap Road begins, going north for three miles to Wear Cove on State 73 between Townsend and Pigeon Forge.

The store at Cades Cove Campground (on the left before you enter the one-way loop) is your last chance to buy food. Though the loop is only 11 miles long and the speed limit is 20, in reality the traffic flows at around 5 to 10 miles an hour, coming to a dead stop whenever an animal is sighted. We had driven about a mile when the line of cars stopped to watch an eight-point white-tailed buck that was grazing beside the road and paying no attention to its audience. A mile farther the cars had stopped again. Hoping a bear was in the vicinity, we asked some people who walked by. "No, two big bucks," they said.

The road has plenty of pull-offs to allow inspecting interesting features. These include pioneer dwellings and old churches from the early 1800s. A treaty with the Cherokees in 1819 opened the cove to settlement. Cabins and farms are sprinkled throughout the cove, and the Cable Mill area provides a study in early mountain communities. A visitors center in a log house has *Foxfire*-type books for sale and local specialties such as stone-ground whole wheat and sorghum molasses. The mill was here all along, but several other buildings were moved to this location from their original settings: a smokehouse, a blacksmith shop, a corncrib, a sorghum mill, barns, and cabins. When we were there, an audience had gathered around an elderly woman in the yard who was talking about daily life in this valley in earlier years.

A drive around the loop provides excellent picnic sites. Many people simply spread blankets in the field for a lunch in the open, surrounded by the lofty mountains. We suggest getting there early and making a day of it (including a picnic), investigating some of the trails and the 18 places of interest mentioned in the tour book. Two other roads provide shortcuts across the valley: Sparks Lane is not far from the entrance, and Hyatt Lane crosses the meadow near the Rich Mountain Road exit.

As always, we hated to leave. It was cool and dark as we drove beside the laurel thickets with trees forming a canopy overhead of green, yellow, orange, and red, backlit by an afternoon sun. And wood smoke was in the air.

If the pioneer sites whet your interest in lifestyles of the 1800s, be sure to take the Tremont Logging History self-guided auto tour. As you're returning from Cades Cove, the road to Tremont—Middle Prong Road—is on the right just before the place where Little River Road comes in from Townsend on the left. It is a three-mile trip that follows an old railroad line to the company town of Tremont, established by the Little River Lumber Company. From 1927 to 1939, logging boomed here, and interesting relics of logging and railroad operations remain. The Great Smoky Mountains Institute conducts workshops here throughout the year on varied subjects from photography to geology, adult backpacking trips, family wildlife weekends, and a wilderness adventure camp for teens. The reasonable fees charged cover lodging, food, and tuition.

One of Ardi's favorite drives is Roaring Fork Motor Nature Trail, which starts just three and a half miles from traffic light 8 in Gatlinburg at Airport Road and takes a five-and-a-half-mile loop at the foot of Mount LeConte. Follow Airport Road and bear right instead of going uphill to a high-rise hotel. Plan to enjoy some hikes on this trip if you're so inclined. For the most part, this drive gives an intimate view of the forest as the boughs of tall trees—huge hemlocks, tall yellow poplars, birches, and black locusts—intertwine above the narrow paved road. The understory holds evergreen rhododendrons and wild grapevines. You will also see an area of downed American chestnut trees that were stricken by a blight. Everything is "up close and personal." You'll find forest animals all around, too, if you look closely.

Occasionally, an overlook reveals a long view. Other "long views" are from a historical perspective. The Ephraim Bales home and the Alfred Reagan place give insights into the hardscrabble life of early pioneers here and how being resourceful enabled them to survive amid great hardships.

As you drive along, a crescendo breaks through whenever you come near the intemperate Roaring Fork with its constantly noisy, lusty, breakneck rush downstream. The road through this loop is winding and has many ups and downs, so it's not for buses and motor homes. In winter it's closed.

Outside the park but just as scenic are two sections of the Foothills Parkway. One part is near Cosby where it connects U.S. 321 with I-40 (you were on it if you left the interstate at exit 443). It goes over Green Mountain and offers great views of the park and Cammerer, Guyot, and LeConte Peaks. The other section is west of the park. It leaves U.S. 321 west of Townsend and goes south for 18 miles on the crest of Chilhowee Mountain to Chilhowee Reservoir. The road offers quite spectacular views from many viewpoints with pull-offs. From the Miller Cove overlook you might be able to see Clingmans Dome; from Look Rock, go across the road and walk a half-mile trail to a lookout tower for unobstructed views in every direction. It doesn't get any better than this! Look for Gregory Bald, Cades Cove Mountain, and Thunderhead.

Sixteen additional miles of the Foothills Parkway have been under construction in two segments and still lack a 1⁶⁄₁₀-mile portion that will link them together. A 10-mile section in Blount County extends eastward from the present western section of U.S. 321 toward Pigeon Forge, and a 5-mile section in Sevier County goes west from Pigeon Forge. If funding is made available, the two will be joined to make a continuous connection between Walland and Wear Valley. The unfinished road is open to hikers, bicyclists, and horseback riders, and is sometimes opened to automobiles for limited dates, as it was for two days in October 1997 during the height of fall leaf color.

## Animals of the Smokies

If any single symbol is most associated with the GSMNP, it is the black bear. Long before Smokey, the U.S. Forest Service bear, made his appearance on the American scene during World War II and became a household name, the Smokies bear was already very familiar to visitors to the park. Not only did tourists often see a live bear, but also its image was promoted through souvenir items sold in gift shops. The animal gained even greater fame some years ago when Zeno Wall, then public-relations manager for the Gatlinburg Chamber of Commerce, toured the nation wearing a realistic bear outfit to promote the city and the park.

Bears tend to live in the more remote areas of the park, although they will also frequent campgrounds or trail shelters. When a bear becomes troublesome, it is removed to another location far from the scene. Park officials always caution visitors that it is unlawful to feed the bears. Leaving food out for them can put humans at risk and lead to habits that ruin the animal.

It should probably go without saying, but we'll say it anyway: bears are wild animals that will attack and have attacked humans who approach too close, crowd them, or get between a sow and her young. Cuddly teddy bears and "Smokey" are not like the real thing. Knowing the difference is important.

Although bears may hang around campgrounds, their life is no picnic. Some years, the nuts and berries on which bears rely to get them through the winter just are not plentiful enough. When this happens, the bears start to roam, and often many are killed. Harm also comes to the bear population from illegal hunting, or poaching. This practice continues because of an international market for bear body parts, primarily used in Asian medicines.

The bear, however, is only one of many animals, big and small, that reside in the park. Some, such as white-tailed deer, have large and healthy populations. In Cades Cove alone are an estimated 750 resident deer. Groundhogs and cottontail rabbits are also commonly seen in places such as Cades Cove. Hikers often spot chipmunks, gray squirrels, and the small mountain red squirrels, nicknamed "boomers." Other animals—red and gray foxes, bobcats, raccoons, opossums, skunks, weasels, muskrats, beavers, and mink—are sighted less frequently. There are also many small rodents that aren't often observed.

Some of the animals that were long ago eliminated have been successfully reintroduced, and ongoing efforts are attempting to bring back other lost species. River otter reintroduction is complete: 140 river otters were successfully placed in the park's streams beginning in 1986. You might look for them in Abrams Creek, Cosby Creek, Little River, or the Middle and West Prongs of the Little Pigeon River, although they are rarely seen during the daytime.

Another reintroduction program fluctuates between success and setbacks. The red wolf, a very endangered species, was first brought into the GSMNP in 1991. It was a historic move: never before had a major predator been returned to a national park. New litters are being born each year, but only a few pups have reached maturity. It will take some years for a verdict on their long-term survival.

The next reintroduction may be elk. As this is written, it looks as if an experimental release of about 50 elk may place the animals near Clingmans Dome Road early in 1999.

Some animals are on the unwanted list, the most notorious being the European wild hog. This exotic was brought into the southern mountains early in the 20th century and eventually invaded the parklands. Wild hogs do serious damage to the ecology by uprooting wildflowers, contaminating streams, and competing with native species over food crops. Park personnel remove hundreds of the animals each year.

The coyote is also a relatively new inhabitant of the park, although its numbers are not yet great here. Unlike the wild hogs, coyotes are not considered a major threat to the park environment, although there is some concern about their impact on the fox population.

If you're a bird-watcher, you'll love the Smokies. The number and diversity of species are impressive. Some stay for the summer or year-round, while others migrate through.

Of the more than 200 kinds of songbirds seen in the park during the year, about 75 take up residence during the summer. One of the first arrivals of the spring is the Louisiana waterthrush, which appears mid-March from its South American winter home. The climate changes related to altitude provide several different zones in virtually the same geographical location. At the higher elevations, you may see birds normally found in Canada or New England. Some birds simply travel vertically with the seasons, moving down the mountains during the winter and going back up in the spring.

The two largest and most spectacular of the park's birds are the golden eagle and the eastern wild turkey. Both were driven nearly to extinction in this area in the early 1900s. The ban on DDT was the most significant step in rescuing the eagle nationwide. The resurgence of the wild turkey population has been greatly assisted by the TWRA in an intensive restocking program that has been going on for years. Birds have been introduced in counties bordering the GSMNP, and with their numbers increasing, many have moved into the park. An excellent place to see them, as with the white-tailed deer, is Cades Cove. Too, hikers often see them as they walk the trails.

Other large birds present are hawks, owls, ruffed grouse, crows, and common ravens. Crows and ravens are cousins, but they can be distinguished in three ways. Ravens are bigger; they are found most often in the high spruce-fir forests; and instead of cawing like the crow, they *croak*.

## Hikes, Nature Walks, and Camping

Trails, trails everywhere: there's hardly a spot in the GSMNP where a trail is more than two miles away (although that two miles may be nearly straight up!). There are short nature walks, hikes to waterfalls, ridges, balds, and mountaintops. There are seasonal wildflower and fall-color hikes, both guided and self-guiding. Some trails allow horses, while others are for foot travel only. Every auto tour offers several hikes along its route. Also, in the Smokies, hiking and camping often go together. Both rationed and unrationed backcountry sites and shelters are available, and there are developed campgrounds, of course.

Any serious hiker will want to have a trail map of the park. It will tell where the trails are and what to do if someone gets injured or lost, or has a bear encounter. It also spells out the hazards to guard against. All of the nearly 100 backcountry campsites in the park are identified. Most of the shelters are on the AT. This trail requires reservations, and all overnight trips require a permit, while camping is allowed only at the designated sites and shelters.

Six developed campgrounds are on the Tennessee side. Off the western Foothills Parkway are Abrams Creek (16 sites) and Look Rock (92 sites). Between Sugarlands and the Cades Cove Loop are Cades Cove (161 sites) and Elkmont (220 sites), and at the eastern end of the park are Cosby (175 sites) and Big Creek (12 sites). Reservations at Cades Cove and Elkmont were suspended in October 1997, so all campgrounds are now first come, first served. The park campgrounds do not have showers.

*Hiking Trails of the Smokies*, a book published by the Great Smoky Mountains Natural History Association, is probably the best hiking guide to this area. It was researched by writers who actually hiked the trails, other writers who developed the human history of the park trails, and geologists. This comprehensive guide also includes a detailed map that identifies each trail by name.

So, where will your next hike take you, and how will you decide?

If waterfalling is on your mind, how about heading down

Little River Road from Sugarlands? We've already mentioned Laurel Falls, which will be on your right (parking lots are on both sides of the road). In mid-May the mountain laurel will be blooming here. Next, you can actually see the Sinks as you drive along. Look on the left after you've gone about 12 miles. Drive another mile and look for Meigs Creek Falls. Hint: there's a long parking lot next to the river.

At the far end of the Cades Cove Loop Road is the trailhead for Abrams Falls. This is a five-mile round-trip, rated moderate, and will take half a day of walking through pine-oak forest on the ridges and hemlock-rhododendron along the creek. The falls delivers a large volume of water into a deep pool (not for swimming because of the undertow).

Another series of falls is on the Roaring Fork Motor Nature Trail. The hike to Rainbow Falls is another half-day, moderate, five-and-a-half-mile loop. LeConte Creek is small, but the water takes an 80-foot free fall. On the way, you may see many wildflowers and mushrooms. The second trail goes to Grotto Falls in a two-and-four-tenths-mile round-trip. This is an easy walk that crosses small streams and goes behind the falls. It is closed in winter. The third falls is called Place of a Thousand Drips. Whether it "drips" or falls depends on what the clouds above are doing. Since it's right on the road, you don't need to hike to see it.

Two other falls hikes are east of Gatlinburg. The trailhead to Ramsay Cascades is in Greenbrier Cove off U.S. 321 on the way to Cosby (exit at traffic light 3 in Gatlinburg and go about six miles to the turnoff). From there, it's a four-mile drive along the Middle Prong of the Little Pigeon River. The trail is a strenuous all-day, eight-mile round-trip hike to the highest waterfall in the park, dropping 100 feet in magnificent cascades. Several people have plunged to their death here, so be very cautious. To see Henwallow Falls, go all the way to Cosby and turn onto Gabes Mountain Trail near Cosby Campground. The hike is a moderate four-and-four-tenths-mile round-trip that takes roughly four hours, going through hemlock, poplar, and rhododendron. The falls is 2 feet wide at the top and fans out to 20 feet wide at the base. The bonus is that you can take a side trip to the base of the falls and get a different view.

By far the best-known trail in the park is the Appalachian Trail. Dedicated hikers from Boy Scouts to John Muir "think-alikes" yearn to make the 2,158-mile trek from Maine to Georgia (and of course walk the top of the Smokies along the way).

At one time you were virtually guaranteed solitude when walking along the Smokies section of the AT. Lea and three companions hiked the western portion of it in 1950, beginning at Clingmans Dome and ending at Deals Gap, following the state line all the way to the western park boundary. They didn't encounter a single person during the entire trip. The trail had already been rerouted to its present location (from Doe Knob down to Fontana Dam), but they followed the old route to Moore Springs and across Gregory Bald.

That sort of situation has long ceased to exist. Today, the AT is heavily traveled, and because of this expanded use, park regulations require that hikers planning to use the Smokies portion of the trail make reservations in advance. It can still be an exciting adventure, but it is no longer a pristine one.

Another popular hiking destination is Mount LeConte, the third-highest peak in the Smokies at 6,593 feet. As the raven flies, it is about eight miles southeast of Gatlinburg. You won't drive there, however, because the only access is by hiking trails frequented by humans and pack llamas. The llamas take supplies to rustic LeConte Lodge on the mountaintop. It's increasingly hard to get lodge reservations, which have to be made at least a year in advance, and preference is given to repeat visitors. There's no electricity, but expect tasty, family-style meals and camaraderie with fellow hikers.

Some people make annual pilgrimages to LeConte. The current record for most visits is held by Paul Dinwiddie Sr., who has made the climb 750 times. An oft-repeated true tale that illustrates the appeal of this mountain is about Jack Huff (the developer of LeConte Lodge), who carried his invalid mother all the way up the mountain strapped to his back in a chair so he could fulfill her wish to see the sunrise from Myrtle Point.

Lea's Knoxville friend David Dickey made an annual trip to LeConte for years and knows all the trails—there are five. He gave us his comments about each.

Alum Cave Trail starts at the Alum Cave Bluffs Parking Area on Newfound Gap Road nine miles south of Sugarlands. The last three miles, from the bluffs to the top of LeConte, are strenuous (the total climb is 2,800 feet). All in all, it's a day's hike, but even better is to have overnight reservations on LeConte.

David says, "This is the most popular route to LeConte, for good reasons. It's the shortest and the most spectacular—cliffs, bluffs, landslides, and a wide variation in vegetation. I like to go up on Alum Cave Bluff Trail and return by another. Of course, this means you have left a car at the end of the second trail or arranged for someone to pick you up there."

This brings us to Bull Head Trail, which begins four miles from Gatlinburg along Cherokee Orchard Road and climbs 4,017 feet in seven miles. David, however, likes to make it a seven-mile journey from the top down:

"My preference for the return trip is, by far," he says, "the Bull Head Trail. In April there is just an overwhelming profusion of wildflowers on this trail, changing in variety from the 6,000-foot level on down to the base of the mountain.

For the most part, this trail is also easier on the feet. There are fewer rocky stretches, and lots of mossy, leafy ones."

The Trillium Gap Trail takes off from Grotto Falls, so the Grotto Falls parking lot on the Roaring Fork Motor Nature Trail is the place to start (the road is closed in winter, though). After the falls, the trail gets steep, passing the headwaters of the Roaring Fork on its way to LeConte. It's a 14-mile round-trip that climbs 3,473 feet.

David comments, "Trillium Gap is similar to Bull Head, with maybe not so many wildflowers but with a half-mile side trail to Brushy Mountain, a heath bald with outstanding views. On the main trail again, beautiful Grotto Falls is a perfect rest stop about three-quarters of the way down."

There is also the Boulevard Trail, which branches from the AT. It may appear to be an easier trail, since it starts at a higher altitude than the others, but, David says, "This is a matter of opinion, for it has many up-and-down meanderings as it drops off the main Smokies crest and then up the side of LeConte, which sits off from the main ridges. It is a pleasant trail, passes within a hundred yards of the spectacular overlook called the Jumpoff, and certainly is cooler than the others due to its sustained height."

Reach the Boulevard Trail by going east on the AT from Newfound Gap. The climb is 1,545 feet, but as David says, you climb more than once.

There's one more trail, the Rainbow Falls Trail, which like the Bull Head Trail starts from Cherokee Orchard Road near Gatlinburg. It is half a mile shorter but climbs the same 4,017 feet. Here is a cautionary note from David: "The Rainbow Falls Trail to LeConte is popular and well known, but it's the one I try to avoid. Avid hikers might like it, and it does have lovely scenic spots such as the falls, but it is rocky, gullied, and rough, not to mention steep. This trail receives wide use, but most casual hikers such as I consider it rugged and strenuous."

Lea agrees with David about the Alum Cave Trail. He has hiked it several times and considers it the top approach, all things considered.

## Smokies Trout Fishing

The Smokies are Lea's favorite place in the state, and it's easy to explain why. He grew up nearby and from boyhood has frequented these magnificent mountains and enjoyed all the pleasures they offer. Paramount among them is the trout fishing. Within the boundaries of the GSMNP are hundreds of miles of streams and rivers that offer excellent angling potential. Some parallel the roads and are easily accessible, but others are in remote areas that require miles of hiking to reach. In other words, you can control the degree of difficulty.

The most convenient of all opportunities are inside the Gatlinburg city limits where there are four well-stocked streams, with portions designated for general fishing, sportfishing, and children only. A daily permit is required, and special rules apply to each category.

Lea prefers less-visited waters, so he often teams up with his friend Jack Snapp of Old Smoky Outfitters, a local fly-and-tackle shop and guide service. They pile into the company's Range Rover and head into the backcountry. Such forays can deliver thrilling bonuses, such as the time when Lea, fishing in a remote stream, looked up to see triplet bear cubs playing nearby.

The GSMNP is one of the last wild trout habitats in the eastern part of the United States. It is also a place where the native brook trout—referred to locally as "spec" (speckled trout)—are protected. These fish prefer higher elevations above 2,000 feet where waters are tiny and where brookies seldom exceed seven or eight inches.

Early logging operations before the park was established polluted half of the stream miles where brook trout lived. An ongoing program is trying to restore their populations to where they are self-sustaining. For this reason, some of the highest streams are closed to fishing. The park fishing regulations specify where these streams are; U.S. Geological Survey 1:24,000 Quadrangle Maps, available at park visitors centers, pinpoint the exact locations.

For fishing, some of the benefits the Smokies provide are a season that's open year-round, the privilege of fishing both the Tennessee and North Carolina portions of the park with a license from either state, and the chance to catch rainbow and brown trout for a gourmet dinner. Both fly-fishing and ultralight spinning are popular, but no bait is allowed: anglers must use artificial lures that have a single hook. There is a daily creel limit of five and a seven-inch minimum length. The possession of brook trout is prohibited.

As for the best trout waters, it's really a coin toss among many high-quality streams and rivers, large and small. Yet, the bigger waters hold plenty of braggin'-size rainbows and browns; and because there's such an immense territory within the huge expanse of the park, you can count on finding plenty of places that provide lots of elbow room.

For those who like to backpack to isolated fishing locations in order to get away from it all, camping permits can be obtained at the Sugarlands visitors center to utilize designated locations. However, anyone going into the backcountry for any reason should carefully study the regulations governing all off-road activities.

This sport and the park locations are thoroughly covered in Lea's book, *The Fly Fisherman's Guide to the Great Smoky Mountains National Park* (Cumberland House, 1998).

## Seasons and Special Events

Smokies visitation has four seasons with hardly a break in between. Winter brings skiers to the slopes above Gatlinburg and frequent snowfalls in the higher elevations—70 inches during a season is not uncommon at Newfound Gap. Spring is many people's favorite for hiking and wildflower viewing, although winter storms can appear even as late as April. Summer brings families, and finding accommodations can be challenging. Fall usage is heavy, too, especially on weekends. Cool nights and changing leaf color make this season especially attractive.

The first single event of the year for nature lovers is in Pigeon Forge in mid-January. It's the Wilderness Week of Nature. There are guided hikes, field trips, slide shows, workshops for nature photography, and—for children—wildlife drawing lessons. Call the Pigeon Forge Department of Tourism for details.

Before that, beginning mid-November and extending through February, Gatlinburg lights up for the winter with its Smoky Mountain Lights celebration, when more than two million lights guarantee not a dark spot in town. Pigeon Forge has its own Winterfest in December with three million lights (we could call all this "dueling lights") and A Smoky Mountain Christmas at Dollywood. Other holiday shows and historical trolley tours showcase both towns.

From March on, in the park and in town, activities are nonstop. Most are oriented toward nature, history, and crafts.

Wildflowers first appear in February, when stems of spring beauty start spreading a petaled blanket on entire hillsides. This show continues through May. By April a whole parade of flower species has joined in, and the annual late-April Wildflower Pilgrimage is probably the most popular event of the year. Visitors join motorcades, guided walks, and photography tours and watch slide presentations.

Late spring and all summer, the calendar is packed with special celebrations, storytelling, crafts and quilt shows, and pioneer life demonstrations. Guided nature and historical walks are very popular, including "school walks" (to a 100-year-old schoolhouse), twilight strolls through old towns, folk "sing-alongs," and "farm walks." Demonstrations include making sorghum molasses and apple butter. Instructional talks focus on wildlife poaching and other topical subjects. Through all the seasons, many presentations describe the wildlife of the park.

There is also an official Smokies' Junior Ranger program for kids 5 to 12 years old. Ask about it at Sugarlands or any campground ranger station. As in the program in the Big South Fork NRRA, the young people fill out a booklet and meet with a ranger to discuss what they've learned, then are awarded a badge. Junior Rangers also have an opportunity to participate in contests and gain additional recognition.

In autumn, with its cool nights and color changes, the walks and talks take a new focus. The forest is preparing for winter, and so is the wildlife. Slide shows tell how pioneers also prepared for the long, cold Appalachian winters. And it is also the time for hayrides in Cades Cove.

"When will the leaves turn?" is a good question, because each year is a little different. We always get clues from media reports that alert the public to the anticipated "best dates." Usually, the last half of October is when color peaks in the Smokies, especially in the lower elevations.

## Will the Forest Survive?

Should we raise a question we're not prepared to answer? Maybe so: the survival of the forest is a critical issue, and this park offers a unique opportunity to study a great variety of temperate-zone forest environments in search of solutions.

Subtle and not-so-subtle changes have occurred in the Smokies since 1934, when this area first became a national park. The name didn't come from the smoky haze that's likely to greet today's visitor looking down from the high elevations, but from the low, well-defined clouds that nestled, in the old days, among the valleys below a clear sky that revealed the distant peaks in sharp detail. How much degradation? In 1948 the visibility was 93 miles, but now it averages 22 miles and is much worse in summer.

Today's culprit is air pollution, and it's destroying more than the view. It comes from above and below: from coal-burning plants to the northwest and southwest, and from auto emissions in the immediate area. It damages many species of trees and causes discoloration on some of them. Every individual who reduces energy use helps to alleviate the problem here and elsewhere.

Did you know that the GSMNP has more than 80 percent of the old-growth forest acreage in the entire eastern United States, with some trees known to be 450 years old? Protecting the park is really protecting a whole element of nature. The enemies that threaten this resource include invasive exotic insects that are on a march of destruction. As we mentioned earlier—kudzu and honeysuckle are two examples—exotics brought into an area usually have no natural enemies present and therefore multiply at alarming rates.

The balsam woolly adelgid has already done a lot of damage, attacking the Fraser firs at high elevations. Only 5 percent of the mature trees in the Smokies have escaped being ravaged by these insects. Hand spraying with insecticide soap is an effective but costly treatment and is being used selectively on this species.

The American beech trees have a new enemy that appeared in the Smokies in 1993: the beech scale insect. The trees stand to be wiped out unless resistant strains develop. Loss of beeches will leave large areas temporarily deforested.

Another insect, the mountain-ash sawfly, has killed great numbers of this tree, which is found only in the higher elevations. And, as if that weren't enough, a pine beetle has killed hundreds of acres of pine trees. A hard winter would slow this destruction.

The gypsy moth and the hemlock woolly adelgid haven't arrived on the scene yet but are within less than 300 miles. The gypsy moth targets broadleaf trees and will be a threat to the mature oak forests. The hemlock woolly adelgid is expected to wreak destruction on mature hemlocks.

When massive areas of forest are destroyed, it isn't just the ugliness of the landscape that is of concern. Both animals and plants depend on the ecological zone's remaining intact, so there is a domino effect that disrupts the whole ecosystem.

All we can say is this: treat the forest kindly, conserve energy, and hope that the scientists who are working on the insect problems will speedily find some effective solutions.

***Where:*** Access the park from Tennessee or North Carolina. Access points in Tennessee are Gatlinburg and Townsend. Exit I-40 east of Knoxville at exit 407 (State 66) and go south to Sevierville, then take U.S. 441 through Pigeon Forge to Gatlinburg. Two alternate routes may have less traffic: from the west, exit I-40 onto U.S. 321 a few miles east of Kingston and go through Maryville, Townsend, and Pigeon Forge; from the east, take I-40 toward Asheville, take exit 435, 440, or 443, and travel west on U.S. 321 to Gatlinburg. From Chattanooga, take I-75 north, exit on U.S. 321, and drive east through Maryville, Townsend, and Pigeon Forge.
***When:*** Year-round. Some roads closed in winter.

*Admission:* Park is free.

*Amenities:* The full gamut that you'd expect in a major resort area, including skiing in winter.

*Activities:* Too many to list, but covered in the text.

*Special events:* Refer to the text.

*Other:* Visitation is heavy. Expect traffic to crawl. Make reservations early.

*For more information:* Great Smoky Mountains National Park, 107 Park Headquarters Road, Gatlinburg, TN 37738. 423-436-1200. Website, http://www.nps.gov/grsm/. Backcountry permits and reservations: 423-436-1231 (daily, 8 A.M. to 6 P.M.).

Appalachian Trail Conference, PO Box 807, Harpers Ferry, WV 25425-0807. 304-535-6331. Website, http://www.nps.gov/aptr/.

Gatlinburg Department of Tourism, 234 Airport Road, PO Box 5, Gatlinburg, TN 37738. 800-267-7088 or 423-436-2392. Website, http://www.Gatlinburg.com/.

Great Smoky Mountains Institute at Tremont, 9275 Tremont Road, Townsend, TN 37882. 423-448-6709.

Pigeon Forge Department of Tourism, 2450 Parkway, PO Box 1390, Pigeon Forge, TN 37868. 800-796-6964 or 423-453-8574. Website, http://www.pigeon-forge.tn.us/.

Accommodations: Gatlinburg, 800-822-1998; Pigeon Forge, 800-251-9100; Townsend, 423-448-6134; LeConte Lodge, 423-429-5704 (one to two years in advance).

Fly-fishing information: Old Smoky Outfitters, PO Box 488, Gatlinburg, TN 37738. 423-430-1936.

# East of "Eden"

East of the Smokies, often described as a kind of "Eden," is the mountainous eastern tip of the state. Tennesseans refer to it as Upper East Tennessee or the Tri-Cities Area, the latter referring to Bristol, Kingsport, and Johnson City. It is bordered by Virginia to the north and North Carolina to the south and east. Quaint little communities with names such as Laurel Bloomery and Flag Pond are tucked away in remote places but are accessible because roads and highways are excellent throughout. Other towns, such as historic Jonesborough, are more mainstream but retain a great sense of a heritage that dates back to the 1700s.

In this region are some of the best recreational opportunities found in the state. There are six TVA lakes: Douglas, Cherokee, Fort Patrick Henry, Boone, South Holston, and Watauga. Each provides anglers, boaters, and swimmers lots of room to pursue their sports. Additionally, there is top-quality fishing for both cold- and warm-water fish in the tailwaters of these reservoirs. Trout fishermen, hikers, campers, and hunters have access to the several hundred thousand acres in the northern portion of the Cherokee National Forest. The upper reaches of the Nolichucky and French Broad Rivers are excellent for canoeing, kayaking, and rafting. Several commercial outfitters offer rental craft and guided trips.

One thing Ardi notices here is that road signs often do not name towns, and they seldom seem to give distances. They simply identify the road itself, as in "Junction, State 173," leaving one to wonder where it might lead and how far that might be. She concluded that in this part of the state those things really don't matter. Whether you're here or "there," you'll be amazed at the scenery in every direction. After all, the mountains did not stop in the Smokies. Their presence dominates this landscape, too.

***For more information on the Northeast Region:*** Northeast Tennessee Tourism Association, PO Box 415, Jonesborough, TN 37659. 423-753-4188, ext. 25, or 800-468-6882, ext. 25. Ask for the "Mountain Heritage Tour" brochure.

## Cherokee National Forest, Northern Division

This part of the Cherokee National Forest consists of great patchwork pieces of land that generally follow the direction of the state line, lying south and east of the cities of Greeneville, Johnson City, and Bristol. These forest patches are unspoiled country. This is not the place of theme parks, water slides, or traffic jams. It *is* the place of nature's theme, tumbling waters, and wild animals (which occasionally stop traffic just by being there).

There are three Forest Service districts. As you travel east from the Smokies, they are the Nolichucky, the Unaka, and the Watauga. Since the properties are somewhat scattered, each district is divided into units. The whole forest is jointly managed with TWRA as the largest and most diverse wildlife management area in the state. It provides nesting and feeding habitats for 150 bird, 140 fish, 43 mammal, 32 amphibian, and 23 reptile species. Black bears are present, and two of the units—the Andrew Johnson near Greeneville and the Unicoi near Erwin—have bear reserves. Deer, wild hogs, red foxes, turkeys, squirrels, ruffed grouse, bobcats, barred owls, ravens, pileated woodpeckers, and timber rattlesnakes are just a few of the animals you might see in the forest.

The trail system in the Cherokee is outstanding, with 275 miles of trails in the northern district alone, plus more than 100 miles of the Appalachian Trail. The AT continues along the state line for the most part on its northward course, dips into North Carolina near Hot Springs, then follows the border again past Roan Mountain and turns west into Tennessee for some 20 miles. It then heads northeast toward Damascus, Virginia.

The recreation opportunities include auto tours, river rafting, swimming, camping, hiking, mountain biking, fishing, horseback riding, and rockhounding. Trails lead to historic sites, mountain overlooks, waterfalls, and trout streams. The Nolichucky Ranger District has five camping and nine picnic sites, plus a shooting range, a boat ramp, and swimming at one location. The Unaka Ranger District has three camping and seven picnic sites; and the Watauga Ranger District has six camping and picnic sites, two shooting ranges, and three boat-launching areas.

All the picnic areas have tables, fireplaces, and trash receptacles. Developed campgrounds are usually open from May through October. Availability is first come, first served. Campgrounds do not have electrical or sewer hookups. Throughout the Cherokee, primitive camping is allowed except where posted otherwise. Primitive camping is free, but fees are charged in the developed campgrounds.

Cherokee National Forest trails do not require permits, but it is always a good idea to let people know your hiking itinerary. Extensive hiking maps (including quadrangle maps with contour intervals) and recreation schedules are available at the three district offices.

Tennessee, unlike its neighbor North Carolina, has only limited resources of semiprecious gemstones. One it does have is unakite, a variety of billion-year-old granite that contains pistachio green epidote, pink feldspar, quartz, and sometimes other minerals, too. It is present in the Unaka mountains—but hard to find—and is not often available in polished stones. Ardi found a slightly different form of it near the North Carolina border southwest of Erwin in the vicinity of Flag Pond. In that rock, the epidote had been altered by natural processes into sausserite and was black instead of green.

People interested in rockhounding should contact one of the Cherokee National Forest district offices first and ask about restrictions. Rockhounding, which means the collection of a few specimens for hobby use, *not commercially*, is generally allowed in the Cherokee, but it is important not to collect them on private land unless permission has been granted by the owner.

*Where:* Along the North Carolina border from the Great Smoky Mountains National Park to Virginia.
*When:* Year-round. Camping generally May through October.
*Admission:* Free. Some day-use and camping fees.
*Amenities:* Developed campgrounds, picnic sites, trails, boat-launch ramps, shooting ranges.
*Activities:* Hiking, wildlife viewing, picnicking, camping, horseback riding, mountain biking, swimming, river rafting, photography, scenic auto tours.
*Other:* Barrier-free access in some locations.
*For more information:* Forest Supervisor, Cherokee National Forest, 2800 North Ocoee Street NW, PO Box 2010, Cleveland, TN 37320. 423-476-9700. Campground reservations, 800-280-2267.

U.S. District Ranger, Nolichucky District Cherokee National Forest, 121 Austin Street, Greeneville, TN 37745. 423-638-4109.

U.S. District Ranger, Unaka District Cherokee National Forest, Johnson City Highway, Erwin, TN 37650. 423-743-4452 or 423-743-5871.

## Erwin National Fish Hatchery

Even if the Erwin National Fish Hatchery weren't at Erwin, we'd find a reason to go there. We'd drive down from Johnson City on I-181 and watch the mountains getting closer and closer and feel the exhilaration that comes with the anticipation of a high mountain adventure.

This hatchery is different from the one at Dale Hollow. It

has a twofold purpose in support of the National Broodstock Program: to supply brood fish for other hatcheries (including the one at Dale Hollow) and to ship eggs to states all over the nation. Fifteen million disease-free eggs are produced annually. The entire operation is dedicated to rainbow trout only, although six strains with individual characteristics and different hatching times are involved.

Brood fish are raised to three- to six-pound weights in the hatchery's 24 raceways, 6 on the lower level and 18 on the upper level. Fish viewing is permitted at some of the raceways and the indoor tanks, but other places are off-limits.

The hatchery has a visitors center and a picnic pavilion, both open to the public seven days a week during daylight hours. The 30-acre property also provides a self-guided nature trail that offers views of ponds and waterfowl. It is an opportunity to walk through a mature forest where some trees are 300 years old and to make nature discoveries.

During periods when the adjacent Unicoi County Heritage Museum is open (seasonally), self-guided audiotapes are available there.

Do plan to look around the area at some of the other interesting places. We suggest taking State 81 to Jonesborough for a scenic drive and then a "more-than-you-can-eat" dinner at the celebrated Parson's Table restaurant in a historic church building just across the railroad track from the courthouse.

*Where:* Take I-181 south of Johnson City to exit 19 at Erwin. Cross the interstate, then turn left at the first stop light onto U.S. 19/23. The hatchery entrance is on the left.
*When:* Year-round. Hatchery open daily. Museum, May 1 to October 1.
*Admission:* Free.
*Amenities:* Hatchery, museum, picnic pavilion, self-guided nature trail.

*Activities:* Guided hatchery tours by request, picnicking, wildlife viewing, photography.

*For more information:* Erwin National Fish Hatchery, 520
Federal Hatchery Road, Erwin, TN 37650. 423-743-4712.

The Parson's Table, 100 West Woodrow Avenue, Jonesborough, TN 37659-1232. 423-753-8002.


## Roan Mountain State Resort Park

The greeting card has a photograph of a grassy mountain bald
with distinctive high-meadow features that are unmistakably
Roan Mountain: rhododendrons blooming in shades of light
red, pink, and purple; a few spruces and Fraser firs thrusting
upward; a backdrop of misty mountains and small, puffy
white clouds. The grasses are bending ever so slightly, bringing wind sounds to mind. It's a view that hikers see from the
Appalachian Trail for 10 miles from Carvers Gap to Big
Hump Mountain. This is the longest stretch of grassy balds
in the world and a place that many believe to be the most
beautiful part of the whole Appalachian Trail.

At 6,286 feet (just 356 feet lower than Clingmans Dome)
the Roan marks the highest elevation in the Iron Mountains,
which divide the two states in this easternmost part of Tennessee. In fact, the mountain straddles the state line, but its
*peak* is in North Carolina. It qualifies as a Tennessee destination, though, with Roan Mountain State Park just 10 miles
away providing the logical base for lodging and activities.

Because of the high elevation, the heaviest visitation at
Roan Mountain is in the summer, and the most popular time
of summer is the last half of June, when 600 acres of catawba
rhododendrons bloom in a natural mountaintop garden. Also
in summer, the park's large heated swimming pool is open
from Memorial Day through Labor Day. Cabins are reserved
well ahead of time for the whole season (however, the camp-

grounds are first come, first served). Weekends are always very busy through October, but in September the park is not heavily visited during weekdays. October, with fall color, brings more people again throughout the month.

Winter attracts another kind of visitor, since this is the only cross-country-skiing state park in the South. The park has three skiing trails for a total of eight and a half miles. A private company gives skiing lessons and provides rental equipment and guided trips to the top of the Roan.

We enjoy staying in the cabins, which are nestled among tall trees and not-so-tall rhododendrons that provide spicy fragrances. The cabins are clean and modern, with fully furnished kitchens and screened porches that overlook small clearings, but there are no microwaves, TVs, or telephones. We find that refreshing.

Mountain weather can be changeable hour by hour, so a day can offer many different moods. Fast-moving, swirling clouds of mist in early morning are dispersed by the sun. It may be hazy for a while, but when rains clear the air, the folds of undulating hills receding for miles in the distance are clearly visible. In other words, when you've seen it once, you haven't seen it all.

Besides the AT, there are U.S. Forest Service trails in both the Cherokee and Pisgah National Forests (the Pisgah is in North Carolina). There are also eight trails in the park, ranging from less than a half mile to four and three-tenths miles. Some lead to high places, while others follow Doe River or smaller streams. Backcountry camping (with campsites but no shelters) is permitted only on the boundary trail system consisting of seven and four-tenths miles of trails. Trail maps are available at park headquarters.

Another trail in the area is the historic Overmountain Victory Trail used by Revolutionary War soldiers on a march from Elizabethton (Sycamore Shoals) to Kings Mountain, South Carolina, where they defeated the British in a battle that reputedly turned the tide of the war. The Overmountain Men camped at Sheltering Rock on the Doe River on September 26, 1780, an event that is reenacted each year on that date.

According to Ranger Walt Stewart, the Doe River, which runs through the park, is one of the best trout streams in the area. It has brown trout, brookies, and some rainbow. Additionally, it is stocked with rainbow every other week from March to mid-June. A special annual event is a trout tournament for kids in May.

The visitors center has memorabilia from the past on display, including prehistoric artifacts. On the wall is an old tavern sign that says:

> *Fourpence the night for bed.*
> *Sixpence with supper.*
> *No more than five to sleep in one bed.*
> *No boots to be worn in bed.*
> *Organ grinders sleep in the washhouse.*
> *No dogs allowed upstairs.*
> *No beer allowed in the kitchen.*
> *No razor grinders or tinkers taken in.*

Other historic places in the park include the Peg Leg Mine site, on which stood an iron-ore mine operated by the Crab Orchard Mining Company in the 1800s, less than a half mile from the visitors center. The Dave Miller Homestead, open to park visitors from Memorial Day through Labor Day, is a farm that dates back to 1870, with the present farmstead built in 1908. It remains now as it was in the early 1900s, with a main dwelling and various outbuildings. Learn here about the rigors and joys of life when farms and families were self-sufficient though virtually isolated.

Interpretive programs and events take place throughout the season, but for nature lovers the Roan Mountain Naturalists

Rally, held one weekend each September, is truly special. It draws people from all over the South and offers nature walks, wildflower hikes, talks, and slide shows conducted by experts.

If mountains are in your blood, you know it, but it's not so easy to explain. These words from the greeting card we described (published by Lasting Impressions, Boone, North Carolina), come close:

"In the mountains, the sun comes up, and then it sets. The time that passes stays in your mind forever."

*Where:* Twenty miles south of Elizabethton. From U.S. 11E between Johnson City and Bristol, turn south on U.S. 19E past Elizabethton to the town of Roan Mountain, then go south (right) on State 143 for three miles to the park.

*When:* Daily, 8 A.M. to 10 P.M. Restaurant open daily June through August and again in October (partial schedule in September). Campground closed November 15 to April 1. Dave Miller Homestead open Wednesday through Sunday, May 30 through Labor Day, 9 A.M. to 5 P.M. Road from Carvers Gap to Rhododendron Gardens closed approximately December 1 through March 31.

*Admission:* Park is free. Modest fees for camping and swimming pool. Cabin rentals by day or week. Senior-citizen discounts for 62 and over.

*Amenities:* Interpretive center, 30 cabins, 2 campgrounds (bathhouses, laundromat), full-service restaurant (May 1 through October 31), picnic shelters, gristmill, pioneer farmstead, swimming pool, tennis courts, ball fields, playground, snack bars, nature trails and Appalachian Trail.

*Activities:* Swimming, fishing, hiking, backpacking, wildlife viewing, photography, picnicking, tennis, cross-country skiing, outdoor field games, guided hikes, and special weekend programs Memorial Day through Labor Day.

*Special events:* Roan Mountain Wildflower Tours and Birdwalks (May), Trout Tournament (May), Rhododendron Fes-

tival (June), three-day Naturalists' Rally (mid-September), Fall Festival (September), Reenactment of Revolutionary War Overmountain Victory March (September 26).
*Other:* Barrier-free access.
*For more information:* Roan Mountain State Resort Park, Route 1, Box 236, Roan Mountain, TN, 37687. 423-772-3303. Cabin reservations, 800-250-8620. Website, http://www.state .tn.us/environment/parks/ then select.

Appalachian Trail Conference, PO Box 807, Harpers Ferry, WV 25425-0807. 304-535-6331. Website, http://www.nps.gov/ aptr/.

## Two Caverns: Appalachian and Bristol

Something old, something new. It's not a wedding we're talking about but two caverns in Upper East Tennessee that we found to be interesting field trips when we were staying at Roan Mountain. We always seem to think of caverns on rainy days (which can occur frequently in the mountains), but when we're incorporating a scenic auto tour in the plan, we opt for nice, sunny weather for the event.

### Appalachian Caverns

Appalachian Caverns, managed by a nonprofit organization dedicated to cave education and preservation, is the "new" one. The cave was 500 million years in the making, but it's been open to the public for a relatively short time—since 1991. The walkways, more than a mile long, are home to more animal life than other caves we've visited. One gray bat colony is estimated at 12,000 individuals. The gray bat is one of five bat species in the cave. There is also an underground river, Muddy Creek, that runs through and contains carp, bluegills, catfish, and turtles. It is called Linville Creek inside the cave.

The tour lasts a little more than an hour and takes you through "the largest great room in a Tennessee cave" according to our guide, Shannon Tignor, who said it is 100 feet wide, 135 feet from the water level to the ceiling, and 1,400 feet long. (Appalachian Caverns and Cumberland Caverns will have to slug it out over this one!) He also showed us a bottomless pool—that is, sonar has not been able to identify the depth. Divers went down  145 feet without reaching bottom. They did find a hole in the rock and an underground lake that they estimated to contain five surface acres. It may turn out to be larger than the Lost Sea.

Several types of rock formations are seen on the tour. The minerals visible include black manganese, white calcite, and rust-colored iron oxide in limestone bedrock. Others, such as very rare butterfly onyx, are present but not where the commercial tour goes. The cave is being explored by an archaeologist, who has discovered animal skeletons and other remains (with evidence that bears and caribou were present) and Indian artifacts, some objects dating back 15,000 years. There is a historical past as well. Two brothers, Jim and John Linville, lived here for several years, and John's journal recounts that period in the early 1800s.

This is a massive cave with 52 known openings and countless chambers, two of which have not been mapped but appear endless, according to our guide. Some rooms are large, even spectacular, definitely worth a look (though not having the richness of formations we've seen in some other commercial caves). This may change. Amy's Dreamland, a recently discovered room having rare and fragile formations, may be opened for public tours in the future.

Three-hour wild tours are offered for the more adventuresome, requiring passing through crawl spaces and doing some strenuous climbing, but revealing some beautiful rooms. These tours require advance booking.

## Bristol Caverns

Bristol Caverns, open commercially since 1944, is five miles south of Bristol. Gary Barnett, one of the owners, gave us an exceptional tour of these caverns, which have an abundance of formations and an interesting history. We were impressed with several elements and appreciated that the lighting was natural, enabling us to see the actual rock colors throughout.

This cave system has been well explored and mapped and is known to be about 78 acres in all. One fairly large section has not yet been commercialized, but long-range plans call for some of it to be opened. The animals here include two species each of cave crickets and spiders, three salamanders (black, Missouri, and hellbender), and an occasional stray bat. Since bats like dark, quiet places, they avoid the cave areas that are lit and where the tours go. This cave, too, has an underground stream, with a water flow that varies according to the seasonal rains.

As we walked through the different levels of the cave, Gary pointed out and explained many types of formations. Stalactites, stalagmites, helictites (stalactites that have become twisted or bent), columns, arches, cave coral, soda straws, flowstone, and rimstone are just some of the formations that together create a fascinating underground environment of cascades, draperies, pools, and other shapes. Some formations resembled giant waterfalls, and others reminded us of simple objects such as tobacco leaves.

One spot, nicknamed Panorama Point, provided a view of all three levels. The lowest level is the youngest at 65 million years, while the upper two levels are estimated to be 200 million years old.

We found an interesting scenic drive from Bristol Caverns back to Roan Mountain State Park that we'd like to recommend. Basically, continue east on 421 across South Holston Lake and cross Delaney Mountain, then drop into Shady Valley. The AT crosses your path just before you descend into the valley. You will climb again and go over Iron Mountain at Grindstone Knob, then down to Mountain City. Follow State 67 southwest past Watauga Lake and turn left onto U.S. 19E at Hampton. You'll discover scenic areas and trails along this route, and you'll go through several parts of the Cherokee National Forest. You will also pass a restaurant on Watauga Lake near the marina that may tempt you with fish dinners.

***Where:*** Appalachian Caverns: off I-81 west of Bristol. Take exit 69 and go south on State 37 through Blountville. Turn right onto Buncombe Road and continue for one and a half miles, then turn left on Cave Hill Road and go half a mile. From the south, take U.S. 11E from Johnson City to Bristol, exit onto State 37 and go north to Buncombe Road.

Bristol Caverns: from Bristol, take U.S. 421 (exit 3 from I-81) south to Bristol Caverns Highway; turn left and follow the signs (five miles total).

***When:*** Appalachian Caverns: year-round. Monday through Saturday, 9 A.M. to 6 P.M. (opens 11 A.M. October 1 through February 29); 1 P.M. to 6 P.M. on Sunday. Closed Thanksgiving Day and from December 24 through January 3. Bristol Caverns: year-round, daily. March 15 through November 14, 9 A.M. to 6 P.M.; November 15 through March 14, 10 A.M. to 5 P.M. Last tour leaves one hour before closing. Closed Thanksgiving and Christmas Day.

***Admission:*** Modest fee.

***Amenities:*** Gift shop (both locations).

***Activities:*** Cave tours (Appalachian Caverns has wild cave tours).

*For more information:* Appalachian Caverns, 420 Cave Hill Road, Blountville, TN 37617. 423-323-2337 or 423-279-7143.

Bristol Caverns, 1157 Bristol Caverns Highway, PO Box 851, Bristol, TN 37621. 423-878-2011.

E-mail, bjmattox@preferred.com

Website, http://pages.preferred.com/~bjmattox/bcave.htm

## Bays Mountain Park and Planetarium

The part of eastern Tennessee between Morristown and Kingsport, reached by I-81 and U.S. 11W, is an area rich in history and natural features. These include Cherokee Lake on the Holston River, Elrod Falls in Hancock County, the historic town of Rogersville, and long Bays Mountain that ends at the Kingsport city limits.

If we lived in this area, we would be spending many days at Bays Mountain Park and Planetarium. It is a 3,000-acre nature preserve with animal exhibits in natural habitats, 25 miles of hiking trails, a 44-acre lake, a planetarium and observatory, an interpretive nature center, a gift shop, and a farmstead museum—in our view, a class act!

From the paved parking lot, we like to head first to the animal habitats. On our last visit we watched a bobcat that had found a baby squirrel that must have dropped from its nest. The squirrel was trying to get away but couldn't crawl very well. Soon the bobcat had it in its mouth and was carrying it away. A raccoon habitat is nearby, but these nocturnal animals, though they can be very entertaining, are usually sleeping during the day.

The otter environment was our next stop. There is a pool, and in it a rock that looks like a doughnut turned on its side. The mother otter would swim through the "doughnut hole" belly up, then right herself. At that point, her two babies would climb on her back for a piggyback ride. This amusing trick was repeated over and over.

At the lakeshore not far from the otters is a waterfowl aviary. There are wood-duck nesting boxes, and we saw several kinds of ducks in the lake. Many of them stay year-round.

The gray wolves, nearly black in appearance, were an addition in 1992—three littermates that included a male and two females. Their ancestors for several generations back were captive-born wolves. It was feeding time when we were there, and a few loud "yoop, yoop" calls brought them running.

A large deer habitat has an elevated platform that provides clear views of that entire area. Among the deer we saw was a large buck with a handsome set of antlers.

The extensive trail system takes hikers around the lake and atop the nearby ridges. Individual trails range from 300 feet to four and eight-tenths miles. Being connected, they easily allow all-day hikes. Free trail maps, available in the park gift shop, help assure that you won't get lost. Along the way, hikers may glimpse deer, beavers, rabbits, weasels, foxes, woodchucks, squirrels, geese, wild turkeys, grouse, herons, hawks, and various kinds of warblers. Some roads are open to mountain bikes, which must first pass inspection by park personnel.

The nature center has an exhibits gallery and a saltwater aquarium on its lower level. The main level has a gift shop, which is also an information center. That's where we met Senior Naturalist Joe H. Taft, who took us to the Steadman Farmstead Museum across the parking lot. It has pioneer tools and implements on display and depicts the mountain heritage of the people and the land.

Bays Mountain Park has a full activity schedule on weekends year-round. These include star watches and programs about bats, snakes, venomous animals, and wolves. You can join wildflower walks in April and May and take barge rides from May until fall. Something special is always offered on weekdays in summer. Choose from barge rides, wolf shows, canoe tours, and moonlight hikes.

Stargazing is another popular activity. The observatory has an eight-inch refractor telescope and several reflector telescopes, with viewing opportunities scheduled periodically. The planetarium in the nature center regularly provides shows, too.

Coming to Bays Mountain is easier than leaving. The signs direct you toward the park, but you could make a wrong turn as you leave and end up looking at more rural landscapes than you bargained for. Our advice: make notes!

*Where:* From I-81 going north, take exit 51, turn right immediately on New Moore Road, then left on Princeton Street. There are several turns, all marked, on the way to Bays Mountain. The final turn is onto Bays Mountain Road.

*When:* Year-round. 8:30 A.M. to 5 P.M. Monday through Friday and until 8 P.M. Saturday and Sunday (opens 1 P.M. on Sunday). Nature Center has the same hours, except it opens at 1 P.M. on Saturday. Park has extended hours (until 8 P.M.) daily June through August and follows Nature Center hours November through February. Closed Thanksgiving, Christmas Eve, Christmas Day, and New Year's Day.

*Admission:* $3.00 per car. $1.50 per person for planetarium shows, barge rides, nature programs.

*Amenities:* Nature interpretive center with exhibits, Discovery Theater, library, gift shop, live animal habitats, aquariums, saltwater touch pool, planetarium, observatory, Farmstead Museum, outdoor amphitheater, nature trails.

*Activities:* Wildlife viewing, hiking, photography, year-round interpretive programs, nature videos, telescope viewing, lake barge rides, canoe tours, planetarium shows, fishing (for people under 16 and over 65 only), picnicking, mountain bike riding (rules apply).

***Special events:*** "Howlings" (most months), wildflower walks (April and May), Fall Color Barge Day (October).
***Other:*** Barrier-free access. No food or drink concessions or machines. Pets not allowed on premises. During snowy weather, call ahead for park conditions.
***For more information:*** Bays Mountain Park and Planetarium, 853 Bays Mountain Park Road, Kingsport, TN 37660. 423-229-9447. Website, http://www.kpt1.tricon.net/Org/baysmtn/.

## Warriors' Path State Park

While Bays Mountain west of Kingsport provides outstanding mountain terrain, Warriors' Path State Park, three miles southeast of this city, has elements just as appealing though different. What the two locations offer in common are opportunities for nature education and appreciation.

You might say Warriors' Path is more recreation oriented. That's true in general. Set on the shores of the Patrick Henry Reservoir on the Holston River, just off I-81, it is an easily accessed destination for fishing, boating, swimming, camping, picnicking, hiking, mountain biking, horseback riding, golfing, and other outdoor activities. It is widely recognized, though, for something quite different: its award-winning programs in outdoor education for schools, educators, and the general public.

Marty Silver, park naturalist, was given the distinguished Roger Tory Peterson Award for Nature Educator of the Year in 1994 and then in 1997 was awarded the James L. Bailey Award for Excellence in Environmental Education by the State of Tennessee. Marty works with around 40,000 students each year from elementary school through college and organizes and conducts education seminars for adults, attracting guest speakers from among the region's most respected naturalists, scientists, and teachers.

The park's free nature-oriented special events open to the public start in January with the Winter Gardening Seminar. Spring Festival, incorporating three days of naturalist-led hikes and workshops, is held in April. From June through August, nature and recreation activities take place daily, Tuesday through Saturday. They include guided hikes, creek walks, historical tours, crafts, games, junior naturalists, and campfire talks. In July the Folklife Festival is a daylong event that features demonstrations of traditional life skills and crafts. Games, contests, and old-timey music add to the festive atmosphere. Nature Nearby is October's offering, an environmental-education workshop for teachers and youth leaders that shows how to use natural classrooms to bring conservation to life. Autumn Outdoors is a two-day event in November that combines a Friday-evening lecture and an all-day Saturday workshop. The appropriate emphasis on a December morning is Adopt-a-Tree Day. (How appropriate to get seedlings just when Christmas trees are being harvested!)

Whether you're interested in special events and nature study or you simply want to enjoy time in the outdoors at your own pace, this 980-acre park has the room and facilities to accommodate your wishes. The modern campground has 135 campsites and modern bathhouses with hot showers, and a check-in station where you can purchase supplies and snacks. Next to the campground is an Olympic-size swimming pool and water slide. Patrick Henry Lake has a marina (which rents paddleboats and fishing boats) and free boat-launching ramps. Modern picnic grounds in several locations provide tables, grills, rest rooms, and shelters.

For hiking, the park offers nearly 11 miles of trails, including the popular Fall Creek Loop and Holston Bluffs. Sinking Waters Trail, recently developed, is a 1½-mile loop through a new area offering excellent views of wetlands and the diverse wildlife attracted to it.

***Where:*** From I-81, exit on State 36 and go north to Hemlock Road (the fourth traffic light). Turn right and continue to the park entrance.

***When:*** Year-round, daily.

***Admission:*** Free. Fees for camping.

***Amenities:*** Campground, golf course, swimming pool, marina, boat rentals, picnicking grounds and shelters, recreation hall, stables, hiking trails, fitness trail, cycling path, playgrounds.

***Activities:*** Fishing, boating, swimming, camping, picnicking, hiking, bicycling, wildlife viewing, nature study, photography, daily summer programs (Tuesday through Saturday from June through August).

***Special events:*** Winter Gardening Seminar (January, preregistration required), Spring Festival (April), Folklife Festival (July), Nature Nearby (October, preregistration required), Autumn Outdoors (November), Adopt-A-Tree Day (December). Free.

***For more information:*** Warriors' Path State Park, 490 Hemlock Road, Kingsport, TN 37663. 423-239-8531 or 423-239-6786. Website, http://www.state.tn.us/environment/parks/ then select.

## Farmhouse Gallery and Gardens

We learned of this place one morning when we were staying at Hawley House Bed and Breakfast in Jonesborough (a place we recommend). Dr. Larry H. Brown and his wife, Deborah, had been to the Farmhouse Gallery and Gardens a few miles south of Johnson City and gave a glowing report. Several aspects intrigued us, and we decided to investigate.

The scenario is this: Johnny Lynch, a wildlife artist, and his wife, Pat, buy a 70-acre farm that they decide to turn into a wildlife sanctuary. It has a 160-year-old log cabin that Johnny wants to preserve, so he makes it his studio and adds a greenhouse. Pat becomes interested in growing, drying, and selling wildflowers and herbal teas. They add other gift items, such as wood carvings, to their gallery which features Johnny's wildlife art. They find artifacts in the surrounding area and display them in glass cases.

Each year they add new elements, such as spring-fed, clear water ponds stocked with trout and special food plots and plants that attract wildlife. They create little waterfalls, walls made of stacked rocks, perennial and display gardens, and wildflower walkways. And they put up squirrel boxes, bluebird houses, purple-martin houses, and bat houses. Their three children—Robin, Trevor, and Amy—grow up and participate in the family business when time allows.

By 1994, Johnny's art has gained in popularity and is advertised regularly in *Wildlife Art News*. Their wildflower gardens are perhaps the state's largest and most diverse among those on private property. An outdoor pavilion is complete. They are working on herb gardens, and they are adding trails through the wooded hills that rise at the rear of the property beyond the fields. They plan three and a half miles of self-guided trails and plan to offer guided hikes to groups. Other group activities already established are seminars, talks, and classes in watercolor painting, pencil drawing, and photography.

That was the situation when we first met Johnny and Pat, and now most of these dreams have been realized. It gets better and better, though. Each year new plants and features are added.

It's hard to pick a best time of year to visit. There is a winter goose population of 40 to 80 Canadas. Wood ducks appear the first of February, use the nesting boxes, and stay until the end of September. At different times, birds appear and stay awhile. These include many kinds of warblers as well as indigo buntings, blue grosbeaks, and scarlet tanagers. There are pileated and several other woodpeckers. May and June are months to see baby ducks and geese. Other mammals include deer, peacocks, chipmunks, squirrels, opossums, raccoons, and foxes. The ponds have trout, bass, bream, catfish, and a good collection of turtles.

In April and May the wildflower gardens are bursting with color. This continues through July and again in the fall. To give you a sense of the variety, just from where we were sitting in the pavilion we could see purple coneflowers, jewelweed, boneset, blue lobelias, thalia, impatiens, cattails, hostas, pink cosmos, ironweed, salvias, black-eyed Susans, daylilies, wild red hibiscus, cardinal flowers, butterfly bush, water lilies, ornamental grasses, bicolor lespedezas, evening primroses, joe-pye weed, Jerusalem artichokes, goldenrod, gloriosa daisies, "sensitive plant" (in a hanging pot), and sedum autumn joy.

Special events are held each year, including an annual Autumn Jubilee and Open House on a Saturday in early October. It features barbecue, "press your own" apple cider, and bluegrass music. Spring events include a Fiddlers and Fiddleheads Festival in April with emphasis on wildflowers and music. Another is Heritage Days and Nature's Ways in May. From 10 A.M. until 6 P.M. the focus is on outdoor cooking, wild greens, old-timey ways, and wildlife and gardening seminars. Pat serves samples of her herbal teas and homemade jellies of elderberry, mulberry, blackheart cherry, and autumn olive.

This is a case where a very nice and talented couple is living their dream and sharing it with others. What they've done is inspiring. It's been hard work, but they have had help from friends who are biologists and wildlife experts and from some state agencies such as the Tennessee Division of Forestry.

Yet, creating a wildlife habitat is something that many of us can do. If a visit to the Farmhouse Gallery and Gardens tempts you to follow the Lynches' example—even if in a smaller way—we suggest contacting the National Wildlife Federation (address follows) or your state NWF affiliate. Making it a family project can be a lot of fun and very satisfying!

*Where:* From Johnson City, go south on I-181 (U.S. 19/23), exit 28, left on Okolona Road to the dead end, then south (right) on Unicoi Drive (the old Erwin-Johnson City highway) for two miles. The gallery is on the left (look for the covered bridge). From Erwin, take exit 23, go right to the dead end, then turn left (north) on Unicoi Drive and go three miles.

*When:* Year-round. Tuesday through Saturday, 10 A.M. to 5 P.M.; Sunday, 1 P.M. to 5 P.M. Closed Monday and Christmas Day.

*Admission:* Free.

*Amenities:* Display gardens, wildlife observation areas, walking trails, ponds, studio-gallery, outdoor pavilion.

*Activities:* Nature walks, photography, wildlife viewing, birdwatching, picnicking, art classes, talks, seminars.

*Special events:* Fiddlers and Fiddleheads Festival (April), Heritage Days and Nature's Ways Festival (May), Autumn Jubilee and Open House (October), catered events.

*Other:* Barrier-free access (some areas).

*For more information:* Johnny and Pat Lynch, Farmhouse Gallery and Gardens, Route 2, Box 112, Unicoi, TN 37692. Phone, 800-952-6043 or 423-743-8799. Fax, 423-743-0796. E-mail, lynch.farmhouse@prodigy.net.

National Wildlife Federation, 8925 Leesburg Pike, Vienna, VA 22184 (Backyard Wildlife Habitat program, same address). 703-790-4000. Orders, 800-477-5560. Website, http://www .nwf.org/nwf/home.html.

Hawley House Bed and Breakfast, 114 East Woodrow Avenue, Jonesborough, TN 37659. 423-753-8869.

# Reading Guide

## *Author's Short List*

There are a few books that we use a lot in our travels around the state and wouldn't want to be without. Other titles included in this short list have been recommended by people we interviewed. As we visited the places mentioned in our book, we were pleased to find so many gift shops well stocked with books just ready to be discovered. Consider this list simply a suggested starting point. Enjoy!

*Backyard Naturalist*, by Craig Tufts. National Wildlife Federation (8925 Leesburg Pike, Vienna, VA 22184), 1993. Paper. A great read that will get you digging and planting.

*Best of the Great Smoky Mountains: A Hiker's Guide to Trails and Attractions*, by Russ Manning and Sondra Jamieson. Mountain Laurel Place, 1991. Paper. These two have been everywhere and tell all.

*Caving Basics*, 3d ed., edited by G. Thomas Rea. National Speleological Society (2813 Cave Avenue, Huntsville, AL 35810-4431; 205-852-1300), 1992. Paper. Before you start caving, read this, join a local grotto, and contact the NSS. Stay safe!

*Cumberland Caverns*, by Larry E. Matthews. National Speleological Society (2813 Cave Avenue, Huntsville, AL 35810-4431; 205-852-1300), 1989. Paper. Reads like a novel. Need we say more?

*The Fly Fisherman's Guide to the Great Smoky Mountains National Park*, by H. Lea Lawrence. Cumberland House, 1998. Paper. OK, so Lea wrote this, but even so, it's the best and most definitive guide on the subject.

*Growing and Propagating Wildflowers*, by Harry R. Phillips. University of North Carolina Press, 1985. Horticulturalist Jenny Andrews says, "Read this."

*Hiking the Big South Fork*, 2d ed., by Brenda D. Coleman and Jo Anna Smith. University of Tennessee Press, 1993. Paper. A well-researched and valuable hiker's guide to this vast region.

*Hiking Trails of the Smokies*, by Great Smoky Mountains Natural History Association (115 Park Headquarters Road, Gatlinburg, TN 37738; 615-436-7318), 1994. Paper.

*Historic Cumberland Plateau: An Explorer's Guide*, by Russ Manning. University of Tennessee Press, 1993. Hardcover.

*Mountain Roads and Quiet Places*, by Jerry DeLaughter. Great Smoky Mountains Natural History Association (115 Park Headquarters Road, Gatlinbutg, TN 37738; 615-436-7318), 1986. Paper.

*National Audubon Society Field Guides* (Birds, Wildflowers, Butterflies, Insects and Spiders, Mammals, Mushrooms, Rocks and Minerals, Trees, Eastern Forests). We take these with us everywhere. So, who has room for luggage?

*Natural Wonders of Kentucky*, by Ardi Lawrence. Country Roads Press, 1998. Paper. Not exactly Tennessee, of course, but Ardi will forgive you for crossing the border.

***Our Restless Earth: The Geologic Regions of Tennessee***, by Edward T. Luther. University of Tennessee Press, 1977. Paper. Geology was never so fascinating to the layperson.

***Our Southern Highlanders***, by Horace Kephart. University of Tennessee Press, 1976. The classic that describes Appalachian mountain people and their culture.

***Sand County Almanac: And Sketches Here and There***, by Aldo Leopold. Oxford University Press, 1949, 1987, 1989. Tops on everybody's list.

***South Cumberland and Fall Creek Falls: A Hiker's Guide to Trails and Attractions***, by Russ Manning and Sondra Jamieson. Mountain Laurel Place, 1990. Paper.

***Tennessee Atlas and Gazetteer***, 2d ed. DeLorme Mapping Company (PO Box 298, Freeport, ME 04032), 1992. Paper. Never tour Tennessee back roads without it.

***The Tennessee Conservationist*** (magazine). Department of Environment and Conservation (401 Church Street, Nashville, TN 37243-0440; 615-532-0060). Great articles and photography, and all the latest news.

***Tennessee Wildlife Viewing Guide***, by Paul Hamel. Falcon Press, 1993. Paper. A necessity if you're looking for wildlife. This book is sold in all Tennessee state parks.

***Wilderness Trails of Tennessee's Cherokee National Forest***, edited by William H. Skelton. University of Tennessee Press, 1992.

# Index

Abraham Lincoln Museum, 227, 230
Abrams Creek, 241, 243
Abrams Falls, 244
Adopt-a-Tree Day, 272, 273
Adventure Guild, 150
Airpark Inn, 4, 5
Alfred Reagan place, 238
Alum Cave Trail, 246, 248
Alum Ford, 106
Alum Gap Camp Area, 154
American Museum of Science and Energy,
    205–7
Amphitheater Trail, 71
Amy's Dreamland, 265
Anderson County Tourism Council, 218
Anderson Falls, 151
Andrew Johnson unit, 256
Andrews, James J., 180
Angel Falls Overlook, 103
Angel Falls Rapid, 103
Animal rehabilitation/shelter, 4, 21, 29, 63,
    177–78
Anthodites, 198
Appalachian Caverns, 264–66, 267, 268
Appalachian Plateau, 97
Appalachian powerhouse, 191
Appalachian Trail (AT), 230–31, 233, 245,
    256, 260
Appalachian Trail Conference, 254, 264
Apple Festival, 52
April Wildflower Festival and plant sale, 176
Aquariums
    Memphis Zoo, 11–16
    Tennessee Aquarium, 161, 163–67
Aqueduct, 136
Arbor Day, 185
Arch Lake, 110
Army Corps of Engineers, U.S., 114
Arts & crafts fairs, 6, 38, 40, 144
"As the Indians Lived", 183
Astronomy programs/star watching, 107,
    229, 270
Audubon Acres, 178, 182–85
Audubon Wildlife Festival, 183
Autumn Colors Celebration, 144
Autumn Jubilee and Open House, 275, 276
Autumn Outdoors, 272, 273
Autumn Steam Excursions, 181, 182

Backcountry camping, 50, 106, 125, 243, 261
Bacon rind, 198
Bagel Peddler, 189
Bald Mountain, 189
Bald River Falls, 190, 193
Bandy Creek, 100, 101, 102, 106
Bandy Creek District, 102
Bandy Creek Riding Stables, 105, 107
Barkley Dam, 48
Barkley Lake, 45, 48, 50, 51
Bats, 70, 264, 266
Battery Place, 179
Battle Above the Clouds, The (painting), 168
Battle Creek, 148
Bays Mountain Park and Planetarium,
    268–71
Bean Mountain, 192
Bears, 64, 239–40, 256
Bee Rock, 133–35
Bell, Montgomery, 78–79
Bicycling, 118–19, 139
Big Bone Cave, 143
Big Branch Creek, 104
Big Creek, 243
Big Creek Gulf Trail, 154
Big Creek Rim Trail, 154
Big Hill Pond, 33
Big Hill Pond State Rustic Park and
    Natural Area, 32–35
Big Pecan Tree, 36–37
Big Ridge, 225
Big Ridge State Park, 224–26
Big South Fork, 98–126
Big South Fork National River and
    Recreation Area (NRRA), 98–108
Big South Fork River, 104
Big South Fork Scenic Railway, 106
Big Valley Loop, 225
Big Valley Trail, 225
Bike World, Inc., 55
Biosphere reserves, 49, 162, 202
Bird Day, 65, 66
Bird Mountain, 125
Bird Seed Sale, 178
Black Canyon, 151
Black Mountain, 129
Blind, gardens for, 24–25
Blue Heron, 106

Blue Hole Falls, 151
Blue Ridge, 187–276
Bluebird Day, 77
Bluebird nesting box building programs,
    31, 70
Bluegrass, 57–58
Bluegrass Jam, 144
Bluff Furnace Segment, 179
Bluff Trail, 168–69
Blythe Ferry/Hiwassee Wildlife Refuge, 173
Boardtree Creek, 154
Boardtree Falls, 154
Boating, 49, 110, 142. See also Canoeing;
    Kayaking; Paddling; Rafting
Bone Cave State Natural Area, 143
Boone, Daniel, 226
Boone Lake, 255
Borum Pond, 83
Boswell Landing, 50
Bottomless pool, 265
Boulevard Trail, 247
Bowater Company, 148, 159, 195
Bowater Newsprint Calhoun
    Operations, 160
Brady Mountain, 129
Bridges
    at Natchez Trace Parkway and
        Corridor, 91
    natural, 102, 108, 109, 154–55
    Oneida & Western Railroad Bridge, 103
    Peters Bridge, 104
    Sewanee Natural Bridge, 154–55
    Walnut Street Bridge, 179
Bright's Grocery, 143–44
Bristol Caverns, 266–67, 268
Brown's Creek Lake, 37
Brushy Mountain, 218
Buffalo Range, 53–54
Buggytop Trail, 155
Bull Head Trail, 246–47
Burgess Falls State Natural Area, 136–37
Burial mounds, 123
Burnt Mill Bridge, 102
Burnt Mill Bridge Loop Trail, 103
Burra Burra Mine, 195, 196
Buzzard Slough, 8
Buzzard's Roost, 139–40
Byrd Creek, 129
Byrd Lake, 129

Cable Mill, 236
Cades Cove, 235–37, 240, 242, 243, 251
Cades Cove Campground, 236
Cades Cove Mountain, 239
Café Etowah, 189

Calfkiller River, 134
Camels, 88
Campout at the Zoo, 89
Candy Flats, 176
Cane Creek Gorge, 139
Caney Fork River, 134, 136, 142
Caney Island Indian Mound, 5
Canoe the Sequatchie, 159
Canoeing, 118, 147, 159, 255
Carter State Natural Area, 148, 149, 155
Cascades, The, 198
Cat Chamber, 199
Cat House Café, 13
Catoosa Wildlife Management Area,
    117–19, 120
Cave and rock paintings, 80
Cave Spring, 151
Caves
    Appalachian Caverns, 264–66, 267, 268
    Big Bone Cave, 143
    Bristol Caverns, 266–67, 268
    Craighead Caverns, 198–200
    Cumberland Caverns, 144–47
    Hazard Cave, 110
    Lost Cove Cave, 149, 155–56
    Raccoon Mountain Caverns, 171, 174
    at South Cumberland Recreation
        Area, 148
    Witch's Cave, 104
Cemeteries, 37
Center Hill Dam, 142
Center Hill Lake, 136, 142
Central Basin, 57
Chanticleer Inn, 168, 174
Charit Creek Lodge, 102, 105, 108
Chattanooga, 160–85
Chattanooga Area Convention and Visitors
    Bureau, 160, 163
Chattanooga Choo Choo complex, 166–67
Chattanooga Choo Choo Holiday Inn, 167
Chattanooga Nature Center, 174–78
Chattanooga Riverboat Company, 167
Cheatham County Chamber of Commerce,
    80, 85
Cheatham Lake, 83, 84
Cheatham Lock and Dam, 83, 84
Cheatham Wildlife Management Area, 77,
    82–85
Cheekwood, 72–77
Cherohala Skyway, 189, 190
Cherokee Indians, 115, 123, 169, 176,
    195–96, 236
Cherokee Lake, 255
Cherokee National Forest, Northern
    Division, 255, 256–58

Cherokee National Forest, Southern
 Division, 188, 190–95
Chickamauga Dam, 161, 163, 176, 178, 179
Chickamauga Lake, 161
Chickamauga/Chattanooga National
 Military Park, 168
Chickasaw Indians, 33, 90
Chickasaw Trail, 27
Children's Heritage Festival, 55
Chilhowee Mountain, 192, 238–39
Chilhowee Reservoir, 239
Chimney Rock, 151
Chimney Tops, 125, 235
Choctaw Indians, 90
Christmas Down by the Lake, 34, 35
Christmas in the Mountains, 126
Christmas on the Mountain, 141
Christmas Workshop, 55
Churches, 37
Civil War sites, 51, 168, 169, 176, 180, 199
Clear Creek, 118, 120
Clear Fork River, 99, 102, 103, 104
Clinch River, 202, 220, 221, 222
Clinch River/Melton Hill reservoir, 203
Clingmans Dome, 235, 239
Cloud Forest, 73
Coal mining, 99, 124
Coke ovens, 156
Colbert, George, 92
Colditz Cove State Natural Area, 104–5
Collier Ridge Loop, 105–6
Collins Gulf Trail, 153
Collins Nature Trail, 143
Collins River, 142, 147, 148
Competitive Trail Ride, 107
Connector Trail, 153
Copper Basin, 195, 197
Copper mining, 189, 195–97
Copperhill, 189
Cordell Hull Lake, 58
Cosby, 243
Cosby Creek, 241
Cotton mill, 142
Cougars, 64, 86
Cove Creek, 115
Cove Lake State Park, 218–20
Covenant College, 169
Crab Orchard Mining Company, 262
Crab Orchard stone, 129
Craft Workshops, 107. *See also* Arts & crafts
 fairs
Craighead, Chief, 199
Craighead Caverns, 198–200
Cravens House, 169, 174
Croft farmhouse, 63

Croft, Margaret and Elise, 61–62
Crooked Creek, 104
Cross Creeks National Wildlife Refuge
 (NWR), 44–48
Cross Mountain, 218
Crow Creek, 148, 149, 155
Crystal Falls, 199
Crystal Palace, 145
Cub Lake, 37
Cumberland Caverns, 144–47
*Cumberland Caverns* (Matthews), 146
Cumberland Color Caper, 107
Cumberland County Chamber of
 Commerce, 129
Cumberland Gap, 226
Cumberland Gap National Historical Park,
 226–30
Cumberland Gap twin tunnel, 227–28
Cumberland Mountain, 228
Cumberland Mountain State Park, 129–31
Cumberland Plateau, 58, 97–185
Cumberland Rapid Transit Rafting Trips,
 104, 108
Cumberland River, 48, 58, 83, 99
Cumberland River Bicentennial Trail, 77,
 82–85
Cumberland rosinweed, 150, 155
Cumberland Scenic Trail, 159–60
Cumberland Science Museum, 58–61
Cumberland Trail, 120, 129, 219
Cumberland Trail Conference, 131, 220
Cypress Grove Nature Park, 29–32
Cypress Knee Loop, 31

Daddy's Creek, 118, 120
Dale Hollow Lake, 112–14
Dale Hollow National Fish Hatchery, 114–15
Daniel Boone Heritage Trail, 228
Dark Hollow Trail, 225
Dave Miller Homestead, 262
David Gray Sanctuary, 184
Day with the Eagles tours, 55
*Dazzling Duck* (amphibious vehicle), 184, 185
de Soto, Hernando, 169, 176
Deep Wells Picnic Area, 70
Delta country, heart of, 29–39
Devil's Breakfast Table Trail, 120
Devils Jump, 101
Dickinson Island, 213
Discovery Trail, 213
Dismal Swamp, 33
Dixie Land Excursions, 181
Doe River, 261, 262
Dog Hole Coal Mine, 151
Dollywood theme park, 232, 250

Douglas Lake, 255
Down to Earth Holiday Party, 214
Downtown Arrow trains, 182
Dragging Canoe, Chief, 169
Draperies, 198
Duck River, 45, 147, 148
Duck River gorge, 92
Ducktown Basin Museum, 195–98
Dulcimer concerts, 107, 185
Duncan Hollow Loop, 105–6
Dutch Maid Bakery, 152, 158

Eagle watches, 4–5, 6, 53, 113, 177, 178
Eagles
  bald, 4–5, 9, 64, 113
  golden, 242
Earth Day Celebration, 214
East Obey River, 115
Eastern Highland Rim, 97, 101
Edge Path, 221
Edwin Warner Park. *See* Warner Parks
Einstein, Albert, 201
Elderhostel, 141
Elk, 241
Elk & Bison Prairie, 49, 53
Elk River, 147
Elkmont, 243
Emory Gap, 125
Emory River, 120, 123–24
Enchanted Forest, 212–13, 214
Ephraim Bales home, 238
Erwin National Fish Hatchery, 258–60
Etowah, 189

Fairview Gullies, 36
Fall Color Barge Day, 271
Fall Color Overnighter, 158
Fall Colors Weekend, 141, 158
Fall Creek Falls, 138–39
Fall Creek Falls Bed and Breakfast, 138, 141
Fall Creek Falls State Park, 137–41
Fall Creek Loop, 272
Fall Creek Thaw, 141
Fall Festival, 264
Fall Festival and Plant Sale, 214
Fall Foliage Week, 162
Fall Steam Specials, 182
Fall Wildlife Weekend, 178
Falling Waters River, 136
Family Living History Experience, 55
Farmhouse Gallery and Gardens, 273–76
Farms. *See also* Historic buildings
  Croft farmhouse, 63
  Dave Miller Homestead, 262
  Greenway Farm, 176–77, 179
  Hensley Settlement of farmsteads, 228–29

The Homeplace-1850, 51–52
Fiddlers and Fiddleheads Festival, 275, 276
Fiery Gizzard, 148, 151–52
Fiery Gizzard Trail, 151
Fish hatcheries, 114–15, 258–60
Fishing
  in Arch Lake, 110
  at Catoosa Wildlife Management
    Area, 118
  in Dale Hollow Lake, 113
  at Gee Creek Wilderness, 191
  at Great Smoky Mountains National
    Park, 248–49
  in the Hiwassee River, 192
  in Lake Isom, 8
  at Land Between the Lakes Recreation
    Area, 49
  in Melton Hill Lake, 221
  at Natchez Trace State Park, 37
  in Pickwick Lake, 42
  in Pickwick Tailwaters, 43–44
  in Poplar Tree Lake, 27
  in Reelfoot Lake, 5, 8
  at Rock Island State Park, 142
  at South Cumberland Recreation Area,
    147–48
  in Travis McNatt Lake, 33
  in Upper East Tennessee, 255
Fishing rodeos, 38, 40, 43–44
Flat Fork Creek, 123, 124
Floating, 147
Flower Press, 31
Flowstone, 198
*Fly Fisherman's Guide to the Great Smoky
  Mountains National Park*
  (Lawrence), 249
Folklife Festival, 126, 272, 273
Foothills Gospel Music Festival, 126
Fort Donelson, 51
Fort Henry, 51
Fort Henry Road, 49
Fort Henry Trail, 49, 51
Fort Loudoun Lake, 211
Fort Patrick Henry Lake, 255, 272
Foster Falls, 151–52
Four Rivers Folk Festival, 52
Fox Creek, 118
French Broad River, 255
Friends of Mound Bottom, 80
Friends of the Nashville Zoo, 89
Frozen Head State Natural Area, 123–26
Fruit Bowl, 151
Fuller, William A., 180

Gabes Mountain Trail, 245
Ganier Ridge Trail, 67

Garden Inn, 133–35
GardenFest, 177
Gardens
  Cheekwood, 72–77
  Cloud Forest, 73
  Farmhouse Gallery and Gardens, 273–76
  Howe Wildflower Garden, 74
  Memphis Botanic Garden, 23–26
  Reflection Riding Botanical Garden,
    174–78
  Rose Garden, 73
  *Seijaku-En*, 23–24
  *Shomu-en* (Japanese Pine Mist Garden),
    75–76
  Swan Garden, 74
  University of Tennessee Arboretum,
    208–11
Gatlin Point, 50
Gatlinburg, 232–33
Gatlinburg Department of Tourism, 254
Gee Creek Wilderness, 191
Gentleman's Swimming Hole Trail, 103
Ghost House Trail, 225
Ghouls at Grassmere, 66
Ginger Bay, 50
Gold mining, 189
Golden Pond, 51
Golfing, 42, 81, 140
Good Earth Festival, 25, 183
Gordon House, 92
Grand Canyon of the Tennessee River, 160
Grand Gap Loop, 103
Granny White Pike, 68
Graphite Reactor, 204, 206
Grassmere Wildlife Park. *See* Nashville
  Wildlife Park at Grassmere
Great Falls, 142
Great Falls Dam, 142
Great Falls Reservoir, 142
Great Indian Warpath, 176
Great Lakes of the South, 220
Great Race, 170
Great Smoky Mountains Institute,
  237–38, 254
Great Smoky Mountains National Park
  (GSMNP), 230–54
  animals of, 239–42
  auto tours of, 234–39
  fishing at, 248–49
  hikes, nature walks, and camping, 242–48
  seasons and special events, 250–51
Great Stone Door, 149, 150, 153–54
Great Stone Face, 175
Great Valley, 187–276
Great Western Furnace, 52–53
Greenbrier Cove, 244

Greenway Farm, 176–77, 179
Greeter Falls, 154
Greeter Trail, 154
Gregory Bald, 239
Greystone Hotel, 232
Grist mills, 78, 221, 224
Grotto Falls, 244, 247
*Growing and Propagating Wildflowers*
  (Phillips), 75
Grundy Forest State Natural Area, 149,
  151–52
Grundy Lake, 156
Grundy Lakes State Park, 156–58
Gum Springs, 169

Hacking, 9
Hall of the Mountain King, 145
Halloween Ghost Stories, 198
Halloween Howl and Monster Bash, 65
Hang gliding, 159, 169–70
Harpeth River, 57, 77–80
Harpeth Woods Trail, 71
Harrogate, 227
Harrow Road Café, 103
Harvest Celebration, 55
Harvest Home, 55
Hatchie swamp river, 2
Haunted Swamp, 176, 178
Haunting in the Hills, 107
Haw Ridge Canoe Trail, 203
Hawkins Cove Natural Area, 149–50
Hawley House Bed and Breakfast,
  273, 276
Hazard Cave, 110
Heath Cove Trail, 209
Hensley Settlement of farmsteads,
  228–29
Henwallow Falls, 244–45
Heritage Day, 185
Heritage Days and Nature's Ways Festival,
  275, 276
Hiking. *See also* specific hiking trails
  at Big Hill Pond State Rustic Park and
    Natural Area, 33
  at Big South Fork National River and
    Recreation Area, 101
  at Catoosa Wildlife Management
    Area, 118
  at Frozen Head State Natural Area, 125
  at Great Smoky Mountains National
    Park, 241–48
  at Norris Dam State Park, 221
  at Obed Wild and Scenic River National
    Recreational Park, 120
  at Pickett State Rustic Park, 108–9
  pocket wilderness, 148, 159

at South Cumberland Recreation
Area, 148
at Warriors' Path State Park, 272
*Hiking Trails of the Smokies*, 243
Historic buildings. *See also* Farms
Alfred Reagan place, 238
Cravens House, 169, 174
Ephraim Bales home, 238
Gordon House, 92
Spring Frog Cabin, 182
Historic Rugby Pilgrimage, 104
Hiwassee Ranger District, 190, 194, 195
Hiwassee River, 191–92, 193
Holston Bluffs, 272
Holston River, 271
Homeplace Wedding, 55
Homeplace-1850, The, 51–52
Honey Creek Loop Trail, 103
Honey Creek Pocket Wilderness, 102
Hood Mountain, 193
Horse camps, 37, 105, 107
Horseback riding, 139
at Big South Fork National River and
Recreation Area, 105
at Catoosa Wildlife Management Area,
118–19
at Gee Creek Wilderness, 191
at Land Between the Lakes Recreation
Area, 51
at Natchez Trace State Park, 40
at Norris Dam State Park, 221
Hot-air balloon weekend, 71
Howe Wildflower Garden, 74
Howlings, 271
Hubert Fry Center, 179
Hungry Hawk Trail, 70, 71
Hunting
at Big Hill Pond State Rustic Park and
Natural Area, 34
at Big South Fork National River and
Recreation Area, 100, 107
at Catoosa Wildlife Management
Area, 118
at Land Between the Lakes Recreation
Area, 49, 51
at Pickett State Rustic Park, 110
at South Cumberland Recreation
Area, 149
at Standing Stone State Forest, 116

I-40 Corridor, sites along, 126–37
Ijams Nature Center, 211–15
Independence Day celebrations, 55, 224
Indian Boundary Lake, 190, 193
Indian Rock, 225
Indian Summer Days, 183, 185

Interpretive programs
at Big South Fork National River and
Recreation Area, 100
at The Homeplace-1850, 51–52
at Lichterman Nature Center, 20
at Meeman Interpretive Center, 27
at Roan Mountain State Resort Park, 262
Iron forges/furnaces, 52–53, 57, 78–79, 81, 227
Iron Mountains, 260

Jack's Branch, 93
Jackson, Andrew, 37, 93
Jackson Branch, 92–93
Jackson Falls, 92–93
Jake Blevins homestead, 102
Jambalaya Jammin', 178
Jewelweed Trail, 29–30
Jim Bailey Nature Trail, 81
Jim Oliver's Smoke House Resort,
150–51, 158
John Muir Trail, 102, 103, 191, 193
Jonesborough, 255, 259
Judge Branch, 125
Junior Naturalist program, 71
Junior Ranger programs, 101, 251
Junior trout tournament, 126

Kayaking, 118, 255
Kefauver Hotel, 189
Kenlake Marina, 53
Kentucky, 49, 51, 53, 101, 106
Kentucky Dam, 41, 48
Kentucky Lake, 2, 41, 45, 48, 50, 51
Kid's Fishing Rodeo, 43
Kildeer Pond, 31
Kiln Room, 199
Knoxville area, 200–217
Knoxville Convention & Visitors
Bureau, 201
Knoxville Zoo, 215–17
Kudzu, 38–40

Lake Acorn, 81
Lake Isom National Wildlife Refuge (NWR),
7–10
Lake Trail, 225
Lambert, Ruby and Leo, 170
Land Between the Lakes (LBL) Recreation
Area, 48–55
Laurel Branch Gorge, 151
Laurel Falls, 236, 244
Laurel Fork, 102
Laurel Furnace and ore pits, 81
Laurel Point, 172
Laurel Trail, 154
Laurel-Snow Pocket Wilderness, 159

Leatherwood Ford Area, 102
Leatherwood Ford trailhead, 101, 103
Leatherwood Loop Trail, 103
Leatherwood Resort & Marina, 47
LeConte Creek, 244
LeConte Lodge, 254
Lemurs, 85, 87–88
Lenoir Pioneer Museum, 220
Leopards
   clouded, 85, 86, 88
   snow, 85
Lewis, Meriwether, 93
Lichterman Nature Center, 20–22
Lincoln Memorial University, 227
Linville Creek, 264
Linville, Jim and John, 265
Little Acorn Trail, 71
Little Gizzard Creek, 151
Little Grand Canyon, 199
Little Harpeth River, 71
Little Owl's Village Site, 182
Little Pigeon River, 241, 244
Little River, 241
Little Sequatchie, 147, 148
L & N depot, 189
Logging, 99, 124, 249
Lone Rock Trail, 156–57
Look Rock, 239, 243
Lookout Creek, 175, 176, 177
Lookout Mountain, 161, 168–70, 173
Lookout Mountain Hang Gliding, 170, 174
Lookout Mountain Incline Railway,
   168, 174
Lookout Tower, 125
Lost Chestnut Trail, 209
Lost Cove Cave, 149, 155–56
Lost Creek, 155
Lost Sea, 198–200
Lover's Leap, 168
Lower Falls, 154
Luther, Edward T., 2

Maclellan Island, 183
McLish Stand exhibit, 93
Madisonville, 189
Manhattan Project, 201–2
Maple Creek Lake, 37
Matthews, Larry E., 146
Meeman Interpretive Center, 27
Meeman-Shelby Forest State Park, 26–29
Meeting of the Waters, 103
Meigs Creek Falls, 244
Melton Hill Lake, 202, 221
Memphis, 10–16
Memphis Botanic Garden, 23–26
Memphis Pink Palace Museum, 16–20

Memphis Zoo, 11–16
Mennonite community, 135
Meriwether Lewis Park, 93, 94
Metal Ford, 93
Metcalf Bottoms picnic area, 236
Middle Tennessee, 57–96
Mileage Collector, 182
Mill House, 129
Miller Cove, 239
Mining, 93, 99, 124, 189, 195–97
Missionary Ridge, 181
Mississippi River Floodplain, 2
Mississippi River Group Camp, 27
Monroe Tourism Council, 189
Monsanto Ponds, 95–96
Monterey, 131
Montgomery Bell State Park, 57, 79, 80–82
Monument Pillar, 145–46
Morris, Sukey, 37
Mossy Ridge Trail, 70–71
Mound Bottom, 77, 79–80
Mount Comfort Church and Cemetery, 37
Mount LeConte, 233, 235, 245–48
Mount Mingus, 235
Mount Roosevelt State Forest and Wildlife
   Management Area, 127–28
Mountain bike races, 107
Mountain bike trails, 51, 105–6, 221
Mountain Goat railroad grade, 150
*Mountain Roads and Quiet Places*, 234–35
Mountain View Hotel, 232
Mountaineer Folk Festival, 141
Muddy Creek, 264
Muddy Pond Mennonite community, 135
Mullen's Cove Loop, 160
Museum of Appalachia, 223–24
Museums. *See also* Farms; Historic
   buildings
   Abraham Lincoln Museum, 227, 230
   American Museum of Science and
      Energy, 205–7
   Cheekwood, 72–77
   Cumberland Science Museum, 58–61
   Ducktown Basin Museum, 195–98
   Lenoir Pioneer Museum, 220
   Memphis Pink Palace Museum, 16–20
   Museum of Appalachia, 223–24
   Ochs Museum and Overlook, 168
   Steadman Farmstead Museum, 269
   Tennessee Valley Railroad Museum, 178
   Unicoi County Heritage Museum, 259
   Wilson's North American Wildlife
      Museum, 131–33

Nantahala Forest, 190
Napier Mine, 93

Narrows of the Harpeth Scenic River, 57,
    77–80
Nashville, 58–89
Nashville Dome, 57, 97
Nashville Wildlife Park at Grassmere,
    61–66, 85
Nashville Zoo, 62, 85–89
Natchez Indians, 90
Natchez Trace, 71
Natchez Trace Parkway and Corridor, 89–96
Natchez Trace State Park, 35–40
*National Audubon Society Field Guide to
    North American Wildflowers/Eastern
    Region*, 193–94
National Catfish Derby Fishing Rodeo,
    43–44
National Catfish Derby Kid's Fishing
    Rodeo, 44
National Environmental Research Park,
    202, 205
National Fitness Campaign Walking
    Course, 130
National Park Service Headquarters, 108
National Speleological Society (NSS), 145,
    146–47
National Wildlife Federation, 276
Native American festivals, 65
Native American skills workshops, 183
Native Americans, 105, 115–16, 134, 153, 182,
    183, 189
    Cherokee Indians, 115, 123, 169, 176,
        195–96, 236
    Chickasaw Indians, 33, 90
    Choctaw Indians, 90
    Natchez Indians, 90
    Shawnee Indians, 116
    Woodland Indians, 79–80
Native Plant Sale, 178
Natural Areas Planning Act, 66
*Natural Wonders of Kentucky* (Lawrence),
    49, 229
Nature Loop, 71
Nature Nearby, 272, 273
Nature Photography Workshop, 107
Nature Station, 53
Nemo Bridge Trail, 120
Neville Bay, 50
New Madrid Fault, 2
New River, 99
Newfound Gap, 247
Newfound Gap Road, 235
Nickajack Dam, 161, 176, 177
Nickajack Lake, 161, 165
Nolichucky Ranger District, 256, 257, 258
Nolichucky River, 255
Normandy Dam, 147

Norris Dam, 220
Norris Dam Marina, 221, 223
Norris Dam Reservation, 222
Norris Dam State Park, 220–23
Norris Lake, 220
North Chickamauga Creek Greenway, 179
North Lake Trail, 67
North Old Mac, 125
North Ridge Trail, 203
North White Oak River, 99
North-South Trail, 51
Northeast Tennessee Tourism
    Association, 255
Northrup Falls, 104
Not So Far A-field Trips, 214

Oak-Hickory Trail, 209
Oak Ridge, 201–5
Oak Ridge area, 200–217
Oak Ridge Forest, 208
Oak Ridge National Laboratory (ORNL),
    202, 204, 206
Oak Ridge Reservation (ORR), 202
Obed Gorge, 120
Obed Wild and Scenic River, 118, 203
Obed Wild and Scenic River National
    Recreational Park, 119–23
Ochs Museum and Overlook, 168
Ocoee Ranger District, 194
Ocoee River, 192, 193
Ocoee Scenic Byway, 188, 190, 192
Oconaluftee visitors center, 234
Ogle's General Store, 232
*Ohmigod*, 121
Old Federal Road, 176
Old Owl Trail, 71
Old Smoky Outfitters, 248, 254
Oneida & Western Railroad Bridge, 103
Oscar Blevins Trail, 101–2
Ospreys, 162, 184
Oswald Dome Lookout, 192
Otter Creek, 118
Otter Creek Road, 67
Otters, 240–41, 268–69
*Our Restless Earth: The Geologic Regions of
    Tennessee* (Luther), 2
Outpost Supply Center, 50
Over the River and Through the Woods,
    176, 178
Overmountain Victory March
    Reenactment, 262, 264
Overmountain Victory Trail, 261–62
Owl prowls, 30, 177, 229
Owl's Hill Nature Center, 76
Oxbow lakes, 18
Ozone Falls State Natural Area, 128–29

Paddling, 104, 191, 192
Panorama Point, 266
Panther Branch, 125
Paris Landing State Park, 50
Park Inn, 40
Parks/recreation areas. *See also* Wildlife
  refuges/nature preserves
  Bays Mountain Park and Planetarium,
    268–71
  Big Hill Pond State Rustic Park and
    Natural Area, 32–35
  Big Ridge State Park, 224–26
  Big South Fork National River and
    Recreation Area, 98–108
  Burgess Falls State Natural Area, 136–37
  Chickamauga/Chattanooga National
    Military Park, 168
  Cove Lake State Park, 218–20
  Cumberland Gap National Historical
    Park, 226–30
  Cumberland Mountain State Park, 129–31
  Cypress Grove Nature Park, 29–32
  Fall Creek Falls State Park, 137–41
  Gee Creek Wilderness, 191
  Great Smoky Mountains National Park.
    *See* Great Smoky Mountains
    National Park
  Grundy Lakes State Park, 156–58
  Hiwassee Scenic River State Park, 195
  Land Between the Lakes Recreation
    Area, 48–55
  Meeman-Shelby Forest State Park, 26–29
  Meriwether Lewis Park, 93, 94
  Montgomery Bell State Park, 57, 79,
    80–82
  Natchez Trace State Park, 35–40
  National Environmental Research Park,
    202, 205
  Norris Dam State Park, 220–23
  Obed Wild and Scenic River National
    Recreational Park, 119–23
  Paris Landing State Park, 50
  Pickett State Rustic Park, 102, 106, 108–12
  Pickwick Landing State Park, 42–43, 44
  Point Park, 168–69, 174, 175
  Radnor Lake State Natural Area, 66–69
  Reelfoot Lake State Park, 2–6
  Roan Mountain State Resort Park,
    260–64
  Rock Island State Park, 141–44
  Ross's Landing Park, 163
  Signal Point Park, 160, 173
  Solway Park, 203
  South Cumberland Recreation Area,
    147–58
  Standing Stone State Park, 115–17

Tennessee Riverpark, 178–80
Warner Parks, 69–72
Warriors' Path State Park, 271–73
Parson's Table, 259, 260
Parton, Dolly, 232
Patrick Henry Reservoir, 271
Patterson Forge, 78–79
Peg Leg Mine, 262
Pelicans, 63–64
Percy Warner Park. *See* Warner Parks
Peters Bridge, 104
Phillips, Harry, 75
Phosphate mining, 93
Photography workshops, 65, 66, 107
Pickett State Rustic Park, 102, 106, 108–12
Pickwick Lake, 41, 42
Pickwick Landing State Park, 42–43, 44
Pickwick Tailwaters, 43–44
Piersol Group Camp, 28
Pigeon Forge, 232, 250
Pigeon Forge Department of Tourism, 254
Pin Oak Lake, 37
Pin Oak Lodge, 37
Pine Succession Trail, 213
Pineapple Room Restaurant, 76, 77
Piney Campground, 49–50
Piney River Trail, 159
Pinnacle Point, 228
Pinnacle Ridge, 225
Pioneer camps, 107, 229
Pioneer Springs Trail, 28
Place of a Thousand Drips, 244
Planetariums
  Bays Mountain Park and Planetarium,
    268–71
  Sharpe Planetarium, 19
  Sudekum Planetarium, 58–61
Pocket wilderness hikes, 148, 159
Point Park, 168–69, 174, 175
Poplar Tree Lake, 27
Pops in the Park, 182
Pot Point Loop, 160
Potassium nitrate mining, 99
Powell River, 220
Prentice Cooper State Forest, 150, 159–60
Project Suet, 31
Pryor, William, 52
Przewalski's horse, 62, 64–65

Quilt festivals, 229

Raccoon Mountain, 161, 162, 171, 173
Raccoon Mountain Caverns, 171, 174
Raccoon Mountain Hawk Watch, 162
Raccoon Mountain Pumped Storage
  Plant, 171

Raccoon Mountain Pumped Storage
    Station, 174
Radnor Lake State Natural Area, 66–69
Rafting, 104, 255
Rail Pond, 96
Rainbow Falls, 244
Rainbow Falls Trail, 247–48
Ramsay Cascades, 244
Ranger Creek Falls, 149
Rappelling, 150
Raven Point, 151
Red pandas, 85, 86, 88
Reelfoot Lake, 2–10, 165
Reelfoot Lake State Park, 2–6
Reelfoot National Wildlife Refuge (NWR),
    7–10
Reelfoot Wildlife Management Area
    (WMA), 5–6
Reflection Riding Botanical Garden, 174–78
Reliance, 193
Revolutionary War sites, 169, 261–62
Rhododendron Festival, 263–64
River Bluff Small Wild Area, 221
River precautions, 122
River Sounds Traditional Music Festival, 55
Roamin' & Restin' (Oakley), 232
Roan Mountain, 256
Roan Mountain Naturalists Rally,
    262–63, 264
Roan Mountain State Resort Park, 260–64
Roan Mountain Wildflower Tours and
    Birdwalks, 263
Roaring Fork, 238, 247
Roaring Fork Motor Nature Trail, 238,
    244, 247
Robertson, James, 81
Rock City Gardens, 174
Rock climbing, 141, 150
Rock Creek, 110–11
Rock Creek Outfitters, 150
Rock houses, 105, 160
Rock Island State Park, 141–44
Rock Point, 225
Rockhounding, 257–58
Rolley Hole National Championship,
    116, 117
Roosevelt, Franklin D., 201
Roost, The, 15
Rose Garden, 73
Rose gentian, 162
Ross's Landing, 183
Ross's Landing Park, 163
Ross's Landing Plaza, 179
Round House Reunion, 6
Ruby Falls, 170, 174
Rugby, 103–4, 108

Rushing Creek Campground, 50
Russian wild boar, 121

Saint Augustine Cisca Trail, 176
Sale Creek, 184
Sandhill Crane Weekend, 172
Saunders, Clarence, 16
Savage Gulf State Natural Area, 152–53
Scottish Highland Games, 65, 77
Seijaku-En, 23–24
Senior Capers, 141
Senior Citizens Shenanigan, 38, 40
Senior Day, 15
Senior walks, 65, 66
Sequatchie, 137–60
Sequatchie County Loop, 158
Sequatchie River, 159
Sequatchie Soar and Flight, 159
Sequatchie Valley, 158–60
Sequoyah, 169
Serendipity Trail, 213
Sevier, John, 169
Sewanee Natural Bridge, 154–55
Sharpe Planetarium, 19
Sharp's Station, 225
Shawnee Indians, 116
Sheltering Rock, 262
Shomu-en (Japanese Pine Mist Garden),
    75–76
Short Mountain, 218
Signal Mountain, 160, 161, 172–73
Signal Point, 172–73
Signal Point Park, 160, 173
Silverbrook Stables, 138
Sinking Waters Trail, 272
Sinks, 244
Skiing, 250, 261
Small Wilds Campsite, 151
Smoke House Restaurant and Trading
    Post, 150
Smoky Mountain Christmas at
    Dollywood, 250
Smoky Mountain Lights, 250
Snap Apple Night, 55
Solway Park, 203
Songbird Trail, 221
South Chickamauga Creek, 182
South Cove Trail, 68
South Cumberland, 137–60
South Cumberland Recreation Area (SCRA),
    147–58
South Holston Lake, 255
South Lake Trail, 68
South Old Mac, 125
South Welcome Station, 49, 51
Southern Belle (riverboat), 164, 167

Species Survival Plan, 85, 216
Spicewood, 125
Spillway Trail, 67
Spring Creek, 193
Spring Escape, 5, 6
Spring Festival, 273
Spring Frog Cabin, 182
Spring Gorge Ramble, 162
Spring Music & Crafts Festival, 104
Spring Wildflower Pilgrimage, 126, 141
Stagecoach Historic Trail, 153
Stamps Hollow, 133–34
Standing Stone Lake, 116
Standing Stone State Forest, 116
Standing Stone State Park, 115–17
Station Camp Horse Camp, 105, 107
Steadman Farmstead Museum, 269
Steele Iron Works, 93
Stinging Fork Trail, 159
Stone Door Camping Area, 153
Strip mining, 203–4
Sudekum Planetarium, 58–61
Sugarland Mountain, 235
Sugarlands, 233–34
Sunset Rock, 169
Swan Garden, 74
Sweden Creek, 148
Sweetwater Branch nature trail, 94

T Wall, 150
Tellicafe, 190–91, 194
Tellico Plains, 190–91
Tellico Ranger District, 190, 195
Tennessee Aquarium, 161, 163–67
*Tennessee Atlas and Gazetteer*, 95
Tennessee Citizens for Wilderness Planning
(TCWP), 202, 203–4, 205
Tennessee Fall Homecoming Weekend,
223, 224
Tennessee National Wildlife Refuge (NWR),
44–48
Tennessee Natural Areas Preservation
Act, 204
Tennessee Ornithological Society, 174, 180
Tennessee Overhill, 188–200
Tennessee Overhill Heritage
Association, 189
Tennessee River, 41, 48, 164, 211, 222
Tennessee River Gorge, 160–85
Tennessee River Gorge Trust, 163
Tennessee River Rescue, 162
Tennessee Riverpark, 178–80
Tennessee Scenic Rivers Act, 203
Tennessee Trails System Act, 204
Tennessee Valley Authority (TVA), 48, 142,
220, 222

Tennessee Valley Railroad, 180–82
Tennessee Valley Railroad Museum, 178
Tennessee Wildlife Resources Agency, 128
Thunderhead, 239
Ticks, 54
Tims Ford Dam, 147
Towne of Cumberland Gap, 227
Trace, The, 51
Tracy City, 151–52
Trail of Tears, 169, 195
Travis McNatt Lake, 33
Tree I.D., 31
Trees of Christmas at Cheekwood, 76, 77
Tremont, 237–38
Tremont Logging History tour, 237
Tri-State Peak, 228
Trillum Gap Trail, 247
Trout Tournament, 263
Tulip Poplar Trail, 208–9
Tunnels
    Cumberland Gap twin tunnel, 227–28
    at Missionary Ridge, 181
    at Narrows of the Harpeth Scenic River,
    78–79
Turkey Bay, 51
Turkey Call Trail, 34
Tuscumbia Trail, 33
Twilight Safari and Reptile Mania, 66
Twin Arches Trail, 102

Unaka mountains, 257
Unaka Ranger District, 256, 257, 258
Unakite, 257
Understanding Animal Talk, 31
Unicoi County Heritage Museum, 259
Unicoi unit, 256
University of Tennessee Arboretum, 208–11
Upper Cumberland Plateau, 98–126
Upper East Tennessee, 254–76
Upper Falls, 154
Utas, 211

Vaughn's Creek, 71
Virgin Falls Pocket Wilderness, 159

Walden Ridge, 137, 158–60, 161, 184
Walden Ridge Trail, 127
Walk on the Wild Side, 89
Walk the Earth, 77
Walk the Greenway, 177
Walker Hall, 182
Walker, James, 168
Walker, Thomas, 226
Walking Stick, Chief, 176
Walleye tournament, 144
Walnut Street Bridge, 179

Warner Parks, 69–72
Warner Woods Trail, 70
Warriors' Path State Park, 271–73
Watauga Ranger District, 256, 257
Water Resources Development Act, 99
Waterskiing, 142
Watts Bar Lake, 127
Wayside Manor Bed & Breakfast, 201
West Tennessee Plateau Slope, 2
Western Highland Rim, 57
Western Natchez Trace, 36
Western Tennessee Delta Country, 1–55
Wetland boardwalk, 176
White Oak Creek, 102, 103
White Pine Trail, 209–10
*White Water in an Open Canoe*, 122
Wild Cave Tours, 171
Wild hogs, 241
Wild turkeys, 36, 242
Wilderness Road Trail, 227, 228
Wilderness Week of Nature, 250
Wildflowers, 34, 68, 70, 74, 100, 125, 148,
    149–50, 176, 193–94, 221
    special events, 65, 66, 75, 77, 126, 141, 177,
    178, 183, 214, 250, 271
Wildlife refuges/nature preserves. *See also*
    Parks/recreation areas
Audubon Acres, 178, 182–85
Blythe Ferry/Hiwassee Wildlife
    Refuge, 173
Bone Cave State Natural Area, 143
Carter State Natural Area, 148, 149, 155
Catoosa Wildlife Management Area,
    117–19, 120
Chattanooga Nature Center, 174–78
Cheatham Wildlife Management Area,
    77, 82–85
Cherokee National Forest, Northern
    Division, 255, 256–58
Cherokee National Forest, Southern
    Division, 188, 190–95
Colditz Cove State Natural Area, 104–5
Cross Creeks National Wildlife Refuge,
    44–48
David Gray Sanctuary, 184
Frozen Head State Natural Area, 123–26
Grundy Forest State Natural Area, 149,
    151–52

Hawkins Cove Natural Area, 149–50
Ijams Nature Center, 211–15
Lake Isom National Wildlife Refuge,
    7–10
Lichterman Nature Center, 20–22
Mount Roosevelt State Forest and
    Wildlife Management Area, 127–28
Nashville Wildlife Park at Grassmere,
    61–66, 85
Oak Ridge Forest, 208
Owl's Hill Nature Center, 76
Ozone Falls State Natural Area, 128–29
Prentice Cooper State Forest, 150, 159–60
Reelfoot National Wildlife Refuge, 7–10
Reelfoot Wildlife Management Area, 5–6
Savage Gulf State Natural Area, 152–53
Tennessee National Wildlife Refuge,
    44–48
Wildwood Lodge, 100, 106, 108, 112
Wiley Oakley Drive, 232
Williams Island Tour, 162
Willow Pond, 72
Wilson's North American Wildlife
    Museum, 131–33
Winter Gardening Seminar, 273
Winter Lights, 15
Winter Wonders Party, 177
Winterfest, 250
Witch's Cave, 104
Wolf River, 2
Wolves
    gray, 269
    red, 241
Wood Duck Lake, 31
Woodland Habitat Trail, 179
Woodland Indians, 79–80
Woodland Trail, 28
Wrangler Camp, 37

Yahoo Falls, 101

Zoos
    Knoxville Zoo, 215–17
    Memphis Zoo, 11–16
    Nashville Wildlife Park at Grassmere,
        61–66, 85
    Nashville Zoo, 62, 85–89
    special events, 15, 89